Ninth Edition

A Handbook of Arts & Crafts

Philip R. Wigg
Professor Emeritus
Bowling Green State University

Jean Hasselschwert
Bowling Green City Schools

Willard F. Wankelman
Professor Emeritus
Bowling Green State University

McGraw Hill

Boston, Massachusetts   Burr Ridge, Illinios   Dubuque, Iowa
Madison, Wisconsin   New York, New York   San Francisco, California   St. Louis, Missouri

McGraw·Hill

A Division of The **McGraw·Hill** *Companies*

Book Team

Publisher *Rosemary Bradley*
Developmental Editor *M. J. Kelly*
Production Editor *Jane C. Morgan*
Designer *Jamie E. O'Neal*
Art Editor *Miriam Hoffman*
Photo Editor *Laura Fuller*
Proofreading Coordinator *Carrie Barker*
Production Manager *Beth Kundert*
Production/Costing Manager *Sherry Padden*
Production/Imaging and Media Development Manager *Linda Meehan Avenarius*
Visuals/Design Freelance Specialist *Mary L. Christianson*
Marketing Manager *Kirk Moen*
Copywriter *Sandy Hyde*

Basal Text *10/12 Times Roman*
Display Type *Cosmos*
Typesetting System *Macintosh™ QuarkXPress™*
Paper Stock *50# Courtland*
Publication Services *Shepherd, Inc.*

Executive Vice President and General Manager *Bob McLaughlin*
Vice President of Production and New Media Development *Victoria Putman*
Vice President, Business Manager *Russ Domeyer*
National Sales Manager *Phil Rudder*
National Telesales Director *John Finn*

Front cover photo: Letraset Phototone
Back cover photos (top): © Paul Barton/The Stock Market; (bottom) © T. Rosenthal/SuperStock

Copyedited by Mary Svetlik Anderson; proofread by Ann M. Kelly

Library of Congress Catalog Card Number: 96–83187

ISBN 0–697–28824–2

Printed in the United States of America

10 9 8 7 6 5 4 3

To the memory of Marietta Wigg

Coauthor, Colleague, and Wife

and

Willard F. Wankelman

Coauthor, Colleague, and Friend

Contents

Preface

Unfortunately another name has been added to our dedication. Willard Wankelman, who has been a coauthor since the inception of this book, is no longer with us. We grieve his passing and are compelled to find a replacement. Jean Hasselschwert has accepted this invitation. She is an experienced art supervisor who has shown promise of bringing many practical insights to the book. Our ambitions are always limited by the prescribed size of the book. There is much that could be added short of a second volume were that possible. However, we think that you will find this latest edition replete with new activities, products, and references.

The book continues to be directed to college art methods instructors, their students, elementary art supervisors, and elementary classroom teachers who direct art activities. Its content is divided into two groupings: general principles of art teaching, which differ from those of most other subject areas, and a variety of art activities selected on the basis of their practicality in the classroom.

As usual, we are indebted to our users, our reviewers, and the staff of our publisher. Users' comments are always welcome, and, even though sometimes contradictory, are always given consideration.

Sally E. Rand
Lansing Community College

Beverly Sanders
Bethune-Cookman College

Darlene Crampton-Fahrenkrog
Concordia University

Dr. Kathy Danko-McGhee
University of Central Florida

C. Morrell Jones
University of Arkansas—Monticello

James L. Burgess
Salisbury State University

Margaret E. (Betsy) Benson, Ed. D.
Augusta Technical Institute

Katherine Glass Kirkpatrick, Ph.D.
Birmingham-Southern College

Art and Teaching

Basic Concepts of Art Instruction

Over the past few decades there has been some revitalization of art instruction. Presumably a good deal of this has derived from college art education programs and their art education majors who have joined school systems across the land. But recently there have been some ominous threats. The federal government has given some thought to the curtailing of its support of the arts. Some of this has come from public servants who strive to be self-appointed censors and some from the public who has voiced outrage against some works given considerable publicity. History proves that this is not a contemporary phenomenon; many historical works now accepted and even admired have evoked wrath. In time, history has a way of pruning its art. Most developed countries have always given more support to the arts than our own, and those countries have managed to survive occasional outrage. It is hoped that this will be the case in the United States.

Additionally, many school systems are now experiencing financial difficulties, and when budget reviews occur, cutbacks often include the arts. We hope that the content of this book will justify continuing support for the arts in school programs. The benefits of art participation are listed under "An Introduction to the Art Activities." We think those benefits are sufficient to warrant support of the arts in any situation. One of your authors remembers the inscription on an art building— "Ars Longa Vita Brevis Est" (Art Is Long, Life Is Short). History concurs; the most compelling key to a historical era is in its art. Our culture needs art too! We should try to pass along a distinguished heritage to future generations.

Art As Part of the School Curriculum

Through the years, as art has increasingly been introduced into public schools as a legitimate subject, opinions have abounded regarding its most effective mode of instruction. These opinions have originated with or been influenced by educational theorists of considerable stature. Their theories have often been at odds, but it has been largely due to their efforts that art has gained, and is gaining, in legitimacy. The old notion of art as a soft playtime therapy is gradually being replaced by the belief that it can be a solid, meaningful subject. This idea is not yet universally accepted, but the trend is in that direction. Strong evidence and support for this can be found in the latest movement known as "discipline-based art education," a movement that seems to be gaining many adherents. This new concept departs from exclusively production-based instruction by adding other areas— aesthetics, art history, and art criticism. These areas may have been with us to a degree, but they are being given new emphasis. The theory is that art can be the focus of study in each of these areas and can be more meaningful to the student. The meaning thus found can be expanded, educationally, into other fields of study and into life experiences.

With this in mind, and if you subscribe to the discipline-based art education theory, the activities in this book should be studied for any correlations with other fields of study or life experiences that can be brought forth. The correlated subjects and other artworks should be discussed and evaluated. In other words, the production of art is not an end in itself. Presumably the goal is to enable students to discuss art with a certain degree of connoisseurship, to be conversant with art of the past and the present to such a degree that they can make comparisons and choices, and to glean information on a wide variety of subjects from such sources. Clearly, art in this context is not a soft subject, nor is it an interlude for the teacher. This theory presumes a greater potential in the student than has been considered in the past.

Attitudes Toward Art Education

Education in the visual arts has had a checkered past. Sixty or seventy years ago there were few public school teachers who conceived of art as a genuinely creative instrument; the majority used art, in a highly regimented manner, as an aid in teaching other subjects. Most career-minded art students went to professional art schools. College art of that time was barely visible. College art courses were usually among the elective curricular offerings and existed largely for art appreciation, although some colleges maintained an artist-in-residence as an obeisance to culture. High schools that offered art courses (usually only the larger ones) offered minimum-credit courses that were taken by many as free rides. At the elementary level, when not subordinated to other subjects, art was often no more than a greatly appreciated therapeutic period of relaxation for the classroom teacher who, in most cases, knew next to nothing about the subject. Children were routinely given stifling and predictable art activities to keep them busy. Art rarely had much educational distinction at any level.

In the intervening years, the picture has changed for the better, though not in every setting. We now have large, well-financed, well-staffed, well-equipped departments and schools of art in many colleges and universities, and their graduates endure rigors of art training equal to those of the professional schools. There are programs of study available to those who wish to be career artists/designers or desire to teach at the college, high school, or elementary levels.

Most elementary teachers now have had some instruction in the teaching of art as part of their college training. Art majors who venture into elementary art generally function as art supervisors, coordinating the art instruction of the classroom teachers. In some cases they make the circuit of several schools and teach the art courses, thus relieving the regular teacher of this duty. People training to teach high school art usually follow a college program that closely parallels that of the professional aspirants. In addition to studio training, they are enlightened by courses in educational psychology, art methods, the exceptional child, public school art, art curriculum, and practice teaching. This educational experience illustrates and reinforces that the art teacher must be a true professional and that art is a serious area of study. Under capable art instruction, students can benefit greatly from their study of art.

The Challenges in Art Teaching

Unfortunately, benefits from the study of art are not easily passed along by the teacher. In addition to being knowledgeable and serious about art education, the teacher must contend with the time lag in art education; although the majority of people have some knowledge and appreciation of most fields, their understanding of art is often somewhat obsolete. Rarely is the average person's exposure to, say, science, matched by his or her exposure to art. After a number of generations of crusading artists and art teachers, the lag is still with us. The lag reverts back to certain notions: (1) that art is a frill—a classroom entertainment of little significance; (2) that art products should be cute or true to life and certainly nonthreatening (passive); (3) that almost any individual's taste is acceptable—certainly not worth challenging—and that any truly reliable standards of art judgment are not likely; (4) that art should not change; it should remain "picturesque," not exceeding the experience or thought level of the viewer; and (5) that art does not, on the whole, provoke any deep thoughts or contain any abiding truths.

All of this is contrary to what the art teacher has been taught, and if the teacher is confronted by these attitudes, troublesome confrontations can result. This impasse can leave the teacher with two options: (1) disregarding the support group (parents and friends) or (2) educating the support group as well as the students. The education would consist of *dis*suading the group of the notions listed in the previous paragraph—a difficult task and probably not wholly achievable. Some effort in this direction would help in providing greater assistance and support for the art students.

The Creative Attitude

A true appreciation of art and the pursuit of art-related activities can benefit all of us and can lead to a better use of our leisure time. This is especially important today because our generation is blessed with more leisure time than any generation in history. In some ways this is good; certainly we all need time to unwind from the fierce competition of the workaday world. Our leisure time is spent on both passive and active indulgences. Some of the time so spent is good for the body, some for the spirit, but unfortunately utter passivity, without any benefits, is far too common in our spare time. Total withdrawal is sometimes a needed therapy, but too little time is spent on the many pursuits available to us that can offer practical rewards, a sense of accomplishment, and a dose of therapy. Such pursuits require varying amounts of original thinking. Since true art is inherently original, it is an activity that has much to offer.

In encouraging originality in art, there can be no place for the kind of teaching that cherishes the comforts of conformity and proceeds on the basis of formula, or predigested information. The only educational system of any value is one that can encourage open-minded curiosity and exploration. Students cannot really think until they are able to experiment with ideas and, by a process involving all their faculties, accept or reject them. Student thinking is often fallible, but mistakes made in the process of earnest searching are much more valuable than the "correct" answers found in the formulas that guarantee a predetermined form of success by placing a limit on the imagination.

Genuinely creative thinking, in any field, is done on an abstract level; it is a product of flights of fancy (of often seemingly ridiculous extremes) unlimited by practical considerations. In science, a realm of utilitarianism, there is a distinct difference between the "pure" and the "applied." Truly creative and significant ideas appear in "pure" science, whereas originality in "applied" science is usually limited to practicality. The most meaningful art forms have been born in an atmosphere of freedom of individual pursuit without the restrictions of usefulness or rules. The proper teaching of art, then, must forget practicality if it hopes to develop any sensitivity to the true nature of art—it must try to evoke an appreciation for things in their own right.

The artist, amateur or professional, finds in art a medium in which he or she can create a world on his or her own terms. In a godlike role the artist can find therapy, solace, pleasure, and catharsis. The basic urge in art probably involves a communication of some kind. Regardless of the personality involved, however, the ultimate satisfaction is that it has forged its way through problems both physical and mental and brought about a conclusion that materializes as something uniquely its own.

Because of the expressive function of art, the basic philosophy of this book is in direct conflict with all practices that tend to standardize and stress application. Classroom use of hectographs, mimeographs, and coloring books discourage inventive and expressive ideas in the development of creativity in students. Oddly enough, the sins of copying are readily recognized and forbidden in most areas of school study, but they are often allowed, and even encouraged, in art. Presumably this situation exists because of two reasons: (1) although it is fortunately in decline, the feeling still persists that art is essentially an imitative or re-creative process, and (2) the establishment of a creative classroom atmosphere involves a separate approach with each member of the class—a far more demanding task than the supplying of copy-work material. The emphasis here placed on creative freedom thus far should not be interpreted as an insistence on complete abandonment or, at best, pure abstraction in art. Regardless of its final form, all art is somehow rooted in nature and is based on a wide variety of individual experiences that are tremendously complex and subject to an infinite number of legitimate interpretations. The great latitude of approach deriving from the subjective character of the field can be, without proper supervision, an invitation to chaos, although discipline is of as great importance in art as in any field. Herein lies one important role of the teacher: that of understanding, assessing, and weighing spontaneity against discipline according to the needs and responsibilities of the individual student.

Where art is used as a tool for the investigation of subject areas such as history, its unique properties are often sacrificed. When this happens, art becomes a mere reporting device. The value of art in a unit of study is always in direct proportion to the emphasis placed on original thinking; when art is made a slave to another study, its essence is destroyed, and it is no longer art. Art should be used to throw fresh light on the academic by revealing hidden values through personal interpretation. In other words, art should operate on the basis of its own principles, not those of the subject being studied. If classroom experiences can be properly tied to creative art programs, both areas of study will be enriched. Art experience can be involved with every field of schoolwork. History, science, geography, literature—all contain material around which art instruction could be organized.

The Creative Impulse

Enthusiasm, in order to be perpetuated, must be shared. Most children have a natural excitement for art. Their first drawings seem to occur instinctively, and the

In decorating each fish, the urge to create has carried this student beyond the limitations of this stereotyped classroom assignment.

works are very enjoyable and meaningful to them. Young people show a natural gift for expression that is unhampered by considerations of style or accuracy in the adult sense. When selected subjects are carefully fed into their absorbent minds and allowed to ferment, they reappear in marvelously fresh interpretations. The ideal art teacher should have the mental flexibility that permits seeing and appreciating things under new and unique conditions. The teacher should also have an evident capacity for excitement that can match that of the student. Good art instruction can be a very remarkable thing—a mutually educative process for student and teacher.

We have spoken of the need for preserving the dignity of art as a basic discipline. If we review the history of art, beginning with the intensely felt drawings of early people, we cannot escape the conclusion that art is an elemental and necessary activity of the human animal. The things put down by prehistoric artists (beasts, weapons, warriors, gods) are formed in a direct manner with natural response to color, rhythm, and texture; the means of art are used in an uncomplicated way showing the close identification of the individual with his or her subject and medium. The same immediacy is apparent when a child begins to draw: the tools (pencil, chalk, crayon) produce great joy as they are introduced, and the drawings created reflect this spirit. A torrent of work pours out representing many things but expressing one mood, that of an intoxicating interest in the marvels of the world. Subjects may change, the form of expression may change, but interest rarely flags until someone in authority begins to question the legitimacy of the images

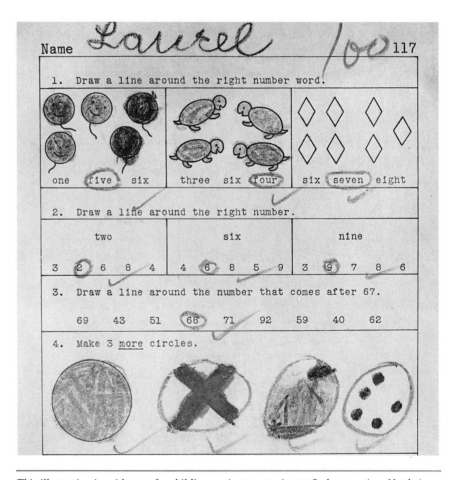

This illustration is evidence of a child's creative urge trying to find expression. Not being satisfied with the simple shapes required as answers, she has used them in creating houses, flowers, and experimental designs.

Chapter One

created by comparing them to adult products. When this happens, the rapport between child and art breaks, adventure ceases, and the work becomes a labored parroting of tired examples.

Admittedly, the child's ultimate process is toward adulthood, but must this natural process be unnaturally accelerated by frustration and inhibition? Does it seem reasonable that accuracy must be substituted for the appreciation of a beautiful color, a bold line, or a vibrant pattern? The need for accuracy, in any event, will make itself felt when the normal child reaches a certain emotional (not chronological) level. When the quest for realism occurs and when the child asks for help, it should be given, not as a manifesto, but as a gift that, if accepted, can coexist with the child's creative resources.

The principles of art are those qualities that, in a very flexible degree and order, seem to be instrumental in making a work seem urgent and readable. When we were children, most of us responded quite naturally to rhythm, variety, repetition, balance, and emphasis—pointing them out seemed a superfluous act. Unfortunately, the aging process and the complexities of society, including social and economic drives, soon supply us with a veneer of sophistication that blunts our responsiveness. We are afraid of failure and consequently shirk the attempt. There are so many opinions on subjects (and particularly art) that we adopt the safest one: we want clear-cut, decisive answers and tangible worthwhile goods—houses, washing machines, televisions—food for the stomach in preference to the psyche. It is no wonder that this materialistic infection can contaminate art to the extent that the principles that should serve to illuminate expression soon become rules which camouflage and disguise.

The Individuality of the Student

When, to what extent, and how are art principles to be applied in supervision so as to avoid the misunderstanding that could easily transmute them into rules? In the first place, children must accept criticism on their terms, that is, when they are prepared to weigh, judge, and apply it. Determination of this readiness must be made on an individual basis by a teacher who understands the personalities involved. Art is a type of personal expression, and any suggestions should be advanced as possibilities to be evaluated in terms of their effect on this expression in the total work. Too many suggestions could easily dilute the individuality of the expression. It may be agreed that a better feeling may be produced through a change of color, that a different placement may heighten the action, that there is too much or too little concentration in certain areas—all of these involving degrees of contrast or sameness according to the general effect intended.

Respect for the individual and his or her ideas is a noble, democratic sentiment and a cardinal code of conduct for the teacher who expects genuine and sustained interest from art students. Maintenance of a Socratic atmosphere of group debate and free evaluation ensures a continuous outlet and discipline for creative impulses. A further requisite is recognition: conscientious effort in art nearly always produces some real merits in a work, regardless of its overall quality. Recognition of these merits should always be given priority in any comments; the younger the child the more emphatic the recognition given should be. As the child develops emotional maturity, criticism may become more pointed and specific but should never be undiluted, nor should it ever include personal prejudice, sarcasm, or ridicule. A consuming interest in art can be completely aborted by a few intemperate words. There are undoubtedly vast resources of potential creativity that have been lost to us because of a well-meaning instructional faux pas.

"Appreciation" has been a much-abused term, one given such a variety of interpretations that it has lost much of its meaning. Artists are reluctant to use it because it implies a kind of clinical detachment from the art object that is alien to the concept of art. In addition, "appreciation" connotes a hushed funereal reverence and a passive acceptance of the assumed verdicts of tradition. This is the antithesis of the ideal classroom atmosphere typified by honest excitement and active inquiry.

Your authors see no justification for the grading of artwork at the elementary level. There are no reasonable standards by which children's art can be judged because it is unparalleled. Undoubtedly they *are* often judged, that is, some are liked better than others because they are seen from an adult perspective. Children are sometimes their own critics, by their own standards, but if they are dissatisfied or frustrated the work is usually ruthlessly discarded. It is difficult or impossible to ascertain this criticism. Really, the important thing is to let the children explore and enjoy themselves. The benefits of their work are mentioned elsewhere in this book. And, as to grades, and contrary to what some administrators may expect, the only reasonable explanation for an unsatisfactory performance would be nonattendance or a determined refusal to participate and these might be somehow rooted in the family. Older, or more mature, students and their conflicts with their growing understanding of reality are discussed elsewhere.

Art As a Subject Area

Our evaluations of art, the things we can learn from art, are valid only if they rise from the same principles of academic freedom associated with other areas of study. The classroom must be a forum for free and open discussion, unaffected by consideration of the things we are supposed to like or dislike. Art, with its rich traditions, deserves respect, but not the deference due the deceased; regardless of its age, art has something to say to us and, consequently, its own form of immortality.

Few subjects can be really understood without actual involvement; this is especially true of art, and even more so when dealing with children. No one can better understand the act of creation than the creator—children are peculiarly equipped to understand because children are *natural* creators, usually needing little encouragement to express themselves enthusiastically. Thus, just as every curriculum should include art, so should that art include its practice. Creativity is a cherished birthright, but as in other fields, it can be lost through disuse. The experiences gained through the continuing practice of art are invaluable as a springboard for the understanding of other forms of art.

Supplementary Teaching Aids

The teacher supervising creative art activities in the classroom should find some help in the principles stated elsewhere in this book, but the actual practice of art can, of course, be supplemented and enriched by a variety of other art experiences. For one thing there is the obvious factual material. Facts, however, should be introduced gradually and interestingly for young people and should *never* be presented as axiomatic. Feeling always has the priority in art, and feeling cannot be legislated or entirely intellectualized. If the teacher fails to make the information exciting or is dogmatic, an atrophy of the senses can set in that is all too common and has deprived so many people of so much pleasure.

The average teacher, even without benefit of specialized art training, is capable of stimulating and perpetuating creativity in children by applying simple principles of psychology. Deficiencies in training become monumentally important only if the teacher is unwilling to acknowledge them openly and admit that he or she can learn something from the students. Professional knowledge of the field should be acquired, but this qualification is of far less importance than the attitude of the person involved. The attitude of the art teacher is always evident in the illustrations with which he or she surrounds the students. A sylvan glade by Corot, a seventeenth-century Dutch still life, or a Blue Boy by Gainsborough may all be goods paintings, but have probably been seen so often that they are taken for granted. It is far better to have something that will attract attention and become a subject of controversy. Nothing is healthier than discourse if it is confined to logical premises; only by arguing a point can we come close to a determination of its validity. Art has never been intended to be taken for granted. A good artwork has always been a product of the controversy raging in the artist's mind, and it has usually aroused some degree of controversy when submitted to the public. By displaying works that are little known or stylistically strange, the teacher can augment the learning process and keep the interest and creative freedom of the art class at a high level. The works displayed should not be the kind of drab, dusty, and unnoticed art too often found in school buildings. Anything not working to stimulate children's sensations will deaden them; there is no middle ground.

If display of artworks is healthy, mere exposure is not enough; there must be the opportunity for *real* viewing, not just a passing glance. Artists are not amused when they overhear people making snap judgments as they race past artworks in a museum; it is evident that people like only what they expect to like. First impressions are often as misleading in judging art as they are in judging personalities. Repeated exposure to an artwork usually produces changed opinions. Every work displayed should be given an honest chance to make its point.

As artworks are seen, discussion should follow. At this point it should be conceded that art is an area in which many schoolteachers are often underprepared and frequently feel insecure in dealing with the subject. If such is the case, the teacher will simply have to learn along with his or her class, finding it a rewarding experience. As a first step in leading discussions, the teacher should be prepared with a preview of the material to be covered. Thus fortified, the instructor should play the role of interrogator, asking the children what the work means to them, what the artist might have intended, why a particular color was chosen, and so forth. Questions of this kind do not call for exact answers; it is enough that speculation takes place and that questions are debated. Ordinarily one has little trouble in getting often remarkably perceptive responses from children.

Enlarging Teacher Qualifications

If the teacher is fortunate enough to find the time to prepare for art as he or she does for other areas, some information on available resources would undoubtedly be appreciated. Any such suggestions would begin with books; in this area the situation has improved greatly. There have been an increasing number of books that address the basic issues in art in ways that are both comprehensible and interesting. A sampler list of resource books as well as other aids may be found at the end of this book. In addition to basic "appreciation" books, there are art history books of various levels of sophistication and books on techniques, educational theory, and biography. The latter are helpful in understanding the artist's experiences; with this, one can begin to understand the measure of the artist's accomplishments.

Encouraging Cultural Awareness

Art history is normally associated with upper-level students, but there is no reason younger children should be excluded from the subject. Indeed, when we consider that art can be related to virtually every other subject, it is clear that its history can be a germinal field for the study of humankind's past. The amazing developments in color slides and prints today make quality reproductions from every period and source accessible to all. Opaque, overhead, movie, and slide projectors are all common items in today's school inventory, featuring great fidelity and ease of operation. Excellent films on art for various age groups are available through many sources.

All of these resources can be used along with or in place of trips to museums. Children are invariably fascinated by exotically unfamiliar forms of expression, and viewing of any kind should always be accompanied by an opportunity for discussion in which there is a prompting of speculation on why the artist works as he or she does. The period and country in which the artist worked will help to account for this and will easily lead into some consideration of the many historical forces that shaped the style. Given advance notice, most museums can supply docents, or guides, who are experienced in explaining works of art to a variety of visiting groups.

Study must be kept within the limits of student comprehension but should be approached in an open-minded questioning manner to which the teacher can contribute some factual material. In such a way, the ageless reciprocity between history and art can be made an enlightening experience for student and teacher. It is also exciting, if somewhat unnerving, to discover the insight and empathy that youngsters display in their reactions to art, qualities that frequently outstrip those of their elders.

There is no place for rote memorization in art history for the young except for memorizing pictures, basic principles, and vocabulary. Precise fact should defer to generalized example, and the provocative and unfamiliar should be given priority over the taken-for-granted. Any information acquired should arise from initial reactions to the works themselves. These reactions should prompt questioning for which the teacher should be prepared; the teacher should, if possible, draw answers out of the pupils themselves through group discussion.

Art history can excite the young into new torrents of creativity, demonstrate that the artist is mirror and barometer of his or her society, and reaffirm that human history is meaningful.

Lastly, why not go to the source itself—the artist? Most communities have artists within reach, and an enterprising teacher should have little difficulty in finding an artist to open the studio or visit a class. Artists are usually very sensitive to

Children are invariably fascinated by exotically unfamiliar forms of expression. . . .
© James L. Shaffer

Chapter One

the interests and needs of children. They also like to talk about art and generally are not reluctant to discuss their own work.

It should not be assumed that suggestions for stimulating interest in art would be applied in the same way or in equal measure to all of the age groups found in the public schools. Greater student maturity carries with it a greater ability to discuss matters logically. The teacher is always best informed on these matters and has the responsibility to exercise ingenuity and judgment in the way things are brought before the class.

The teaching of art has already been alluded to in general terms. The references largely dealt with attitudes, motivations, and assessments. These matters are of critical importance because they are most instrumental in establishing the "personality" of the classroom. Needless to say, and risking redundancy, that personality should be open, informal, exciting, and optimistic, and should foster experimentation and discussion.

Although a classroom that has these attributes is certainly a good candidate for success, there must be some regimen that is the result of planning, effective execution, and control. An art class can easily degenerate into chaos without competent supervision.

Nevertheless, a regimen should not be misconstrued as regimentation. Creativity cannot flourish when administered with an iron hand. The art teacher's function is often a balancing act that fosters free expression within some parameters of order. The key to this is, of course, planning—planning not so different from that practiced in other areas of study. The tool for this is, probably to no one's surprise, the venerable lesson plan. Certainly this tool is familiar to the experienced teacher, but reference is made to it here for the benefit of those who have not had this advantage and to reinforce the idea that it can be used successfully in organizing an art program.

Lesson plans have taken many forms; this one is offered as an example and may be modified as necessary:

Project Title

1. Behavioral Objectives
   How may this project be related to some theme or another area of study? How can it be made relevant to the child? What growth of knowledge or understanding can be facilitated by the project? Are there mechanical skills to be learned? What kind of preparation is necessary? What kind of response is sought from the students?
2. Materials
   What kind of supplies are needed? How much of this can be provided by the student, and where can he or she find it? Is it readily available? What classroom equipment is necessary; can it be used safely?
3. Motivation
   How can the project be related to student interests? If interest is not present, how can it be stimulated? Field trips, discussions, audiovisual material, natural sources, and new media are possible ways to arouse interest. Do *not* ask the students what they want to do today!
4. Procedure
   A step-by-step breakdown of the technicalities of the project in easily understood terms. Examples: How to hold scissors correctly; how to knot a thread; how to fold a piece of paper. Logically sequence the project from beginning to end. Do *not* insist on everything being the same in the final product!

5. Assignment

What further use, if any, can be made of the product? Do not overemphasize utility; most art exists simply to be seen, understood, and enjoyed.

Examples: Explain to your parents how your puppet was made, think of a name for your puppet, think of a story to go along with your puppet.

6. Evaluation

a. Self

A critique of the project in terms of how it was taught and how it might be improved. Examples: Were the directions understood? Could everyone see? Was it a rewarding learning situation? Was independence of thought stressed? Was the project appropriate to the developmental level of most of the class?

b. Students

How did the class respond? Was enthusiasm mixed? Were instructions followed without difficulty? Did the students make the hoped for correlations? Was the project too easy or too difficult? Were the students pleased with their work?

It may be noticed that we have omitted specific age levels for the projects contained in this book. We have done so not out of neglect, but because we feel that the individual classroom teacher is the best judge about his or her students' capabilities. Children's motor skills and comprehension levels do not correlate neatly with chronological age. The teacher may be confronted with classes of mixed maturity, and this may necessitate mixed assignments. The challenge will be to present and guide the students through the material in a way that can create a meaningful interplay that is not demeaning to any segment of the class.

Most of these projects can be handled by a variety of age levels. Where exceptions exist, they are generally self-evident. Sometimes teacher trainees express the fear that certain projects are beneath the dignity of their students. It should be pointed out (and can be illustrated) that most great artists appreciate the direct approach of children's art, that many deliberately adopt childish styles, and that practically all of them regard children's art with great appreciation and often envy. Pablo Picasso, one of the most influential artists of the twentieth century, frequently reverted to a more simplistic, naive, and unsophisticated manner of working. He also employed art media that might be considered elementary, such as wax crayons and linoleum cuts. Nothing was beneath his interest; after all, it's not what you use, but what you do with it.

The Art World of the Child

Each child is a personality separate and distinct from all others. He or she is an incalculably complex product of a combination of formative influences that can occur only once.

Despite the many individual qualities, the child passes through definite cycles of development that are common to other children. Although these cycles are an inevitable part of growth, it is impossible to predict the time of their appearance or their duration. Stages are often cataloged according to chronological age, but this is only a measurement of convenience; actually, **development is geared to emotional maturity, which varies from child to child.**

It is very important for the teacher to understand and recognize cycles of child development as illustrated by the artwork created. Each cycle is characterized by certain abilities and attitudes, to which the art activities of the individual should be geared.

The following section is taken from the book *The Artist in Each of Us* by Florence Cane, a pioneer in new methods of art education and art therapy. Her experiences with children at all levels preeminently qualify her to speak on the characteristics of creative growth:

> Throughout the first seven years of a child's life, physical growth and muscular activity are predominant. During this period the child draws chiefly in lines (one dimension). The production is characterized by quantity. The child will not be interested in developing the many pictures he or she rapidly draws. At this stage the average child gets pleasure from scribbling and revelling in color regardless of form. A few children do develop further and begin to express their ideas more clearly.
>
> In the next period, roughly from the ages of seven to fourteen, the child develops sensations and feelings as well as the ability to observe the world. He or she becomes interested in two-dimensional form; quality asserts itself over quantity. The pupil works more slowly and is more demanding. Each picture must satisfy himself or herself as well as his or her companions. The child needs the approval of others, caring more about achieving goals. The child wants to learn how to do better. He or she still has the unconsciousness of a child, but is beginning to mature. The ages of ten to fourteen are a very free-flowing time before conflicts begin.
>
> The third period, roughly from fourteen to eighteen, includes adolescence. This period, initiated by the awareness of the third dimension, is coexistent with the pupil's deepening consciousness. Thought emerges and mixes with emotion. Self-criticism at this age becomes severe and, if the right direction is not given, the boy or girl may stop work altogether because of dissatisfaction with his or her efforts.

From Florence Cane, *The Artist in Each of Us,* 1983 revised edition. Copyright ©1983 Art Therapy Publications, Craftsbury Common, VT. Reprinted by permission.

Manipulative Stage

When children first discover art materials, they will explore endlessly, usually producing results that are unintelligible by average adult standards (see figs. 1.1 and 1.2). For children the joy of discovery is what is important; they are interested in seeing just what effects the media will produce. At times children give every evidence of regarding art as a very serious business, and at other times they will shriek with joy. Children frequently accompany their explorations with stories of some kind, but the subjects of these stories are rarely recognizable in their work. Children are always completely absorbed and are having fun, but are also perfecting coordination, discovering the world through new correlations, and learning the possibilities of new materials.

Symbolic Stage

As children continue to experiment, they will eventually discover their ability to produce likenesses (fig. 1.3). The images are not at all sophisticated and may seem crude and inaccurately observed. Actually, visual correlations are not important, and observation is very keen in terms of experience with things. The logic in the work is in terms of what is known about the subjects. For example, the scale of an object or person is in proportion to the importance attached to it.

FIGURE 1.1   *A collage titled "Just for Fun" by a five-year-old child.*

The child's interest in space in strictly limited to the flatness of the working surface. Things are freely rearranged according to an instinctive feeling for design and because they make a more tangible representation of the child's experiences with them. In figure 1.4 the sun is moved to the ground level, the man's hat is floating near the top of the page, and the mouth is made extremely large (because he was calling his son). In the symbolic stage, the child often uses recognizable images, but only as a means to an end—the end in this case being self-expression.

If the teacher insists on realism for its own sake, the expressive role of art is lost. The child has no comprehension of or interest in realism per se. Figure 1.5 is a standard hectograph picture in which the creativity of the child is limited to the application of color to prefabricated adult images. Figure 1.6, on the other hand, has been freely produced by the child on the basis of his or her own observations and decisions. It represents a child in a playground, with slides and swings floating in the sky. Figure 1.7 shows people getting into a boat. Figure 1.8 represents a rabbit in a box.

Representations of trains are made in the next reproductions (figs. 1.9 and 1.10). The first drawing has been made in tempera paint and the second in pencil. The pencil drawing combines the most representative views of train and tracks, the train being in profile, and the tracks as if seen from above. Both are aspects of the subjects that are most frequently observed. No effort has been made to integrate them into one common viewpoint. The tempera painting shows rain falling. The sky is represented by a symbol, a stripe across the top of the page. Such symbols are common in child art and, as far as the children are concerned, are perfectly adequate. Because of the use of such symbolic devices, the artwork of the young is usually very simple, having been abstracted down to a few essentials. It is an excellent example of brevity. It exemplifies expressive use of color; colors are used fearlessly and fully in context with the mood of the artist. (See fig. 1.11.)

Realistic Stage

With increasing maturity, usually beyond the age of eight, children become more factually oriented (fig. 1.12). They become more conscious of adult prototypes and with

FIGURE 1.2   *"House with Decoration" by a four-year-old child.*

FIGURE 1.3 *"Roy Had a Cold and Had to Stay in the House."*

FIGURE 1.4 *"A Man Calling His Son."*

FIGURE 1.5 *A hectographed adult image.*

FIGURE 1.6 *"A Child in a Playground with Slides and Swings."*

their increasing coordination begin to wonder about their ability to produce things more realistically. Children are, however, still children and unable to cope with adult standards. If the teacher preaches the virtues of realism at this emotional level, the results can be disastrous. It is far better to point out that professional artists do not feel impelled to work realistically and that expression is the main purpose of art.

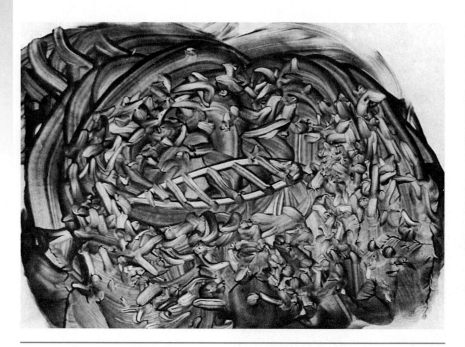

FIGURE 1.7   *"People Trying to Get into a Boat." A finger painting by a five-year-old child.*

FIGURE 1.8   *"A Rabbit in a Box."*

FIGURE 1.9   *Representation of a train made with tempera paint.*

Chapter One

FIGURE 1.10 *Pencil representation of a train in profile with tracks as if seen from above.*

FIGURE 1.11 *"Crossroad." Learn to understand and recognize what the child is thinking by learning to understand what the child is trying to convey in his or her work. Notice the bird's-eye view of the crossroad combined with profile views of the houses and automobiles.*

As children grow into adolescence, misconceptions about the proper place of realism and technique become magnified. (See fig. 1.13.) It is a period of insecurity in which they gradually become aware of the vast complexities of the world and their own limitations in relation to them. Youngsters become thirsty for factual knowledge. Actual information about things is important before attempting to draw them. This is a very critical period for student and teacher alike. The child's feelings of inferiority call for constant encouragement and sympathetic understanding. It is important that young artists be guided in such a subtle way that they feel they are finding their own answers; this will buoy up self-confidence. More than any other, this level of development calls for teachers with a good background in art,

FIGURE 1.12   *"Three Sailboats."*

FIGURE 1.13   *In this illustration the child is beginning to show some awareness of the distances that separate objects from each other but is still unable to relate things in terms of their usual proportions.*

who understand the field so well that they can constantly provide a stimulus through the introduction of new materials, techniques, and illustrations. It is important for children to see, with their own eyes, that artists have always been most successful when they have remained true to themselves, when they have evolved a truly personal style based on a thorough knowledge of the styles of other artists.

Dealing with Variable Talents

"Variable talents," as used in the context of this section, refers to art ability above or below the classroom norm in quality. *All* children need tender, loving, and patient guidance. We cannot say that any child deserves more than another, but with exceptional children the emphases may change. The gifted child may require an unusual amount of *guidance*, whereas the child with below normal ability needs the teacher's *patience* more than anything else.

We have identified the developmental cycles of a child's creative growth (manipulative, symbolic, realistic). Although all children move through these cycles, some do so more quickly than others; this is one of the characteristics of the gifted child. It is not the *only* hallmark of exceptional talent, however. Gifted children absorb and correlate material much more quickly than average children. They have more to say and say it in an original manner. Very often they are impatient with the general classroom assignments and wish to move ahead to something more challenging. The manipulative and symbolic stages rarely create any unusual difficulties for the art teacher. The child and teacher most often experience problems when the child arrives at the *realistic* stage. At this stage children are not only more sophisticated in their concepts, but they desperately want to draw with visual accuracy, to do things that "look like" something. Children experience frustration when they compare their works with adult products. The teacher must encourage and motivate children who arrive at the realistic stage earlier than their peers. The teacher must assure these children that skill in realistic drawing will improve with time and that extreme realism is *not* the only factor in quality art. Evidence that the child is on the threshold of the realistic stage includes the following:

1. Indications of space and depth, usually through overlapping.
2. Some accuracy of scale and proportion.
3. Equating higher levels on the page with distance.
4. Attempts to show action.
5. Efforts at composition.
6. Shading to show solidity.
7. Attempts at perspective.
8. Light and dark patterns.

Most classroom teachers have not had enough art experience to counsel their students in such matters, but students may lose interest in art if the teacher does not assist them. If an art supervisor is available, it would certainly help to draw that person into a greater collaboration with the student; also, there are sometimes artists in the community with whom a relationship can be established. If this kind of help is not available, the teacher might indulge in some study in order to upgrade his or her knowledge of art. These children need help but not the imposition of unachievable objectives; they seek criticism, but too much can be devastating—clearly, a delicate matter.

We have not designated or created any specific activities for the gifted child because the principle determinant for the gifted child is perceptive, sympathetic, and enlightened guidance. Yet, there are some ways in which the activities in this book can be adapted to satisfy the exceptional talent of the gifted child. First, it may be simply enough that the child does a superior job with the activities. Then, if *this* is not enough, the activity may be enlarged, complicated, or made more meaningful and challenging. If *that* is not enough, the child could be allowed to work on an entirely different activity from the rest of the class, possibly as the result of his or her own choice. (This does smack somewhat of elitism and might cause resentment; the teacher is the best judge of this action.)

Another alternative for the gifted child could involve municipalities that have museums or art clubs offering weekend opportunities for art work and supervision. Often this supervision is of a highly professional level; beware that frustratingly adult standards are not imposed on the child.

In contrast to the gifted child, the child with below normal ability may be affected by mental deficiency, physical impairment, emotional disturbances, or a combination of these factors, which may result in a slower pace, a shorter interest span, or a startling deviation from the expected pattern of activity. Because motor skills are often inadequate, art activities requiring motor skills are superb training for these children but they should be kept at a simple level. Sometimes a visual or auditory handicap has been unrecognized—the teacher should be alert to this possibility and should notify parents if a handicap is suspected. Emotional disturbances frequently result from difficult family situations or from sexual dilemmas. Sometimes the root cause of the problem can be subtly elicited from the child, but if not, an inquiry (*very* subtle) should be made. If there is any sign of child abuse, it must be reported to the proper authorities. Generally the resolution of such problems is beyond the teacher's reach. One avenue of discovery and help may lie in art therapy, a burgeoning field. Certified art therapists are available; in their hands art can often be a healing activity. Parents are frequently reluctant to acknowledge their children's problems *if* they are aware of them. They may also disavow any blame in domestic settings that adversely affect the children. Parent-teacher relations can become strained in such situations and must be treated with great delicacy; otherwise the welfare of the child is overlooked. Sometimes the only recourse is to place the child in the hands of a professional counselor or therapist, with parental permission.

Positive and Negative Suggestions on Creative Art Teaching

The following remarks are intended primarily for the classroom teacher who has little specialized instruction in the methods of teaching art. If the suggestions often seem contradictory, it is because no exact recommendation can be provided for every situation, nor can every situation be anticipated. Effectiveness in art teaching, as in any other form of teaching, eventually focuses on the individual teacher's judgment and taste. These comments should therefore be regarded as suggestions, not admonitions. They are included to suggest some of the effective methods and attitudes that are peculiar to the field of art. Perhaps the most important of these is the reminder that an art class is a workshop of ideas and materials, not a standard lecture recitation situation. In such an environment, overguidance is probably worse than underguidance; rules, formulas, and the "tried and true" are of little value.

negative suggestions

Avoid the imposition of a subject unless the child is completely without ideas; if so, merely suggest, don't prescribe.

Don't create the impression that art is merely busywork or a time filler. Don't set the wheels in motion and turn your attention to other matters.

Don't be surprised by the ideas that pour out of the efforts of the very young, and don't criticize them, even if they prove embarrassing. The children are merely reflecting the events around them and their reactions to them.

Don't worry about the objects drawn or the method of depiction until the students reach an age level at which it is natural for them to seek help.

Don't hover over children who exhibit anxiety over the outcome of their work.

When using student works as examples, avoid extremes of praise or faultfinding.

positive suggestions

Allow the child free rein in expression; art may be the means to several goals to the young artist. Some are:

1. A feeling of self-confidence in having control of materials.
2. A means through which self-expression can be fostered more fully than in other media.
3. A way of better understanding the world and one's place in it.
4. The satisfaction (rarely obtained these days) that comes with the expression of the basic creative impulse latent in all of us.

Use art as an integral part of the day's activities. Demonstrate an active and sincere interest in the things being done.

Understand that children create emotionally and intellectually. Their works are illustrative of their deepest feelings and, as such, are deserving of sympathetic understanding, not criticism.

Children are only interested in demonstrating the reality of the mind and emotions, not the reality of outward appearances.

Children need a certain degree of privacy; give them a feeling of independence.

Children are sensitive people, show equal appreciation and concern for all members of the class.

positive suggestions

Give students of all ages opportunities to have contact with art products. Show universality of taste. Let children develop a long-lasting appreciation of art based on their considered judgments, but see to it that honest consideration is given in every case.

Relate your art instruction to those things that are part of the child's own experiences.

Encourage children to show and explain their work to others in the class, thereby creating an atmosphere of mutual interest.

Maintain certain standards in regard to the care of materials and the cleanliness of work area and person.

Attach fundamental importance to creativity and individual thinking.

Teach the child to develop taste by making use of good design principles in bulletin boards and other displays. Emphasize the art concepts of the twentieth century wherever possible.

Point out correlations and relationships in artworks and between art and other fields. Help make art a vital part of an awakening process.

If you have had any experience in art that gives you confidence, do your own art teaching. Elementary art is primarily a matter of guidance and encouragement. You can provide this for your own students better than anyone else if you take the trouble to acquaint yourself with the fundamental art concepts.

Encourage pictorial ideas based on personal activities.

Lend sympathetic assistance to those who don't know where to go with their work. Children expect and deserve help occasionally; this in art is usually a matter of motivation by "talking it over."

Stress the use of class art problems that involve a minimum of instruction. These should stimulate the student's appreciation for visual effects and afford an opportunity for exploration.

negative suggestions

Don't limit the child's art consumption to the styles for which you may happen to have a personal preference.

Don't always expect students to show enthusiasm for subjects that are totally unrelated to their own lives.

Don't isolate pupils from each other or discourage a certain amount of conversation if it is of a constructive nature.

Don't let freedom of expression lead to abandonment of good work habits.

Discourage copying and reliance on rules and formulas whenever possible.

Avoid the use of trite, unimaginative, and outdated pictures and materials in the classroom.

Art should not be pigeonholed and isolated from other areas. Its concern is humankind and total existence.

Don't relinquish your responsibility in the teaching of art to another person, unless that person's credentials as an art teacher are clearly superior to your own.

Don't expect precise, accurate, academic drawings of stereotyped objects. Such drawings have limited value only for more mature individuals.

Don't expect complete self-reliance from immature children, or feel that their ideas will be inexhaustible.

By all means, avoid the use of ready-made art techniques, such as coloring books, number painting, etc. Such devices slam the door on sensitivity and originality, and make art a lifeless, mechanical routine.

negative suggestions	positive suggestions
One cannot expect identical or even very similar results from the diverse personalities normally encountered in the classrooms. Don't demand conformity.	Treat each child as a unique personality. Encourage the child to reveal himself or herself in the art, and try to understand the child and his or her problems better from this revelation through his or her work.
Don't work on a student's project, unless the student asks to see something demonstrated, and do not, if you draw on the work, make it a formula to copy.	Let children do their own work; give them the immense satisfaction that comes from having been solely responsible for the conception and execution of a piece of work.
Don't discourage conversation and a certain degree of class motion.	Expect and encourage greater informality during the class art period. Real art is a matter of expression and cannot flourish under duress. It depends on a contagion of the spirit and a free exchange of ideas.
Don't create the impression that art is child's play in its entirety, or that creation is always unalloyed fun.	Permit students to grapple with problems occasionally. Let them see that the degree of success is often in direct proportion to the amount of perspiration expended, and that the greatest artworks frequently seem simple only because the artist has had the judgment and patience to reduce things to elementals.
Don't lavish praise on children to the extent that they begin to expect acknowledgment of their genius.	Use constructive criticism. Instead of saying "that's bad," try to find a solid solution or imply that something else might work better.
Don't always confuse results with intentions. Accept results if they turn out well, but point out that there comes a time when end products are not enough.	Be honest with yourself and your students. Admit to them that the happy results of the art projects occur as an accident or as a result of the special disciplines of the projects.
Don't try to force gifted or low-ability children into the same mold as the average-ability children. Try to set up special activities for those whose talents are extraordinarily great or small.	Allow children to progress according to their abilities.
Children should not be "turned off" when they are beginning to respond, nor should they have time for distractions.	Ration the time according to the complexities of the activity.
Don't always expect ideas to flow in a torrent. There are fertile and infertile creative periods in any person.	Use all available visual aids that are of good quality. These will serve as an effective stimulus.

Leading Questions

The Socratic method is often used to stimulate thinking and, on occasion, to challenge certain attitudes. Provocative questions can be subjected to consideration and debate. This interplay could be usefully employed among teachers and among teachers and their more mature students. Some examples of leading questions follow:

What is the frequency of your visits to museums and/or art exhibits? (Most likely *in*frequently)

How often do you listen to music? (most likely *much* more often)

Do you generally judge a piece of music on its reproduction of natural sounds? On its "message"? What? Could, or should, art be judged similarly?

Do you think a sunset could be beautiful if there were no one around to view it? Is the beauty within us? What is its source?

Do you prefer movies with happy endings? Does this have anything to do with the overall quality of the film? Should the mood or subject matter of an artwork dictate our evaluation of it?

Do you admire designs in home furnishings or clothing? Can you admire nonfunctional designs in an artwork? If not, why not?

Do you feel that you have had a special talent in each of your required fields of study? If you could handle these without special talent, could you create art without the special talent that many people think is required? Who is the "king" of rock music? The father of the atom bomb? The father of "modern" art? Are we regrettably uninformed on some subjects?

Do you, or have you, found disagreement with your parents on matters of taste? Could we be imprisoned by our generation?

Doubtless one could think of similarly venturesome questions.

Definitions of Art

All of these definitions are and have been argued, but it may probably be assumed that each has some essence of what we think of as art. Different definitions may more properly apply to certain types or styles of art.

1. The expression of human experience (Dewey)
2. The formal expression of a conceived image in terms of a given medium (Cheney)
3. Intuition (Bergson; Croce)
4. An expression controlled by a certain aspect of the mind
   a. Emotion (Tolstoy)
   b. The will (Nietzsche; Freud)
   c. The intellect (Aquinas)
5. The making of a form produced by the cooperation of all the faculties of the mind
   a. Significant form (Bell)
   b. Eloquence (Burke)
   c. Unexpected inevitability of formal relations (Fry)
   d. A unified manifold which is pleasure giving (Mather)
   e. A diagram (or paradigm) with a meaning that gives pleasure (Listowel)
   f. That which gives pleasure apart from desire (Aquinas)
   g. Objectified pleasure (Santayana)
6. Imitation (Note: what is imitated?)
7. Right making; skill (Note: skill at making what?)
8. Propaganda. Emphasis on communication rather than expression. Implies some conscious effort to influence conduct.

Some, if not all, of these are obviously subject to interpretation. Their introduction would most often spark a lively debate. There is no unanimous agreement on any *one* of them!

Art, Aesthetics, Art History

We generally think that we can recognize art when we see it but, as can be seen from the previous section, it has had many divergent definitions. What is art for one person may not qualify as art for another person. The nature of art history seems self-evident; it is a vast subject with occasional new discoveries and frequent reinterpretations. Aesthetics, according to one dictionary reference, pertains to the appreciation or criticism of the "beautiful." It is a compound of objective analysis, psychology, sociology, and philosophy of art. Aesthetics is a complicated subject on which much has been written and little totally resolved! This is particularly true with the introduction of the term "beauty." Definitions of beauty have changed with the times, and are changing radically in our lifetimes. In some circles beauty is regarded as obsolete.

The average teacher does not need total immersion in the study of art history and aesthetics. Some study, however, will yield benefits in the classroom. It will teach more discrimination in the selection of artworks to be displayed in the room and will provide the teacher with information to be dispensed on the origins of those artworks. Additionally, the accumulated knowledge will give some foundation for the discussions of art (as recommended earlier in the book).

Art history is objective, but aesthetics is subject to a variety of opinions. In some instances the discussions might alter opinions as to the value of a work, but one must be careful not to *impose* values. Younger children will probably decide on favorites independent of any explanation, whereas older students may be inclined to change their opinions, particularly as regards recent art, as the artist's intentions are made clear. Examination of ethnic and geographically exotic art is interesting and should be encouraged. We think such studies will be fascinating and instructive to both the teachers and their pupils!

Most of us associate art with beauty and *expect* art to be beautiful even if unable to define what that beauty is. In the previous section of this book, a definition of art is not easily found—beauty is equally elusive. It has meant different things to different people through history. The field of aesthetics evolved in an effort to find an answer to that critical and confounding question: What is beauty?

Historical cultures have had their own concepts of beauty and our contemporary responses to them vary. For the ancient Greeks, beauty was in the idealized human form and, in most cases, we can accept this as beauty. We can also accept the somewhat revised Roman version of Greek art, although it is sometimes too realistic for us. Medieval art is still indigestible for many of us, but Renaissance art is almost a seminal type of beauty for a great number of our contemporaries. Raphael, for instance, is the epitome of this kind of beauty, though some find it overly saccharine. A good deal of the art following the Renaissance is reasonably acceptable until stumbling blocks were erected during the nineteenth century.

During that century preceding our own, there were many momentous changes in art that confounded the public (and many artists who clung to the old ways). Impressionism, generally looked on with favor today, found a hostile audience. The Postimpressionism that followed experienced only slightly mitigated hostility. With the advent of Cubism, Expressionism, Abstraction, Futurism, and the other "isms" of the twentieth century, the separation between innovative artists and the layperson became an ever-widening abyss. The accelerating changes in every phase of our lives were paralleled by unavoidable corresponding changes in art and most people were not able to adapt to them. The practical results of change (automobiles, washers, television) could be appreciated but nonutilitarian art changes were not easily accepted. There is a ray of light, however; our technology has made all forms of art (artistic beauty?) accessible and it seems that some of the barriers to expanded taste have gradually eroded.

Let us see what aspects of art history have been at least mildly repugnant: Greece—generally liked, but nudity displayed; Roman—less idealized, the *un*pleasant coexisting with the pleasant; Medieval—a rather alien language of art to many, but considered "beautiful" by some; Romanticism—the occasional violence and unfamiliar settings are thought by some to be distasteful; Postimpressionism—radical change of styles from those preceding, frequently depressing instead of exalted subjects; Cubism and other "isms" (many quite different from each other)—no visible subject matter, seemingly inept and irrational, satirical and impenetrably personal.

But what is liked? Judging from the above we like, first of all, the familiar—an inheritance of taste from family, friends, and associates. We like the understandable, even though there is frequently little effort to understand the nonunderstandable. Perhaps, above all, we like certain subjects that can be recognized. They must also be reasonably familiar and understandable, acceptable to our peers, somewhat idealized or sentimental and "pleasant" as opposed to moody or threatening in their themes.

If *subject* is so important to us, it merits further investigation. Regrettably, as with art and beauty, subject is another term that is almost undefinable. Superficially subject designates objects, themes, and persons. There is also subject in abstract art, though less visible. In such art, the subject may be simply an idea or a particular use of an element or elements. For most laypersons the subject needs to have the instant recognizability of those objects, themes, or persons because beauty is often judged by this re-presenting.

There are qualifying factors, however. As stated before, the subject should be moral, pleasant, or uplifting. But a complication enters. What if we have a work that meets these criteria but is badly executed? Would it be beautiful? On the other hand, imagine a work that has none of those criteria but is expertly executed; could it be beautiful? Many great artists have created (beautiful?) works based on gross subjects. And, surely, not all persons, even of similar backgrounds, would agree on the beauty of a given subject.

There are conclusions to be drawn from this: Beauty, to the beholder, must be based on the artist's vision, skill, and interpretation of a subject irrespective of the nature of the subject. Additionally, the observer must be endowed with similar gifts, in some degree, to detect and appreciate the beauty; it is a two-way street. The emergence of a new style, or a new way of looking at things, in art can produce some consternation and a period of evaluation. Thus, we must often have the consensus of sensitive experts through the years to finally affirm the merits of artworks, and, ultimately, the public may be willing to accept this assessment. The average person does not have the background of an expert, but he or she can view visual art, study it, and learn from it, and, in the process, advance his or her understanding and taste. Yes, beauty is in the eye of the beholder, but we must ask what lies behind that eye. It was once said of an artist that "he only has an eye, but what an eye!" An interesting comment with an equally interesting implication; obviously there must be more than the eye involved in the creation and appreciation of beauty.

Beauty, whatever it is, does not seem to be universally sought in much of today's art. Many artists are in revolt against idealistic or comfortable subjects and refined technique. There are styles of intense realism in which such considerations might be inappropriate. The artists who produce such work might conceivably consider it beautiful (although they would be unlikely to use the term), but it would be an alien type of beauty for many of us. Perhaps beauty is ripe for redefinition.

Safety in the Art Classroom

In recent years, people have become increasingly aware of the danger of pollutants in the environment. This concern has now extended into the classroom. Although we have always been dimly conscious of the need for safety, the scope of the dangers was little known, and there was never a systematic study of the effects of the use (more often misuse) of materials in the educational system. This situation is now being remedied. Various agencies are imposing regulations and limitations on the use of supplies and equipment thought to contain hazards. In art, the first awakening to this need occurred at the professional, college, and university levels. Artists and art students were using, without restraint or protective devices, such threatening materials as resins, lacquers, acids, and solvents. The unfortunate result was an increase in injuries and deaths.

Although the more dangerous and toxic items are not ordinarily found in the elementary and junior high schools, there are still enough dangers to indicate the need for caution and careful supervision. In some states (California, Tennessee, Oregon, Illinois, and Florida), legislation has been passed that bans the use of toxic art materials in the elementary school classroom.

Dangers can arise from unexpected sources, and there is a need to disseminate information on these sources. The Center for Occupational Hazards is performing this function by collecting reports on hazardous substances and practices. The information gathered is circulated by means of books, lectures, and articles in regular publications such as the *Art Hazard News*. Subscriptions to the periodicals published by this group are recommended for all school systems. Certainly, the *Art Hazard News* is a must for art teachers. Subscriptions may be obtained by writing the center at 5 Beekman Street, New York, NY 10038.

One article in the *News* so clearly illustrates the incipient dangers that it is reproduced here in its entirety. It is entitled "The Young at Art" and was written by Monona Rossol, M.S., M.F.A., the Information Center Director. It is, of course, only one of many articles available on the subject.*

Some of the most important and interesting calls received at the Center for Occupational Hazards are those from Poison Control Centers asking for our help in determining the ingredients in art materials. The frequency of these calls has increased greatly since November 1979, when our service was added to the list of resources on POISONDEX—the computer-generated poison control identification and management system available to nearly 900 Poison Control Centers in the U.S. and Canada. An examination of some of the calls received by the Center for Occupational Hazards demonstrates the need for continuing and increasing efforts in disseminating art hazard information.

The most common calls from Poison Centers involve ingestion of an art material by a child. Among them are calls about children who have eaten artists' paints. One toddler chewed through a tube of flake (lead) white oil paint; another child ate dyed crystal paper (for transfer dyeing); still another ate the colored knobs from the ends of the center spikes of artificial flowers; and a number of children have eaten a variety of materials related to ceramics, such as glazes and stains.

Almost a third of the calls we receive from Poison Control Centers involve ceramic materials. Besides those about children, others have been about adults. One woman accidentally inhaled a powdered ceramic stain which spilled into her face when she tried to retrieve its container from a high shelf. Another call concerned a 58-year-old woman with an irregular electroencephalogram which her doctor attributed to her use of manganese dioxide as a clay colorant.

Chapter One

Then there are miscellaneous calls: a boy, with lead-poisoning symptoms, who had the habit of chewing the ends of his oil paint brushes while he worked; a girl with suspected cyanide poisoning from a silverplating accident; two complaints about fumes from heat-pressing decals on polyester T-shirts; a series related to an outbreak of dermatitis among young adults who attended a face-painting party; a question about inhalation of smoke from burning ironwood and newsprint; an inquiry about fumes from using dye strippers (to remove dye from fabric); a boy who accidentally injured his eye with a colored copy pencil; and a 17-year-old boy who, for some reason, chewed a considerable quantity of "Dippity-Do" dyed paper.

Poison Control Centers usually call us when they lack information about ingredients in a particular art material which may be affecting someone's health. Although we often can provide this information, in many cases it is not readily available. In a number of instances, Poison Control Centers have called us after they have been unable to reach the manufacturer at the address on the product label because the company has moved or changed its name. In these cases, calls to large art suppliers or to trade magazines which advertise similar products have been useful. Often tracking down a manufacturer can take a day or longer. In one case, we never have been able to find the company, and we believe it is likely that the firm was very small and has gone out of business. We have had equally bad luck in reaching foreign manufacturers.

A day or longer in answering Poison Control calls is sometimes far too long. When a call involves accidental ingestion and when emergency room personnel are standing by for ingredient information, we do not have time to track down elusive manufacturers. In these cases it is sometimes possible to use other label information to narrow down the number of likely ingredients. For instance, if a product is known to contain organic solvents and the label also states that the product is inflammable, we can eliminate many solvents because only a limited number are inflammable. Sometimes the label's directions for use will contain clues about ingredients. For example, some ceramic products are called glazes, but the directions show that they are not to be fired but are to be applied to the finished ware and left to dry. This information means that the product is not actually a glaze, but a varnish or paint material. But the directions on a container of true ceramic glaze, too, can be useful. By combining information about the firing temperature, the type of kiln in which the glaze is to be fired, and the glaze color, we can narrow possibilities of actual compounds in the glaze.

Using label information to guess about ingredients is not ideal. And we resort to this step only when better information is not available.

There is no substitute for accurate knowledge of a product's ingredients. Some simple rules can help artists and others avoid situations in which ingredient information is unobtainable.

1. Don't buy unlabeled products or products whose labels are damaged or covered by price stickers.
2. Keep label information with the product at all times. Do not transfer products to unlabeled containers, remove labels, or allow spills to obliterate labels.

3. Write to manufacturers for Material Safety Data Sheets and other toxicological data. At the time of purchase ask the supplier for any additional product information he might have.
4. Keep a file of package inserts, directions, Material Safety Data Sheets, and other collected information. Make sure that the file is kept in good order and is handy in case of accident.

Although these rules apply especially to situations where young children might come in contact with art materials, our file of Poison Control calls suggests that accidents involving art materials can happen to anyone, no matter what age. Every studio, whether used by the young or old, warrants such vigilance.

One cannot, in every case, anticipate and forestall accidents. With some simple precautions one can make the classroom a safer place to work. The teacher must always be vigilant while overseeing a class in which dangerous situations can develop; even a pen point can cause a puncture wound. Scissors should always have blunted tips. Small children should use draw tools for linoleum cutting. Even simple tools can cause damage. It would be wise to take inventory to determine whether tools should be altered or replaced. When possible, materials should carry the label CP or AP indicating certification by The Art and Craft Materials Institute, Inc. The label certifies the nontoxicity of the item. In California, Tennessee, Oregon, Illinois, and Florida (where the use of toxic art materials in the classroom is banned), labels listing acute and chronic health hazards are mandatory on all art and craft products that contain toxic ingredients. Other labels may warn of danger, and if material is seen to be or suspected to be dangerous, it should be stored in an inaccessible, locked storage area.

In the ideal situation, a school nurse should always be available during school hours. The teacher should establish a close working relationship with the nurse, making him or her aware of the perils that can accompany an art program. Therefore, the nurse can see that appropriate medical supplies are stocked. Parents should be queried as to any known allergies the children may have. This information should be on file for emergency treatment.

In most cases, troubles arise as the result of the following:

1. Inhalation. This trouble suggests the need for adequate ventilation, particularly where fumes and gases are involved.
2. Ingestion. Materials used should be nontoxic and carefully monitored while in use. Children love to put things in their mouths.
3. Absorption. Some materials can be absorbed through the skin and affect internal organs. Aprons, gloves, and sometimes even goggles must be worn.
4. Electrocution. Cords and plugs should be inspected. All electrical equipment must be grounded properly.
5. Burns. These can result from the careless use of irons, stoves, and molten materials, as well as acids and alkalis.

The Department of Health Services—State of California has developed a list of acceptable art products to be used in the elementary classrooms. This forty-page list entitled "Art and Craft Materials Acceptable for Kindergarten and Grades 1–6" and the California guidelines for the safe use of art and craft materials in schools are available from the Center for Safety in the Arts as a public service. The cost is minimal and includes any updates done by the California Department of Health Services during the year following your purchase. To obtain this material, write to the Center for Safety in the Arts, 5 Beekman Street, Suite 1030, New York, NY 10038.

The Center for Occupational Hazards offers a wealth of information on hazardous materials and practices. Obviously, space forbids the inclusion of all of this information; we can, however, reproduce a partial list of art materials too toxic for use in public schools:

lead-containing materials

- Lead-pigmented paints and print-making inks
- Enamels fired onto metals (except Vitrearc brand)
- Lead glazes, ceramic glaze chemicals, and lead fruits

asbestos

- Sculpture stones, soapstones, steatite, serpentine, greenstone
- Asbestos gloves and other products
- Some talcs used in some glazes, white clays, and slips
- Instant papier-mâchés
- Vermiculite

aerosol spray cans

- All aerosol sprays are too hazardous except for outdoor use or in ventilated spray booths

materials too toxic for children under twelve

- All solvents, such as mineral spirits, turpentine, and solvent-containing rubber cements, glues, shellacs, paints, inks, and permanent felt-tip markers
- Oil paints
- Ceramic glazes and enamels
- Paints or pigments in powdered form and pastels
- Photographic chemicals
- Wallpaper paste

known or suspected carcinogens

- Some solvents like benzene, carbon tetrachloride, and chloroform
- Some ceramic glaze chemicals including chrome oxide, chromates, and uranium oxide
- Some paint and print-making pigments including barium yellow, chrome yellow, diarylide yellow, lithol red, molybdate orange, pthalocyanine blue and green, strontium yellow, and zinc yellow

There is also a recommended safety reading list for schools; all are published by the Center for Occupational Hazards:

articles (a partial listing)

- *Electric Kiln Emissions and Ventilation*
- *Health and Safety in Schools*
- *Teaching Art to High-Risk Groups*

data sheets (a partial listing)

- *Are Public School Art Materials Safe?*
- *Art Painting*
- *Asbestos Substitutes*
- *Ceramics*
- *Children and Art Materials*

- *Children's Art Supplies Can Be Toxic* (lists products authorized to bear the CP Certified Products Seal and the AP Approved Products Seal of the Certified Products and Certified Labeling Bureau of the Arts and Crafts Institute, Inc.)
- *Craft Dyeing*
- *Labeling Problems of Arts and Crafts Materials*
- *Lead Glazes and Food*
- *Safety Rules for Power Tool Operation*
- *Silk Screen Printing Hazards*
- *Silver Soldering*
- *Stained Glass*

miscellaneous

- *Health Hazards in the Arts and Crafts* (a 16½ × 20 inch multicolored wall chart, with hazards and precautions)

Use of the Computer in Art

New technology has always been exciting to artists because of their interest in experimenting and using new ways to communicate. The computer is certainly one of the most important advances in technology and is starting to be used in the field of art. The capabilities of the computer change by the minute and new software becomes available every day. Because of the rapid development and improvement of this tool, it may take some time before it becomes evident which particular aspects will be judged the most important to the artist.

Before educators include the computer in the list of media, some questions they will need to ask are:

1. Are there enough computers to accommodate the class?
2. What is the computer's capacity?
3. What software is compatible with the computer?
4. How much money is available to spend on software?
5. Would students be able to use the computer and programs as a reinforcement tool for the information taught by the teacher?

There are programs for drawing, painting, and animation available. Some of the titles are:

Dabbler Paint Program is an electronic paint program, simulating natural mediums, that combines interactive art tutorials with graphic technology.

Sketcher 1-0 is a gray scale paint program that simulates the tools and textures of natural media with special image-editing capabilities.

Fine Artist Software has a complete palette of colors, a selection of brushes, and a lot of background colors and patterns. Choose from over 100 clip art images or create them. Compatible with *Creative Writer Software*.

Paint Toolbox includes 38 activities that deal with shape, color wheel, balance, dominance, perspective, distortion, and some animation.

Blazing Paddles is an all-in-one illustrator. Paint with a variety of brushstrokes, airbrush, and insert ovals, lines, rectangles, texture, and shapes to create pictures. Color mixing allows over 200 textured hues. It includes 5 text fonts and 10 shape tables.

Kid Pix 2 introduces the world of computer graphics that can be used across the curriculum. Very simple on-screen tools and tool options feature their own sounds and include "wacky brushes" and rubber stamps.

Take 1 Deluxe is an animation tool for creating computer movies.

The CD-ROM selections in art history include *History Through Art Series:*

Ancient Greece	Ancient Rome	Middle Ages	The Renaissance
The Baroque	The Enlightenment	The Romanticism	The Modern Era
The Twentieth Century			

Galleries and museums are beginning to put some of their collections on CD-ROM so that a great deal of information is available on a small disk. Some available now are: *Great Painting from Frick Collection; Art Gallery CD from the National Gallery, London; Ancient Egyptian Art–Brooklyn Museum;* and *Master Works of Japanese Painting–Etsuko and Joe Price Collection.*

Effective Use of Display Areas and Bulletin Boards

Bulletin boards can make learning a pleasure for children by surrounding them with stimulating and decorative displays. All areas of school study can profit by a creative presentation of subject material.

Display areas should be changed frequently to maintain student interest, with the frequency of change depending upon a great many intangibles; the interest period of pictorial matter is generally shorter than that of a more technical nature. The teacher will have to sense the saturation point and make arrangements for new displays. He or she should make sure that out-of-date material is removed immediately, and that items of timely interest are posted promptly.

In addition to their usefulness in the classroom, bulletin boards can announce events and record activities of general interest. In so doing, they also help to enrich halls and corridors and intensify school spirit.

The effectiveness of a bulletin board, regardless of its content, depends upon its arrangement. Arranging a display on a bulletin board is a design problem that includes consideration of size, shape, color, texture, light and dark, variety, balance, and repetition.

The following brief suggestions will be of some help in developing a successful display.

1. Harmonize the shapes to be placed on the bulletin board with the structural lines of the board as shown in the illustration directly below.

2. The busyness of the arrangement confuses the basic purpose of a bulletin board: communication.

3. The background area around the shapes placed on the bulletin board should be as interesting as the shapes themselves.

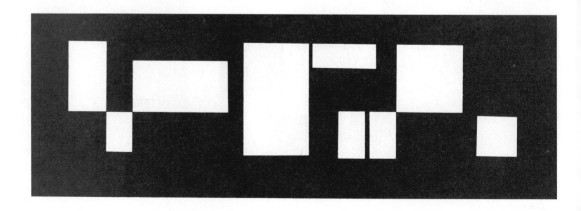

4. Always allow a larger margin at the bottom than at the top or sides. This principle also applies to the matting of pictures (see pp. 330–334).

5. One color or texture distributed throughout the display can serve to unify the bulletin board. This is easily accomplished by mounting the subjects on a particular color or textured surface.

6. Think of the space to be decorated as if it were a scale, and *balance formally* or *informally* as shown.

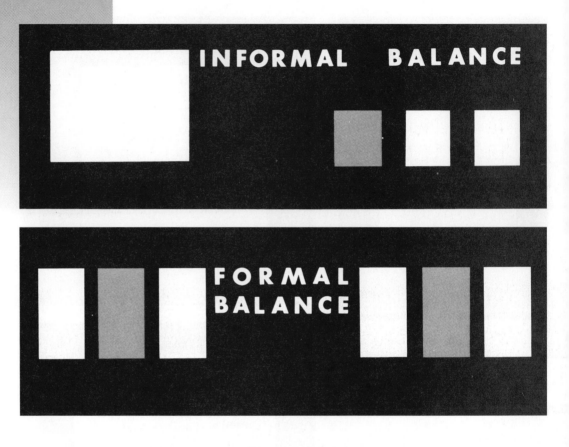

7. If lettering is to be incorporated in the display, it should be legible and concise—one or two words, a short phrase, or a short question. A title is of little value if it cannot be read quickly. Lettering should be considered an integral part of every display, but avoid lettering that must be read diagonally or from top to bottom.

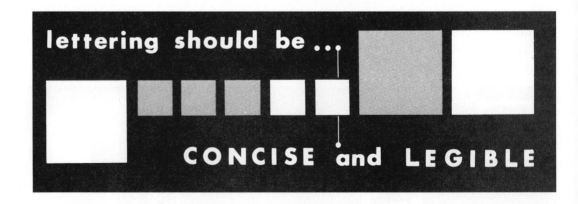

8. If lettering other than horizontal must be used, make it read from the bottom up. (See the following illustration to avoid any misunderstanding.) The style of the lettering should also be kept simple.

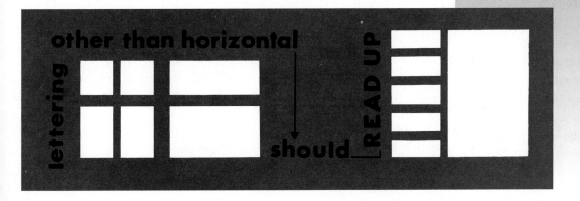

9. Colored string, yarn, or ribbon can be tacked or pinned into place to control the desired eye movement by leading the observer through the arrangement.

10. Group the material to be displayed on the bulletin board by topic or related subjects.
11. Bulletin boards lend themselves to the display of every school or extra-curricular activity. However, if classwork or artwork is to be displayed, be sure each child is represented.
12. Displays do not have to be limited to flat items; shadow boxes, paper sculpture, or any other three-dimensional objects may be attached to the board and may be included as part of a display merely to create variety and attract attention.
13. It is better to have no board at all than to have one that is overburdened. Allow comfortable intervals between notices or displays.

2 Design

The Elements of Art

The elements of art are line, shape, value, texture, and color. Line does not exist in nature, but the artist uses it to define the edges or boundaries of objects. This is often referred to as "outline." Lines may be long or short, thick or thin, and dark or light (value). They may also possess color and may be straight, angular, or curved. The character of a line is determined by the drawing instrument such as pencil, pen, or brush. All of the factors cited have certain compositional functions. They also have expressive properties, particularly when augmented by color. Lines can be used to suggest texture and value through squiggles, hatching, and cross-hatching. The comparative values, thicknesses, and directions can also promote the appearance of space.

Shapes are outlined or filled-in areas. They may be rectilinear (straight lines), curvilinear (curved lines), or a combination of the two. When an artist uses shape, whether or not he or she is attempting to reproduce something, there is normally a search for balance, related directions, and controlled importance (through size, value, shape contrast, location, and color). Shapes may indicate space through those same means or by using traditional perspective. Different shapes have traits that can produce emotional reactions.

Value refers to degrees of darkness or lightness. All of the other art elements exhibit value. Value can describe objects, create shapes, and suggest space. The value of an object (local value) could most likely be affected by highlights and shadows that are values in themselves. Dark values in an artwork can project a mood of gloom, mystery, and menace, while light values are more cheerful and less threatening.

Line

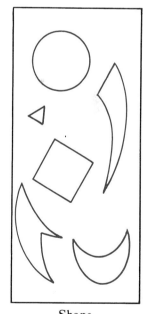

Shape

The Elements of Art Structure

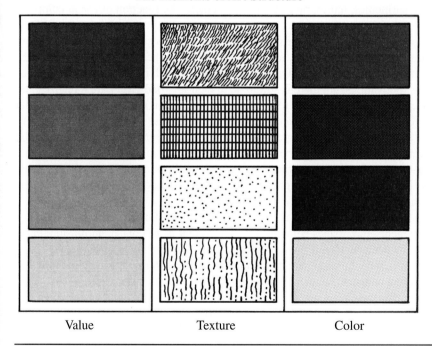

| Value | Texture | Color |

These are extremely simplified examples of each of the art elements; they may further consist of the following. Line: Angular, zig-zag lines; curved spiral, circular, serpentine, or any combinations of these types; Shape: Square, triangle, octagon, oblong, circle, oval, free-form; limitless possibilities and combinations; Value: Numerous variations from snow-white to pure black; Texture: Simulated (copied from rugs, wood, towels, grass, etc.), invented (entirely the product of the artist's imagination), abstract (freely interpreted from existing textured surfaces); and Color: An infinite number of hues with their numberless variations of value and intensity.

Texture has four categories—actual texture is the way the surface of a real object looks and feels, simulated texture is the artist's attempt to re-create that effect, abstract textures are simulated textures modified for artistic reasons, and invented textures are created (rather than re-created) by the artist. Selections from this group can lend reality, warmth, decoration, and psychological qualities to an artwork.

Color is produced by the light waves reflected by an object (in art, pigments). They are warm or cool, light or dark, and they have varying degrees of brightness (intensity). We all react emotionally to different colors; in various situations they can appeal to us or repel us. Contrasting colors are exciting, but harmonious colors are calming. The artist can use color to reproduce natural effects, to attract attention in varying degrees, and produce spatial suggestions (bright colors advance, and dull colors recede).

The elements of art are mixed and controlled by the artist so that they work in concert to transmit his or her responses to persons, places, and things.

Visual Composition

Each artwork is unique, with its own set of unique design problems, and good design is, in large part, a thing instinctive in the artist. Nevertheless, there are some guiding principles of which we need to be reminded periodically, and which, if repeated often enough, can become a part of the artist's instincts.

Design is perhaps more accurately called "composition." The artist works with elements (lines, shapes, values, textures, and colors)—sometimes representing recognizable subjects, sometimes not—just as the music composer works with notes, harmonics, tempi, rhythms, and dynamics. The function of *visual* composition is to make the material legible, interesting, and expressive of the artist's feelings about the subject. The artist's "form" (total composition) may be directed by logic or instinct. Some artists are more cerebral than others; their work is dissected and analyzed as it develops. Other artists seem to work more out of their subconscious motivations, but there is still logic to their artwork. Every artist realizes that there are limits to his or her format (the area on which the artist works) and that this surface becomes an arena of visual forces that must work to his or her advantage. Things must be tied together so that they lead comfortably from one to the other, and there must be assurance that an appropriate amount of emphasis is given them—all of this while working for pictorial equilibrium, or balance. Obviously, these goals are not easily reached; a well-designed work is the result of considerable alteration.

To achieve *balance* the artist must have some feeling for the visual weight of the elements and images being drawn. The weight is, of course, an illusion, but it is real to the artist. Visual weight derives from size, lightness or darkness, placement, general configuration, and complexity. A large shape is usually (not always, depending on what else the artist does to it) heavier than a small one, a dark shape heavier than a light one, a shape at the lower part of the drawing heavier than one at the top, and some shapes, simply because of their character, are seemingly heavier than others. These factors may be intermingled in an image, increasing or reducing the apparent weight. One cannot put such factors into the scales, so the artist must develop some sensitivity to the weight represented. Once this sensitivity is achieved, it is possible to scan a work and respond to its balance or imbalance. Balance is generally sought and can take two forms: symmetrical balance or asymmetrical balance. In symmetrical balance similar or identical images are given similar or identical placement on either side of a work. This is a rather simple and often monotonous form of balance. In asymmetrical balance unlike images are given dissimilar placement in such a way that a total feeling of balance is produced.

When placing the images, other design criteria must be observed. It is possible that although balance has been achieved, placement has caused some images to lose some of the importance they deserve; in other words, the relative dominance has been disturbed. Relative dominance refers to the degree of significance the artist attaches to each image. Obviously if everything is of equal importance, the work is difficult to read and the artist's message is lost. Dominance is manipulated by the same factors that create weight: a larger image is interpreted as being more important, and so forth. When balance is achieved but relative dominance lost, the artist must go back to the drawing board. He or she must juggle the factors until the needs for balance and relative dominance are both satisfied. By now it can be seen that composition is not unlike a game; not an easy one, but one that is very rewarding if the answers are found. In this "game" the artist creates his or her own problems, each of which is unique, and experiments until the problems are solved. This problem-solving function necessitates some sacrifices for the benefit of the total image.

Assuming that problems of balance and relative dominance have been solved, there remains the task of relating the imagery in terms of the observer's perusal of the work. Although the observer may not be aware of it, the artist *directs* this perusal. Transitions are created between areas of interest. The directions implicit in these areas may be, or can be made to be, participants in this directional sweep, augmented by newly introduced passages. When this final matter is settled to the artist's satisfaction, presumably we have a work that attracts the observer's attention, which is then comfortably directed from point to point, each point occupying its own importance scale in the work.

This discussion has isolated compositional problems in such a way that it seems that there is a predictable sequence to them. On occasion, the artist may direct his or her attention to each individual problem, but usually the problems are

Balance Diagram

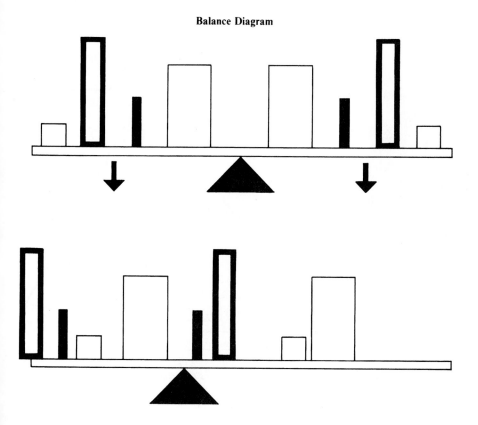

considered en masse. So we find that the development of a work is not usually intellectual or methodical, but instinctive, with the artist's feeling for rightness directing the proceedings.

Harmony and Variety

The two most important factors in composition are harmony and variety. Harmony refers to sameness, and variety to difference. The composition may be unbalanced in favor of one or the other, but both must be present to some degree. Harmony leads to close relationships and, when overused, dullness. Variety creates excitement and, in the extreme, chaos. Any of the elements illustrated thus far may be modified in various ways to produce either harmony or variety. An example in color might be a scheme that is largely made up of reddish hues (harmony) or one that utilizes clashing colors or all the colors in the rainbow (variety). In dealing with shapes one could devise some that are entirely made up of straight lines (harmony) or straight and curved lines (variety). The characteristics of the elements just cited are among their physical properties; there are many that can be manipulated. If harmony and variety are appropriately blended to suit the expressive needs of the artist, it can be said that the work is *unified*.

It would probably be foolish to show concern for the design abilities of the very young, for the verbalization of such a concept would be unintelligible to them. Most young people already have a good instinctive sense of design that is frequently lost with the advancing years. It has already been noted that maturity is a variable and that the realistic stage, when reached, can present many problems. One of the problems is that, in their preoccupation with realistic imagery, young people may lose contact with their compositional needs. If this occurs, it may be advisable to point out (without neglecting the importance of good drawing) that "likeness" is not the only answer in creating good art. Competent artists realize that visual reality (likeness) often has to be adjusted or reevaluated for effective composition. Those who are gaining competence in realistic drawing do not usually welcome or see the need for such sacrifices. It requires a great deal of diplomacy

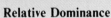

Relative Dominance

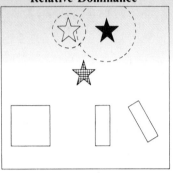

The circles represent the areas of attraction of the stars. The black star circle is larger because that star, because of its contrast, is more dominant. The rectangle on the right has more dominance than its size justifies because it is tilted. All elements or images have degrees of attraction because of factors such as these.

Venus and Adonis. Titian. National Gallery of Art, Washington Widener Collection, 1942.

This diagram demonstrates the basic movements of the preceding work. The eyes of the observer are directed along these paths. Secondary movements or relationships could also have been indicated.

to convince such persons that the real aim of art is the expression of something that cannot be communicated by faithful copying, no matter how skillfully it is done.

The Development of an Artwork

Every artwork has the illusion of a certain amount of space, whether planned or unplanned. This spatial illusion is the product of the elements listed previously and the images they create; dark lines move ahead of light lines, large shapes move ahead of small shapes, bright colors move ahead of dull colors. Artists use these physical properties of the art elements to control the space in their works. When art elements are close together in space that space is called decorative space. When art elements are separated, the space is either shallow or deep space. Other devices used for space control are size, position, overlapping, transparency, interpenetration, sharp or diminishing detail, converging parallels, and linear perspective.

Any attempt to impose compositional concerns on young children would be fruitless. Children produce exciting and expressive images but the images lack the coherence of a mature work. Only as children mature does the importance of composition become reasonable—and that very slowly. People involved in personal creativity can evoke this realization most successfully.

For the sake of interest, here is the way an artwork *may* develop; works do not always develop in the same order. An artist must begin with an idea, or germ, that will eventually develop into the concept of the finished artwork. The idea may be the result of aimless doodling, a thought that has suddenly struck the artist or a notion that has been growing in his or her mind for a long time. If this idea is to become tangible, it must be developed in a medium selected by the artist (clay, oil, paint, watercolor). The artist not only controls, but is controlled by, the medium.

Through the medium the elements of form emerge, with their intrinsic meanings. These meanings may be allied with a representational or nonrepresentational image; in either case, the bulk of the meaning will be in the form created by the elements.

While working on the artwork, the artist will be concerned with composition, or formal structure, as the most interesting and communicative presentation of the idea is explored. During this process abstraction will inevitably occur, even if the work is broadly realistic; elements will be added, eliminated, or generally edited. The abstraction happens with an awareness, and within the parameters, of the principles of composition.

As the creative procedure unfolds (not always directly, neatly or without stress and anguish), the artist fervently hopes that the result will be unified. This refers to the culmination of everything being sought in the work. Put simply, it means that every part not only fits, but that each one contributes to the overall content or meaning. At this point, however arduous or circuitous the artist's route, the work is finished—or is it? Having given the best of themselves artists are never sure of this! Perhaps the perspective of a few days, months, or years will give the answer. How fortunate are the grade-schoolers, that they can just pitch in and avoid such worrisome matters!

To learn about the many considerations involved in striving for compositional unity in art, it is recommended that the reader study some of the many books on the subject. Prejudice dictates that a reading list be headed by *Art Fundamentals,* produced by the publisher of this book, and written, in part, by one of the authors of this text. Details on this and other recommended books can be found in the Art Resources section.

Through the exploration of 2-d and 3-d media, older or more talented students may discover, select, and transform ideas from personal experience into subject matter in their artworks. They thus learn art concepts and art vocabulary from practical experience. When these students study their own artwork or historical artwork, they learn how art critics, historians, and society have perceived artworks and thus improve their ability to express themselves.

The elements of line, shape, color, value, and texture have been discussed in some detail; the compositional concepts include balance, pattern and repetition, rhythm and movement, unity, emphasis, and contrast and variety. Some of these are germane to certain activities and, in some cases, these are pointed out. The objectives of the activities may be expanded because of the choice of subject and the emphasis placed on different aspects of the lesson.

An Introduction to the Art Activities

The activities in this volume are so named because they produce action and as an alternative to the term *problems,* a term often associated with art assignments. Problems are usually assigned as a specific segment of art for which a solution is sought, and the solution is often found through an intellectual process. Fine art is produced by using varying degrees of the intellect and the intuition, the proportions depending on the artist, the work, and the difficulties encountered. Although there is some amount of problem solving involved in these activities, more for some children than others, the balance in this book would favor intuition. Younger children do not ordinarily intellectualize their works. In supervising very young artists, it is wise to provide motivation and enthusiasm, allowing their instincts to guide them; as the students grow older or show evidence or precocity, reason will come into play.

All children are different; they cannot always be accurately classified by age, grade, or any other standards. They also respond differently to art and with different degrees of creative maturity (see "The Art World of the Child," pp. 12–13). Students within the same class may be at different stages of development, the manipulative, symbolic, or realistic stages. Some may be exceptional in art, some in other fields. Certain activities will be more challenging or more interesting to some students than to others, but most of the activities will be received by all with some degree of enthusiasm and will have some benefits for all. With creativity having such elastic boundaries for such a wide range of individuals, the teaching of art requires a flexible and sensitive teacher.

Thus we have not graded the activities in this book, nor have we identified the rewards to be identified with each of them. The benefits are related to the emphasis and type of emphasis given the activity by the teacher, and most of the benefits are self-evident.

Nevertheless, we have listed the general benefits associated with the use of these activities—not the individual activities, but the activities as a whole. We hope that you can identify them with the needs of your particular situation:

Appreciation: Showing a deserved degree of regard for a product or performance based on an adequate understanding of the difficulties involved.

Concentration: The stretching of the interest span. Focusing on a particular task without being unduly influenced by distractions.

Conceptualization: Foreseeing the results of certain actions. Planning in one's mind's eye. The thought and its subsequent portrayal.

Cooperation: Relating to and contributing to social growth. Constructive teamwork. Productive participation.

Correlation: The ability to see, understand, and exploit relationships between things. May include relationships between certain areas of art and other subject areas.

Dexterity: Neuromuscular coordination; eye-hand control. The ability to handle physical tasks.

Family relationships:	Children usually like to represent their family and direct their work toward it. They expect a positive response from relatives.
Individual growth:	Improvements in behavior, attitude, and performance in matters both personal and social.
Interest in nature:	Children usually show an automatic interest in natural items or occurrences. This can be enhanced and exploited by the teacher.
Perception:	Not just looking at, but *seeing* things with a degree of accuracy. Noting certain things beyond the obvious.
Resourcefulness:	The motivation and energy required to develop ways of problem solving.
Self-esteem:	An outcome of individual growth. Recognition of one's ability to perform things and perform them with confidence. Self-awareness of skills and abilities. The teacher's positive remarks are especially helpful here. Pride, but not to excess.
Social growth:	Adapting one's responses to those of other people. Thinking of one's efforts as part of a *total* effort. Cooperating unselfishly in group activities.
Stability:	Acceptance of constructive criticism without rancor, such criticism being made only as adequate maturity is reached; rarely applies to younger children.

Color

3

The Spectrum

Color can be an immensely complicated field of study. There are many color theories, some of them devised for specific conditions or applications of color. Fortunately, the readers of this book need only a basic understanding of the color principles that artists and physicists have given us.

In dealing with the color of light, we can see that its rays are divided into constituent colors as they pass through a glass prism. This array, known as the spectrum, demonstrates violet, dark blue, blue, green, yellow, orange, and red as well as other colors invisible to the naked eye.

The colors we detect in objects are visible because these are the only colors reflected back to our eyes; the rest are absorbed by the surface of the object. This is, of course, also true of the media used by the artist, whether that be chalk, watercolor, oil paint, pastel, or tempera. When a ribbon of red oil paint is squeezed from the tube, the paint reflects only the color red back to our eyes.

Color inherently fascinates all of us and particularly children, who are as fearless in its use as they are with any medium within reach. Most of us are aware that colors affect us psychologically, and this means that color selection is of primary consideration in creating the mood of an artwork. Young children seem to know this instinctively, and in any case, it is foolish to burden them with such considerations; however, when one deals with children on the threshold of the realistic stage, it might be appropriate to point out the symbolic and expressive properties of color.

Color Relationships

Many colors come prepackaged, and many people use the colors just as they find them, "direct from the tube." On occasion this may be appropriate, but in doing so consistently one misses the opportunity to learn something about color relationships and the fun that comes from mixing colors. It is always a delight to see what happens when colors are added to each other. Experimentation should not be discouraged, but there should be some *planning* of the color mixtures; only through methodical mixing can one get some idea of the infinite color possibilities.

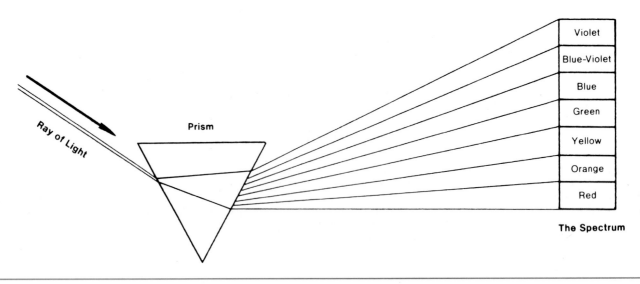

The rays of red have the longest wavelength and those of violet the shortest. The angle at which the rays are bent, or refracted, is greatest at the violet end and least at the red.

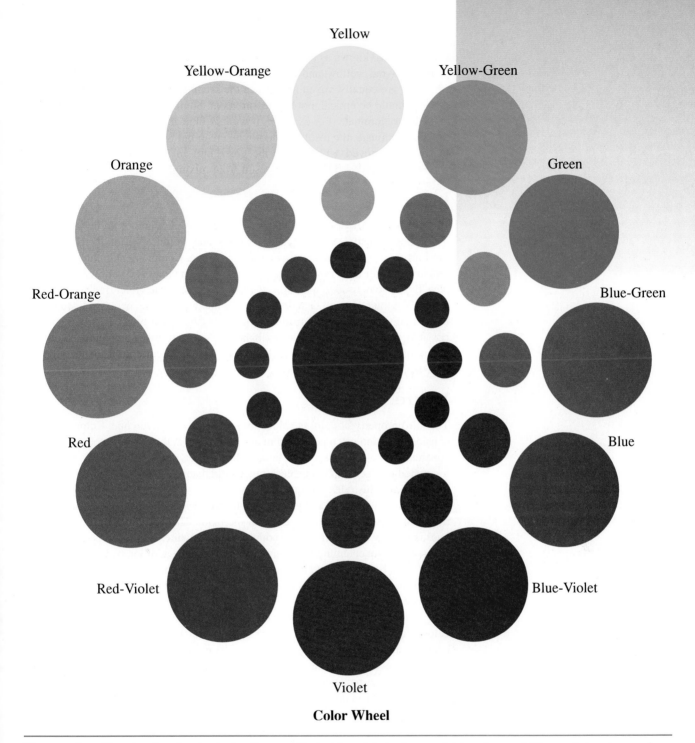

Color Wheel

The outer ring of hues has the primaries *(red, yellow, and blue) and* secondaries *(green, violet, and orange). Were we to insert new colors appropriately between each of these, they would be called* tertiaries. *One could continue doing this "ad infinitum," as there is no limit to the modifications of hues.*

As the hue moves inward it is being neutralized by its complement (the hue directly opposite on the wheel) until it reaches a neutral, or gray. As in the case of the hues, intensities can be infinitely modified. This is also true of values; each of the hues or its intensities could receive increasing amounts of white and/or black (not shown).

Hue

Colors are also known as hues. The basic hues from which all others evolve are the *primaries*—red, yellow, and blue. The first step in this evolution occurs when the primaries are equally mixed to produce the *secondary* hues. The equality of color mixing should be optical, not by measurement. Some hues are stronger than others and tend to dominate. For example, if we mix blue and yellow for a green and let the blue dominate, the result would not be green but blue-green. This would mean that we had moved a bit beyond the green into an *intermediate* hue. The color wheel illustrates the hues that can result from mixing.

Intensity

Hue can be modified in its *intensity* or brilliance. A pure hue could be said to be at maximum intensity. Anything added to this hue would affect its brightness, but most artists use a complement when dulling a hue. Complementary hues are those directly opposite each other on the color wheel, with violet and yellow being examples. If the violet used to neutralize the yellow is not a true violet (red and blue balanced), the intensity will be reduced, but the hue will change, being inclined to lean toward either orange (too much red) or green (too much blue). It is theoretically possible to achieve a true gray by balancing out any two complements, but the nature of pigment used in art media is such that different complements will produce somewhat different grays.

Value

The third property of color is value—the darkness of a given hue. Color value is a consideration too often neglected in art. In looking at the color wheel, it should be apparent that yellow is much lighter than violet, and if the wheel were photographed in black and white, each hue would display its own characteristic value. The diagram illustrates this quite clearly.

The pattern created by the use of value contrasts in a composition is an important factor in the effectiveness of the work. The darkening and lightening of hues is usually accomplished by adding black or white. It is theoretically possible to do so without changing the intensity, but in fact, the addition of any color to hues will change both value and intensity to some degree. In some cases hue is changed as well; some black additives result in a greenish hue. The characteristics of media vary, even according to manufacturer, and are not entirely predictable.

To confirm what has been said here and, in the process, learn something of color relationships, it is recommended that a color wheel be attempted along with experiments in both intensity and value. There are limitless possibilities, so great in fact that even in hue, the colors produced are so many that there can be no standard identifying names for them, although they can be seen to be reddish, bluish, or whatever. By neutralizing and darkening and lightening these hues, the possibilities expand almost geometrically.

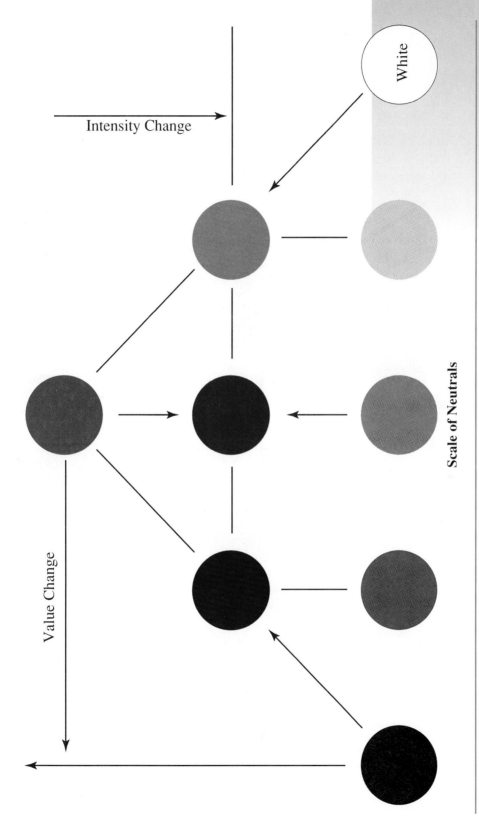

Intensity Change

Value Change

White

Scale of Neutrals

The red at the top of the illustration is presumably at spectrum intensity (pure red). As we move down one step we can see that the red has been slightly neutralized in its intensity. If we move right we can see this neutralized red has had its value changed by the addition of white; moving to its left it becomes darker (black added). The bottom circle (two steps below red) represents the ultimate neutralization of the red; this, in turn, moves toward white (right) and black (left).

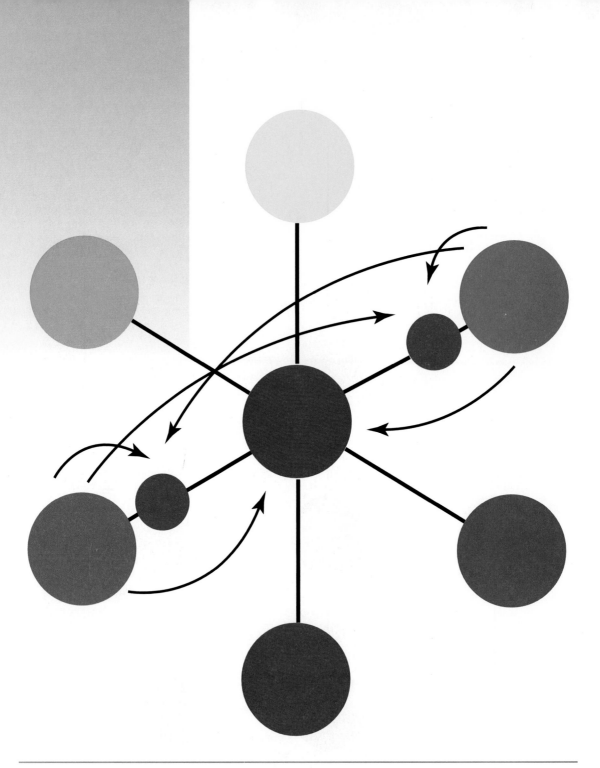

These two diagrams (above and on p. 49) illustrate the four means of changing the intensity of color. (1) In the diagram on p. 49, as white (a neutral) is added to bright red, the value is changed, but the resulting color is lowered in intensity. (2) In the same way, the addition of black to bright red creates a dark red closer to the neutral scale because the intensity is changed. (3) When a neutral gray is added to the spectrum color, the intensity is lowered, but the value is neither raised nor lowered. (4) The diagram on this page indicates change of intensity by adding to a color a little of its complement. For instance, by adding a small amount of green to red, a gray red is produced. In the same way, a small amount of red added to green results in a gray green. When the two colors are balanced (not necessarily equal amounts), the resulting mixture is a neutral gray.

Chapter Three

White

High light

Yellow

Yellow-Orange

Light

Yellow-Green

Orange

Low light

Green

Red-Orange

Medium

Blue-Green

Red

High dark

Blue

Red-Violet

Dark

Blue-Violet

Violet

Low dark

Black

This chart shows the value of each of the hues illustrated at maximum intensity (not neutralized). It can be seen that pure yellow is the lightest of the hues, corresponding to "high light"; red-orange is somewhat darker, matching up with "medium" value. Violet is the darkest of the hues shown (low dark). Any changes in any of the hues would move them up (lighter) or down (darker) on the value scale.

A "hands-on" study of color should begin with the painting of a color wheel consisting of at least twelve hues (yellow, yellow-orange, orange, red-orange, red, red-violet, violet, blue-violet, blue, blue-green, green and yellow-green). Following this procedure, each hue should be taken through a number of modifications of its value and intensity. © *James L. Shaffer*

Color Schemes

Once the many possibilities are appreciated, selection of color schemes can begin. Artists utilize color according to their own feelings. Excitement can be the product of a complementary plan, while relative calm is the result of analogous hues (those hues near each other on the color wheel). Colors can be warm (red, orange, yellow) or cool (blue, green, some violets). The color temperature is another ingredient in the mood evoked. Sometimes artists use triadic schemes; the primary triad is red, yellow, and blue; the secondary triad is orange, green, and violet. Other triadic systems with similar hue separation are, of course, possible.

Split complements are often utilized; this entails the use of a hue plus those colors to either side of its complement on the color wheel.

Some artists stay fairly close to *local* hues (the hues normally associated with objects), but they are rarely entirely literal in their transcription of color; nature is entirely too complex to treat with complete fidelity. Those artists closest to nature

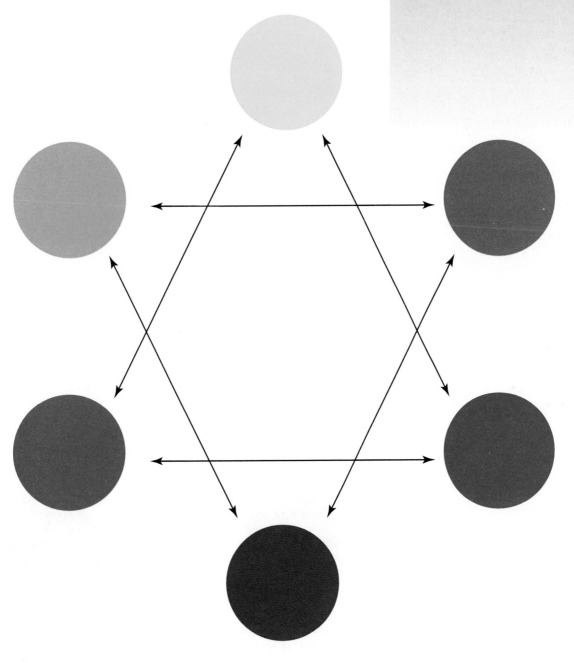

Triadic Color Interval
(Medium contrast)

are termed *naturalists,* and those who distance themselves somewhat are called *realists.* Other artists find that natural colors are inadequate for their needs. Such artists use non-local hues (green faces, purple cows, etc.); the hues are employed to achieve decorative, symbolic, or expressive effects. Despite the differences in their artistic goals, these artists are collectively known as *expressionists.*

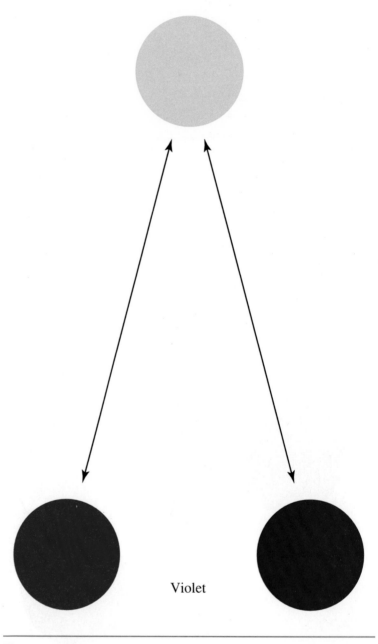

Violet

This example shows yellow and its split complementary colors, red-violet and blue-violet, on either side of yellow's complement violet.

Lettering and Calligraphy

Principles of Lettering

Lettering and manuscript writing is an art that must conform to certain principles in order to be attractive and legible. There is no better time to learn these principles than in the formative years. There are many types of lettering, and these are capable of many types of expression (speed, action, dignity, beauty, for example). However, the beginner should not venture too far from the simpler forms of lettering; and for this reason, only the fundamental rules of the Gothic letter structure are illustrated here. A variety of lettering can be created from this basic type, as is indicated in the accompanying illustration.

Lettering is one of those rare areas in the field of art where definite rules seem justified. To improve lettering and manuscript writing, a few simple guides are listed. Each of these guidelines is subject to variation in more complicated styles, such as italic (slanted) or script.

It is recommended that a rough layout of the letters be done in pencil before inking. Full consideration should be given to the forms of the letters, size, placement of words on a page, and spacing between letters and words. Those who want a satisfactory appearance but who cannot find the time for hand lettering may want to consider lettraset or press-type.

 Caution: Some of the activities in this chapter call for the use of X-acto knives. Extreme care and supervision must be utilized whenever X-acto knives are used. Safety instructions should be given before **EVERY** use of the knives. X-acto knives are now sold with safety caps, but separate caps may be purchased for older knives. Heavy corrugated cardboard should always be placed under the paper or material being cut. The X-acto knife is held like a pencil, with the fingers holding the knife on the textured ring. The slanted, sharpened edge should be directly over the line to be cut and the position of the knife or the paper should be changed if the line changes direction. Keep the fingers of the holding hand out of the way of the blade, usually above the cutting area. Remind students often to check themselves and the position of the knife and their hands.

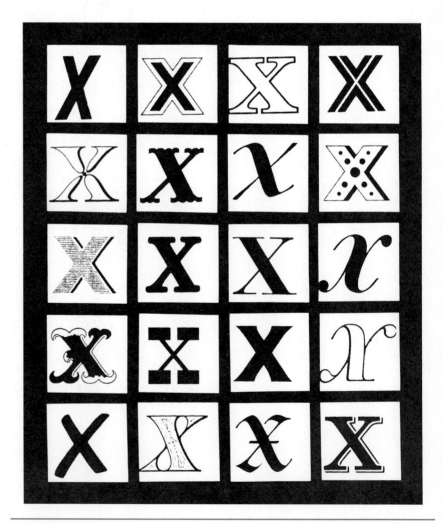

A basic letter with numerous variations.

Ink or Felt Pen Lettering

procedure

supplies

1. Ink
2. Lettering pen and pen holder, or felt pen
3. Paper
4. Ruler
5. Pencil

1. The axes of all Gothic letters are perpendicular to the line upon which they rest and are of uniform thickness.

PERPENDICULAR | perpendicular

2. Capitals, or uppercase letters, are all the same height—usually two spaces high for children.

ABCDEFGHIJKLMN
OPQRSTUVWXYZ·
1 2 3 4 5 6 7 8 9 0

3. Capital letters are of three different width groups—wide, average, and narrow.

Narrow Letters

EFIJLT

Wide Letters

GMOQW

There are no serifs or dots on the basic Gothic letters I or J, as indicated above, unless used on all letters.

4. A serif is a cross stroke on the end of the individual lines of a letter. (When serifs are used, they must be used on *every* letter.)

COLOR ART CRAFT

5. Horizontal line intersections generally should be above or below the middle of the letter for greater legibility.

Letters with horizontal line intersection above the middle:

B E F H X

Letters with horizontal line intersection below the middle:

A G K P R Y

6. Correct spacing is absolutely necessary to make lettering or manuscript writing legible and attractive. Measured spacing produces a lack of unity in lettered words. Spacing should be done with feeling for the *area between* the letters. When lettering, leave the width of an average letter between words.

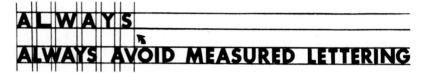

7. Lowercase, or small letters, are usually divided into thirds for the convenience of young children.

abcdefghijklmnop

qrstuvwxyz

8. The lowercase Gothic alphabet can be divided into three families of letters: Short letters

aceimnorsuvwxz

Letters with ascenders

bdfhklt

(Note that the letter t extends only halfway into the top space.)

Letters with descenders

gjpqy

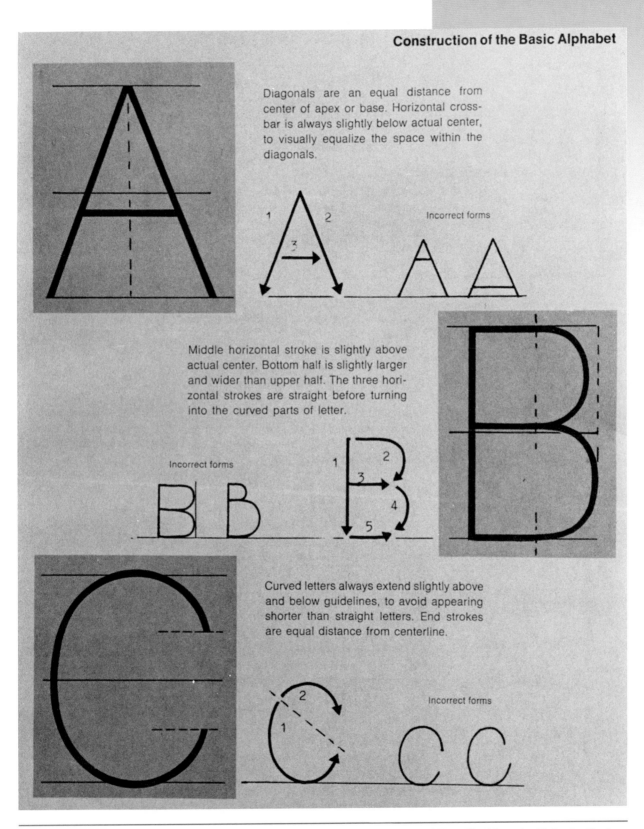

Diagonals are an equal distance from center of apex or base. Horizontal cross-bar is always slightly below actual center, to visually equalize the space within the diagonals.

Incorrect forms

Middle horizontal stroke is slightly above actual center. Bottom half is slightly larger and wider than upper half. The three horizontal strokes are straight before turning into the curved parts of letter.

Incorrect forms

Curved letters always extend slightly above and below guidelines, to avoid appearing shorter than straight letters. End strokes are equal distance from centerline.

Incorrect forms

From "Construction of the Basic Alphabet" (pp. 4–12), "The Tools of Calligraphy" (p. 112) in Hand Lettering Today *by Abraham Switkin. Copyright © 1976 by Abraham Switkin. Reprinted by permission of HarperCollins Publishers, Inc.*

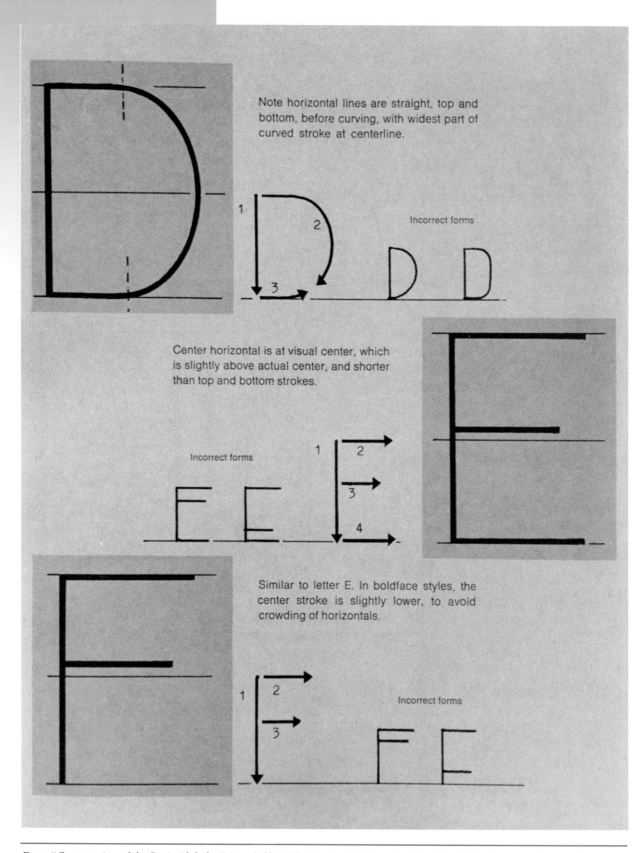

Note horizontal lines are straight, top and bottom, before curving, with widest part of curved stroke at centerline.

Incorrect forms

Center horizontal is at visual center, which is slightly above actual center, and shorter than top and bottom strokes.

Incorrect forms

Similar to letter E. In boldface styles, the center stroke is slightly lower, to avoid crowding of horizontals.

Incorrect forms

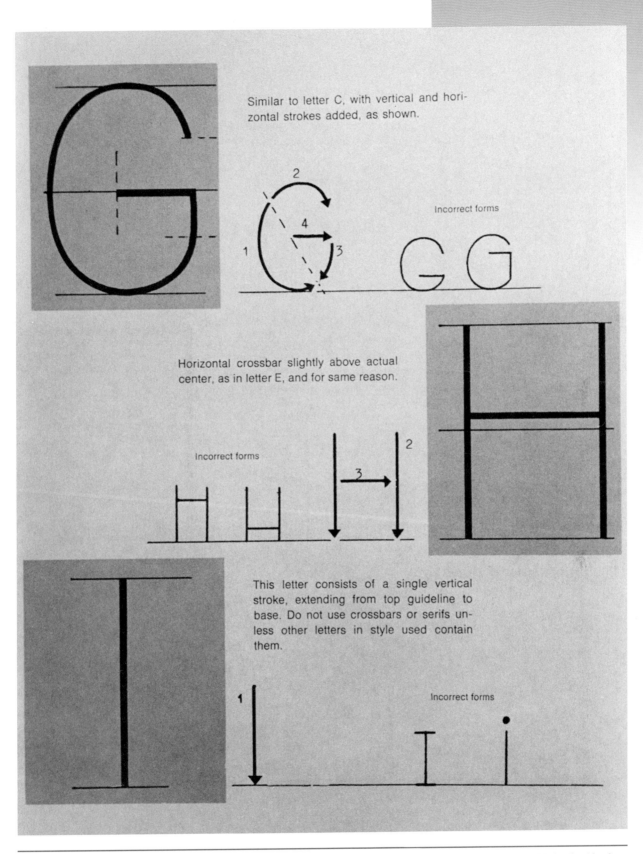

Similar to letter C, with vertical and horizontal strokes added, as shown.

Incorrect forms

Horizontal crossbar slightly above actual center, as in letter E, and for same reason.

Incorrect forms

This letter consists of a single vertical stroke, extending from top guideline to base. Do not use crossbars or serifs unless other letters in style used contain them.

Incorrect forms

From "Construction of the Basic Alphabet" (pp. 4–12), "The Tools of Calligraphy" (p. 112) in Hand Lettering Today *by Abraham Switkin. Copyright © 1976 by Abraham Switkin. Reprinted by permission of HarperCollins Publishers, Inc.*

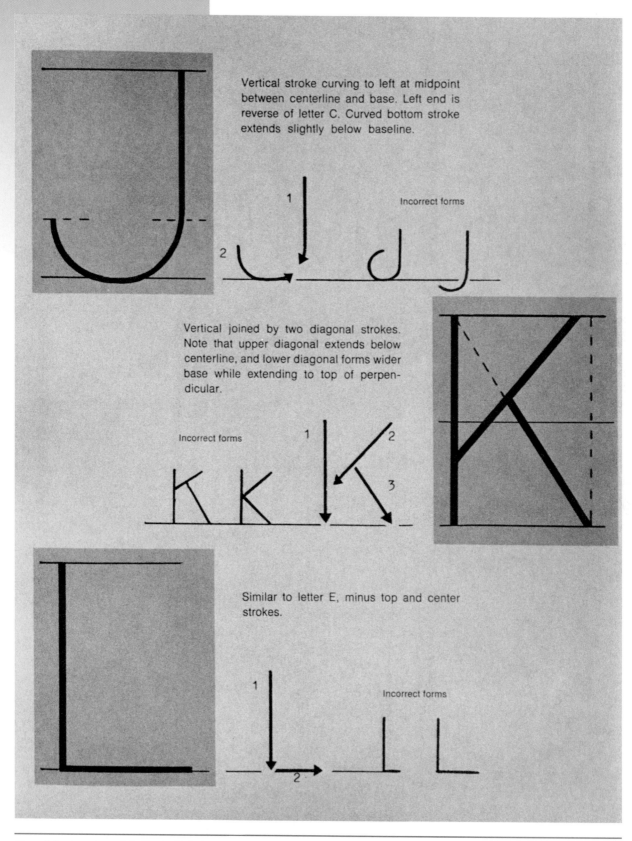

Vertical stroke curving to left at midpoint between centerline and base. Left end is reverse of letter C. Curved bottom stroke extends slightly below baseline.

Incorrect forms

Vertical joined by two diagonal strokes. Note that upper diagonal extends below centerline, and lower diagonal forms wider base while extending to top of perpendicular.

Incorrect forms

Similar to letter E, minus top and center strokes.

Incorrect forms

From "Construction of the Basic Alphabet" (pp. 4–12), "The Tools of Calligraphy" (p. 112) in Hand Lettering Today *by Abraham Switkin. Copyright © 1976 by Abraham Switkin. Reprinted by permission of HarperCollins Publishers, Inc.*

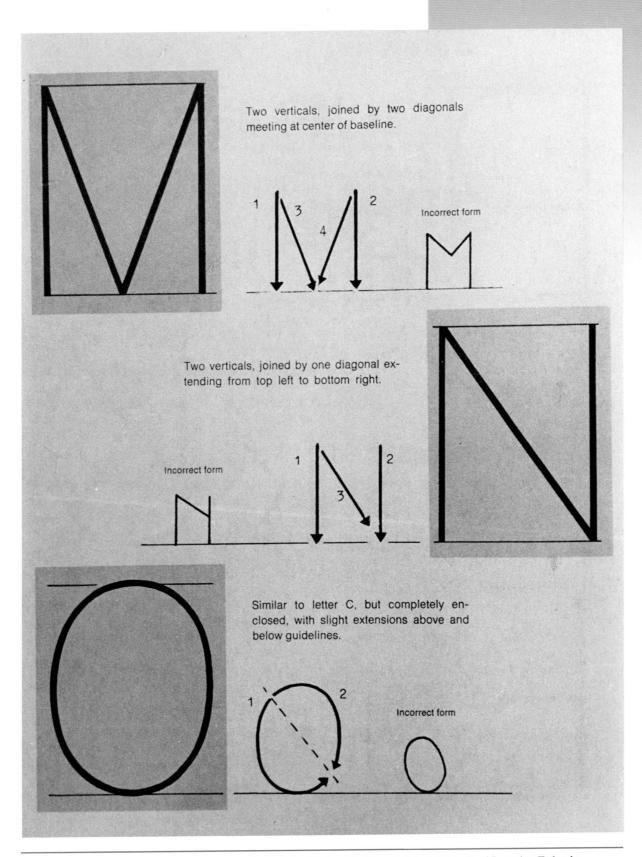

Two verticals, joined by two diagonals meeting at center of baseline.

Incorrect form

Two verticals, joined by one diagonal extending from top left to bottom right.

Incorrect form

Similar to letter C, but completely enclosed, with slight extensions above and below guidelines.

Incorrect form

From "Construction of the Basic Alphabet" (pp. 4–12), "The Tools of Calligraphy" (p. 112) in Hand Lettering Today *by Abraham Switkin. Copyright © 1976 by Abraham Switkin. Reprinted by permission of HarperCollins Publishers, Inc.*

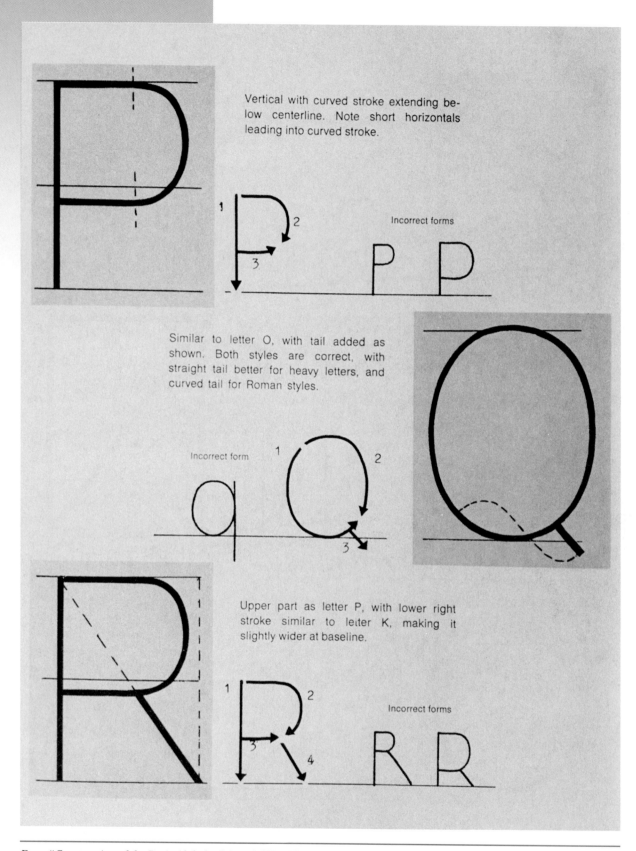

Vertical with curved stroke extending below centerline. Note short horizontals leading into curved stroke.

Incorrect forms

Similar to letter O, with tail added as shown. Both styles are correct, with straight tail better for heavy letters, and curved tail for Roman styles.

Incorrect form

Upper part as letter P, with lower right stroke similar to letter K, making it slightly wider at baseline.

Incorrect forms

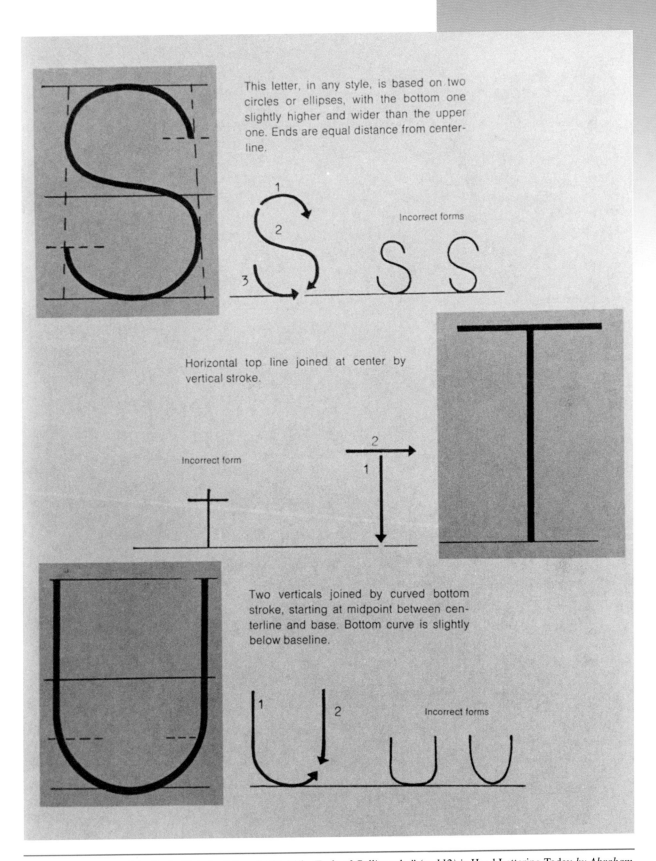

This letter, in any style, is based on two circles or ellipses, with the bottom one slightly higher and wider than the upper one. Ends are equal distance from center-line.

Incorrect forms

Horizontal top line joined at center by vertical stroke.

Incorrect form

Two verticals joined by curved bottom stroke, starting at midpoint between centerline and base. Bottom curve is slightly below baseline.

Incorrect forms

From "Construction of the Basic Alphabet" (pp. 4–12), "The Tools of Calligraphy" (p. 112) in Hand Lettering Today *by Abraham Switkin. Copyright © 1976 by Abraham Switkin. Reprinted by permission of HarperCollins Publishers, Inc.*

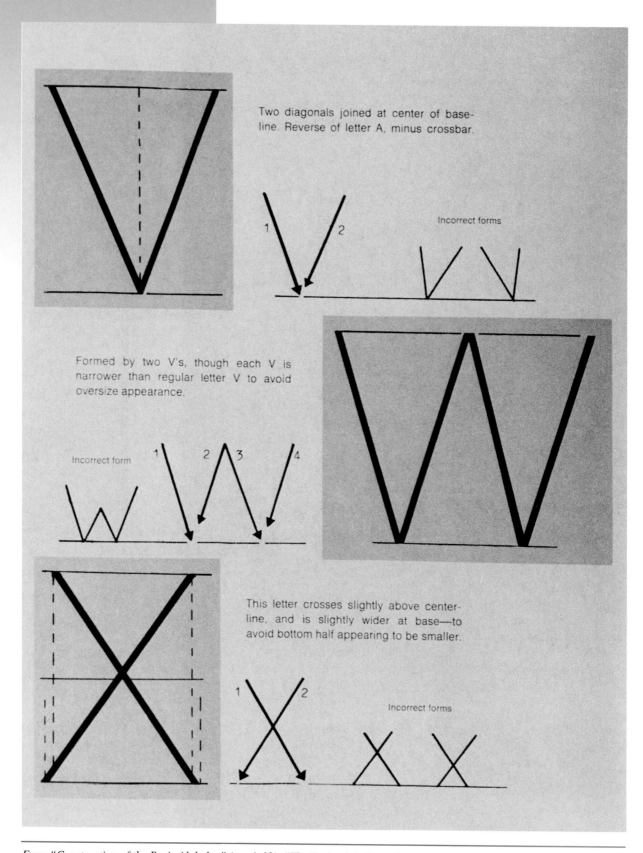

Two diagonals joined at center of base-line. Reverse of letter A, minus crossbar.

Incorrect forms

Formed by two V's, though each V is narrower than regular letter V to avoid oversize appearance.

Incorrect form

This letter crosses slightly above center-line, and is slightly wider at base—to avoid bottom half appearing to be smaller.

Incorrect forms

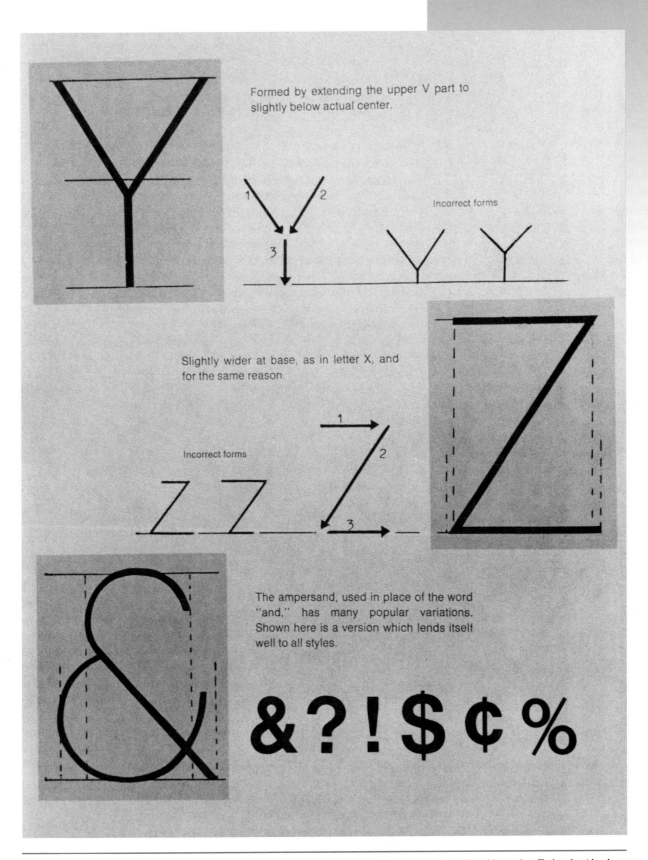

Formed by extending the upper V part to slightly below actual center.

Incorrect forms

Slightly wider at base, as in letter X, and for the same reason.

Incorrect forms

The ampersand, used in place of the word "and," has many popular variations. Shown here is a version which lends itself well to all styles.

&?!$¢%

Cut Paper Letters

procedure

1. Cut a number of strips of paper measured to the height of the proposed letters (Ill. 1).
2. Although all of the letters are of the same height, they are divided into three widths: wide, average, and narrow. The wide letter is a square and is made by folding the bottom corner up against the top of the strip and cutting along the edge of the triangle thus formed (Ill. 2). Cut a considerable number of these shapes (Ill. 3).
3. The average width letter is made by cutting away a portion of the square (Ill. 4). Cut a number of these of the same width.
4. The narrow letter is made by cutting another portion from the average width letter. Cut a number of these of the same width (Ill. 5).
5. A supply of shapes for each size letter has now been provided. The paper size must be selected according to the width of the letter chosen and can be cut according to the instructions that follow.
6. **Use safety scissors if possible.**

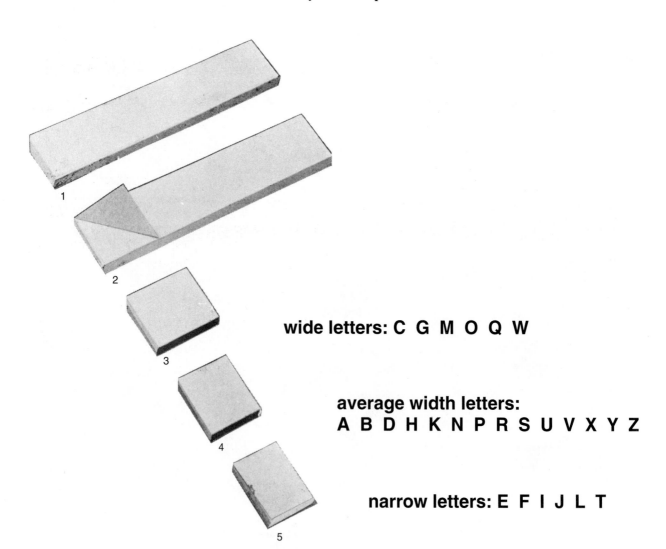

wide letters: C G M O Q W

**average width letters:
A B D H K N P R S U V X Y Z**

narrow letters: E F I J L T

average width letters:
A B D H K N P R S U V X Y Z

The top of the letter A must be cut half as wide as the final thickness of the letter.

Fold in half and cut around the corner to form the curved edge of the letter (Ill. 1).

Fold top edge to middle crease and cut opening as illustrated (Ill. 2).

Fold bottom edge up to the bottom of the top opening and cut larger opening, as illustrated (Ill. 3).

Unfold and cut out triangle. The bottom of the letter B will be larger than the top (Ill. 4).

Fold bottom edge up and cut opening and corners.

The crossbar of the letter H must be cut half as wide as the final thickness of the letter.

The first two "K's" (Ills. 1 and 2) are cut by folding; the third is not folded (Ill. 3).

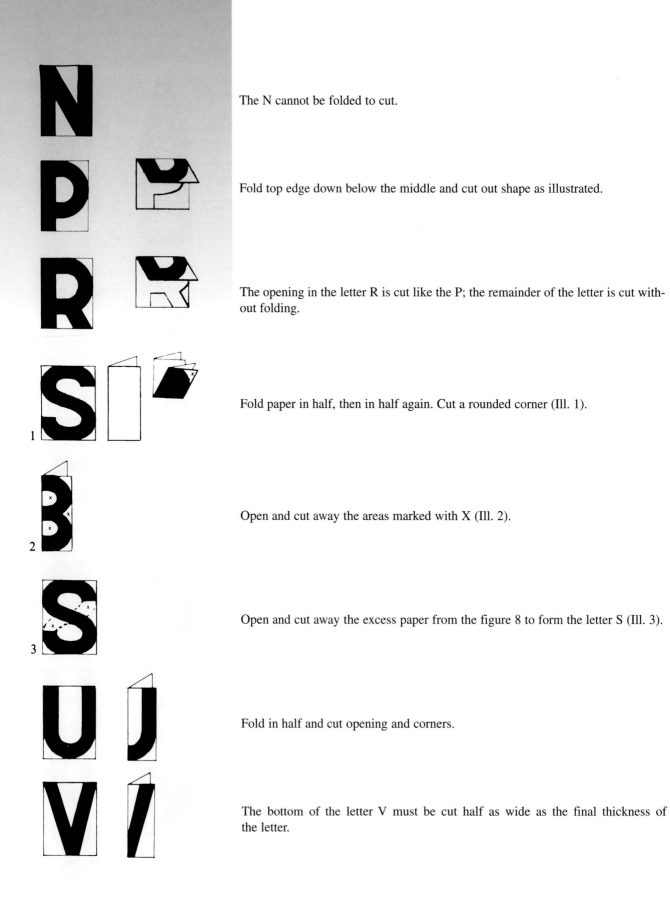

The N cannot be folded to cut.

Fold top edge down below the middle and cut out shape as illustrated.

The opening in the letter R is cut like the P; the remainder of the letter is cut without folding.

Fold paper in half, then in half again. Cut a rounded corner (Ill. 1).

Open and cut away the areas marked with X (Ill. 2).

Open and cut away the excess paper from the figure 8 to form the letter S (Ill. 3).

Fold in half and cut opening and corners.

The bottom of the letter V must be cut half as wide as the final thickness of the letter.

The center of the letter X must be cut half as wide as the final thickness of the letter.

The stem of the letter Y must be cut half as wide as the final thickness of the letter.

The Z cannot be folded to cut.

narrow letters: E F I J L T

Shorten the middle arm of the E. The middle arm of the letter E must be cut half as wide as the final thickness of the letter.

For the F, shorten the middle arm and remove bottom leg. The middle arm of the letter F must be cut half as wide as the final thickness of the letter.

Cut to match thickness of other letters.

The letter J is a narrow letter but is cut like the letter U.

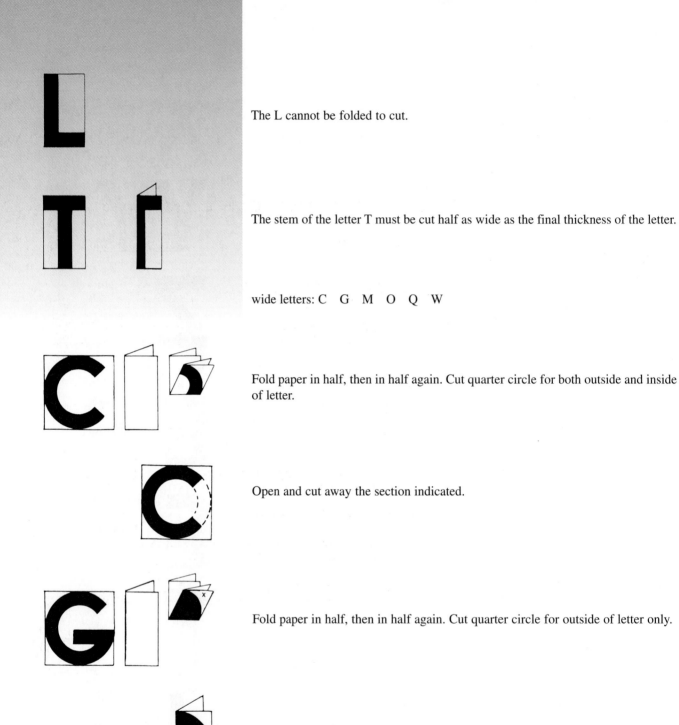

The L cannot be folded to cut.

The stem of the letter T must be cut half as wide as the final thickness of the letter.

wide letters: C G M O Q W

Fold paper in half, then in half again. Cut quarter circle for both outside and inside of letter.

Open and cut away the section indicated.

Fold paper in half, then in half again. Cut quarter circle for outside of letter only.

Unfold and cut out openings in the areas indicated.

Open and cut away the parts indicated.

The middle bottom of the letter M must be cut half as wide as the final thickness of the letter. The sides of the M are vertical. The middle of the M should go to the bottom.

Fold paper in half, then in half again. Cut quarter circle for both outside and inside of letter.

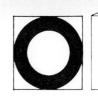

Fold paper in half, then in half again. Cut as indicated.

Open and cut away the extra tails; or cut like the letter O and add a separate piece for the tail.

The middle top of the letter W must be cut half as wide as the final thickness of the letter. The sides of the W slant. The middle of the W should go to the top.

The top or bottom of the following letters can either be pointed or flat, but all must be of the same style when used together in forming a word. Pointed letters should extend either above or below the line.

AA VV NN ZZ
WW MM

Simple three-dimensional lettering is interesting to use and easy to make.

Fold a sheet of paper so that it is twice the height of the intended letter. Fold the paper in half again if the letter can be folded to cut. Make sure when cutting that each letter is held together by some part of the fold.

Mount the bottom of the letters on a poster or bulletin board—the spring in the paper will give the top half a three-dimensional effect.

Chapter Four

Paper Strip Letters

procedure

1. Cut paper strips of uniform width.
2. Form the letters as illustrated, adjusting the paper to the desired size. Cut off the excess portion of the strip, if any.
3. Glue the parts of the letters as necessary.
4. Apply glue to the bottom edge of each letter in turn, and fix in place to form desired words.
5. **Use safety scissors if available.**

s u p p l i e s

1. Paper
2. Scissors
3. Paste or glue

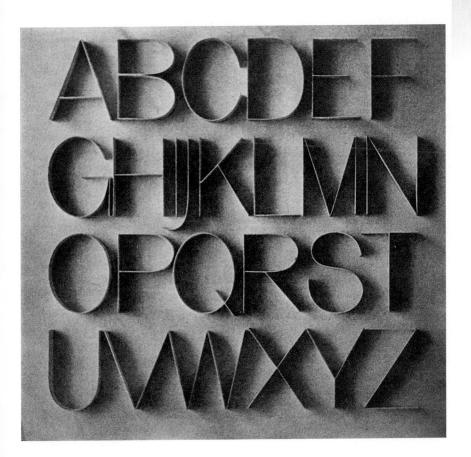

1. Tilt drawing table. (Very helpful, but not essential)
2. Drawing board. (May substitute for above; about 16 inches × 20 inches)
3. "T" square. (Adjustable crosspiece and raised plastic edges are helpful)
4. Paper. (There are many types; experiment. Illustration board usually works well)
5. Pencils. ("F" type)
6. Erasers. (For both ink and pencil; also a kneaded type)
7. Pen holders. (Whatever is comfortable)
8. Pen points. (Fine-pointed, hard and rigid, soft and flexible)
9. Brushes. (Sables are best; they should have fine points)
10. Tempera paint. (Black and white for retouching)
11. Compasses. (One for pencil and one for ink if possible)
12. Ink. (Permanent and waterproof)

Calligraphy

Calligraphy is simply the art of beautiful writing. It is a manual art in contrast with printing, which is a mechanical process. The term printing is often mistakenly used for writing; another term, lettering, is more appropriate. The words calligraphy and lettering are often used interchangeably, although, in most cases, people think of calligraphy as being more florid and elegant. Calligraphy is cursive, the letters being connected as in standard handwriting; in lettering there is usually no connection. Earlier generations may remember their handwriting instruction in which particular emphasis was placed on this skill; more recently this has been somewhat neglected. We are probably most familiar with calligraphy through manuscripts of the Middle Ages, Islamic script, and the brushwork of Asia (principally China and Japan). In the case of the former, calligraphy is considered a pure art.

The invention of printing and the use of movable type made inroads on calligraphy, but a revival occurred in the nineteenth century as a form of protest against industrialization. Most contemporary calligraphy is mistakenly called lettering; it may be done with brush or pen. Even lettering has been considerably aborted by the introduction of "press-type," in which printed letters can be adhered to a sheet through rubbing.

Such Western calligraphy as exists today is generally less flamboyant than that of earlier years. The initial letters in the Book of Kells (Irish, A.D. 800) for example, while beautiful, are virtually illegible. Much modern lettering is associated with commercial applications and requires great legibility as well as impact. The florid style is largely passé.

Most calligraphy, whether with pen or brush, depends on carefully controlled pressures to produce swelling and tapering lines. Asian artists hold the brush upright in contrast to Westerners who hold the instrument at an angle. Earlier masters used black carbon, iron-gall, bistre, and sepia inks. The writing was done with quill, reed, and metal pens as well as brushes. There are specific metal points designed for calligraphy. Many of the pens in use today do not contain a permanent ink; it will fade badly if left exposed to the light. Furthermore, most household pens do not have points with the needed flexibility.

Lettering and calligraphic surfaces are very important, and not all of the paper available today is suitable. Generally the work is done on a smooth surface such as illustration board, although some artists prefer a slight "tooth" (texture). The ink will not penetrate some papers; in others it has an unfortunate tendency to spread. Historical surfaces included parchment, vellum, and wood paneling. Occasionally a ground was painted over the surface to prepare it for the work. If permanence is a factor, the work should be done on paper that has a pure rag content and that is of neutral pH (acidity). Most papers are made of wood pulp, which tends to discolor and deteriorate with the passage of time.

Ordinary handwriting, or chirography, is first taught in the elementary grades. Instruction usually begins with script, or manuscript, writing. By the time the student is in third or fourth grade, the writing becomes cursive with slanted and connected letters. Either kind can be done with distinction; if particularly skillful and beautiful, the latter could be called calligraphic.

The Tools of Calligraphy

Pens specially designed to reproduce the italic style of handwriting:

Speedball Lettering Pens

Speedball Steel Brush

Mitchell Round-Hand no. 0

Mitchell Italic

Osmiroid Broad Oblique

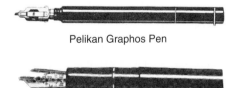

Pelikan Graphos Pen

Platignum Broad Italic

The Pens   These, of course, are the basic tools. There are many kinds and styles of flat pens available today, and each comes in a variety of sizes, or width of nib.

They fall into two categories. Each has its own characteristics as to weight, length and degree of flexibility. It is essential that you find the style of pen which permits you the greatest ease in handling.

The first kind are the nonautomatic feed pens, the most popular of which are the Speedball C series, in 7 sizes. They are inexpensive, easy to use, with much flexibility. They do, however, require frequent filling and, unless the automatic feed is used, can be troublesome, since the ink flow is not controlled. Included here, too, are the steel brushes, which are flexible layers of metal, up to 3/4" wide, allowing letters up to 6" high. Other nonautomatic pens are shown, each with qualities of their own. It is advised that you obtain one of each make and find which suits you.

The automatic-feed fountain pens have the big advantage of controlling the ink flow, so important in any work requiring uniform strokes.

The Osmiroid pen is an automatic feeder, and is useful to those preferring a short nib and an edge that is not as sharp as the Speedball nib.

The Pelikan Graphos has a longer and more flexible nib than either of above, with a very thin and sharpened edge. It is easy to clean due to a swivel-edge top layer.

The Platignum is the most popular of the fountain pens for lettering calligraphy. It lies midway in length and weight, with a well-sharpened edge, in a variety of widths up to 1/8", which allows for a letter one inch high.

It will be necessary for the serious student to experiment with all or most of these pens before finally settling on the pen and holder which are most comfortable in your hand.

Higgins
Pen Cleaner

From "Construction of the Basic Alphabet" (pp. 4–12), "The Tools of Calligraphy" (p. 112) in Hand Lettering Today *by Abraham Switkin. Copyright © 1976 by Abraham Switkin. Reprinted by permission of HarperCollins Publishers, Inc.*

It should not be necessary for relatively inexperienced artists to delve too deeply into letter styles. The basic styles are five in number: Roman, Italic, Gothic, Script, and Block. There are many possible variations on each of these and, as progress is made in the mastery of the basic styles, the artist can move on to more complicated styles. There has always been, and is today, a ready market for skilled lettering and calligraphy, but it is a skill not easily acquired. There are many books on the subjects, some of which can be found in the Art Resources section of this book.

The Tools of Informal Script

Red sable rigger

Red sable pointed tip

Smaller red sable pointed tip

Fountain pen (for a smooth, firm line)

Calligraphy pen (with different-sized flat nibs)

Grease pencil (for texture)

Under the big top

thrilling adventures

children of all ages

Lions, tigers, and bears

The Circus

| Beginning of written forms | Fifth Century | Seventh Century | 900 A.D. |

From Lettering Art in Modern Use *by Raymond A. Ballinger. Copyright © 1952 by Van Nostrand Reinhold Company. Reprinted by permission of the publisher.*

From THE ART OF HAND-LETTERING *by Helm Wotzkow. © 1952 by Watson-Guptill Publications. Reproduced by arrangement with Watson-Guptill Publications, a division of BPI Communications, Inc.*

This is an example of Islamic calligraphy. It is the opening of the surat Maryam (Mary), from al-Qandusi's twelve-volume Quran, which was completed in 1849. The poem in chikeste script (1893) was transcribed by Mahmud Khan (Iran). (From Khibati, A., Sivelmassi, M. The Splendour of Islamic Calligraphy. *New York: Rizzoli International Publications, 1976.)*

Lettering and Calligraphy

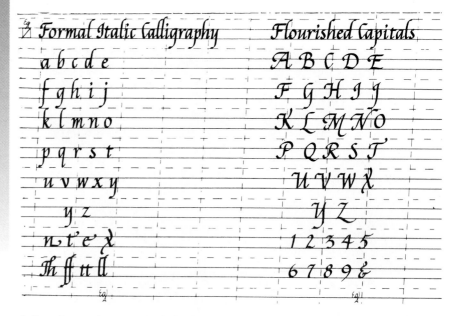

Calligraphy samples. Courtesy of Elmer Girten.

Five pen widths equal height of lower case letters.

The pen nib must be kept at a constant 45° angle at all times.

Thick Med. Thin The square point can make three thicknesses of lines. Only the change of direction of the pen should produce the three lines of various thicknesses.

NEVER TURN THE PEN!

Example:

Thin Med. Thick Med. Thin

Capitals are not as high as ascending letters.

The slant of the lower case letters should be a constant 7° angle. Note the dotted verticle lines on the practice sheet.

The release stroke on eleven of the lower case letters should always be at a 45° angle.

Numbers are slightly taller than the lower case letters.

Courtesy of Elmer Girten.

Illumination

Illumination refers to the drawing and painting of independent illustrations in the margins, and the embellishments of initial letters. The patterns and letter flourishes are usually done in bright colors and gold with great decorative freedom. Initial letters of medieval manuscripts were often incorporated in a comparatively large picture, which might be devotional, domestic, or floral. Illumination was one of the major art forms, especially in the early Middle Ages, and through this medium important traditions of art from classical antiquity were transmitted.

procedure

1. Draw a frame around the edge of the paper.
2. Select one Gothic letter and draw it carefully on the paper so that is touches at least two of the frame lines.
3. In the space around the letter arrange plant life, animals, birds, people, and patterns.
4. Add color to the design.
5. Metallic acrylics, temperas, and markers are available and are wonderful to add to the design.

supplies

1. Pencil and eraser
2. Tempera paint, acrylic paint, watercolors, or markers
   Metallic markers are great to use.
3. Heavy paper

Ceramics

Nature of the Clay Medium

Clay (simple dirt, to many!) is a material of organic and mineral composition. It exists in several forms and grades, some of practical application. Clay is malleable when wet, retains water, and holds together when dry. The earliest humans made clay pottery. Ancient hieroglyphics inscribed in clay still exist. Many brick and adobe building structures have been made of clay. White clay is used commercially as a coating for paper.

Making Clay

Any local clay can be easily transformed into pliable clay for classroom use by the following method. This same method is used in reconditioning any unfired clay.

procedure

1. Break the moist clay into small pieces, and allow them to dry thoroughly.
2. Place the pieces of dry clay into the cloth bag and pound them with the hammer or mallet until they are almost a powder.
3. Fill the container half-full of water and pour the broken or powdered clay into it until the clay rises above the surface of the water. Moist clay will not disintegrate when placed in water, so be sure it is bone dry and broken into pieces. The smaller the pieces, the more quickly the dissolving process will take place. This process is called *slaking*.
4. Allow the clay to soak for at least an hour. This period will vary according to the size of the pieces.
5. Stir the clay thoroughly with a stick or the hands until all the lumps are dissolved. This clay mixture is called *slip*.
6. Pour the slip into the second container through the sieve to remove any foreign matter, and allow it to stand overnight. If there is any excess clear water, pour it off.
7. Remove any excess moisture by placing the clay on the plaster slab. Allow the water to be absorbed until the clay can be kneaded without sticking to the hands.
8. Store the clay in a container with a lid, or cover the container with a damp cloth. Small amounts of clay can be kept moist by using plastic bags or aluminum foil.

supplies

1. Local or commercial water-base clay
2. Two containers for mixing clay (galvanized or plastic buckets, crocks, earthenware crocks, etc. A tightly fitting lid is desirable.)
3. Hammer or mallet
4. Cloth bag
5. Sieve or piece of window screen
6. Plastic bags or aluminum foil for storing clay
7. A plaster slab is ideal for absorbing excess moisture from the clay

Suggestions on Handling Water Clay

1. Pliable clay should be kneaded (wedged) to remove all air bubbles before working.
2. Clay objects should dry slowly to prevent cracking. Thinner forms will dry more quickly than thicker forms. The thin form may be wrapped with a damp cloth to equalize the drying.
3. Cover the clay objects with a damp cloth or paper towels and wrap in a plastic bag or place in a zip-lock plastic bag to slow the drying process or to keep the clay moist from day to day.
4. Cut the clay with a wire; an opened paper clip works well.
5. Moist clay will not adhere to dry clay due to shrinkage.
6. Clay appendages, or details that are to be added to pots or figures, must be of the same consistency as the piece to which they are to be attached. The two areas that are to be joined should be scratched or scored with a sharp tool, and covered with a slip (liquid clay) or wet slightly before being placed together. Then, the joints should be fused into one piece with a smooth tool or the fingers.
7. Holes may be made in flat pieces by pushing soda straws through the moist clay. Holes can be carved or pierced while the clay is leather-hard.
8. Dry clay objects (unfired clay is called greenware) must be fired to a temperature of at least 1500 ° F, or 830 ° C, to be hardened. An electric kiln is the best method for firing. However, the primitive open campfire method can be used.
9. Glaze can be applied to bisque (a piece of clay that has been fired once is called bisque) by dipping, spraying, or with a brush. The piece is then refired. All glaze must be wiped from the bottom or the foot of the piece with a sponge or cloth before firing.
10. A simple, low-fire glaze can be purchased commercially.
11. If no kiln is available, the greenware can be finished by waxing, painting with enamel, shellac, or varnish, or with tempera or acrylic paint. Varnish, shellac, or clear plastic spray, either matte or glossy, can be applied over tempera or acrylic paint for permanency.
12. Overhandling of the clay will cause it to dry rapidly, which in turn causes cracks or crumbling.

Clay Modeling

procedure

method a

1. Beginning with a basic shape of the object to be modeled, squeeze or push the clay to form the features (arms, legs, head, for example). Think of the object as a whole, rather than separate parts.
2. Between working sessions, wrap the clay piece with a moist cloth or paper towels and place in a plastic wrap or zip-lock bag to retain plasticity.
3. Allow the piece to dry slowly at room temperature.
4. Check for firing details.

method b

Beginning with a basic shape of the object to be modeled, use a modeling tool to carve away all unnecessary parts until the piece is formed.

method c

Beginning with a basic shape as in method a, additional parts may be added if correct methods are used. Both parts should be scored at the place of attachment, wet with one finger dipped in water and after they are pressed together, the edges are smoothed together with the use of the finger or a tool. (Scoring means to scratch the clay in two directions with a sharp tool such as a wire to make the surface of the clay look like a window screen. This technique must be used if separate pieces are to stay together.)

Local or commercial water-base or self-hardening clay. For small projects, Crayola Model Magic or Fimo could be used.

Clay may be formed with fingers, hands, and tools (tongue depressors, wood blocks, modeling tools, etc.).

Clay Decoration

Clay can be decorated by pulling or pushing it into a new shape. This can be done by using fingers or hands or by paddling with a piece of wood. Designs can also be carved into leather-hard clay with a sharp tool. Wire loops on a stick are also used to carve patterns.

Fingers were probably the first things used to make designs into the surface of a still wet vessel. Natural objects such as stones, pieces of bone, shells, and sticks were used to make interesting patterns. These things are still used and many more objects have been added to the list; utensils such as craft sticks, tongue depressors, pencils, forks, knives, nuts, and bolts and any other thing that can be pressed into or dragged across the clay to make a design. Stamps can be designed and made by filing, sawing, or drilling into small pieces of wood or the ends of dowels. A piece of moist clay can be made into a stamp by pulling and elongating one end to make a handle, flattening the opposite end and pressing simple tools into the flat end. After the stamp has dried and been fired, it can be used over and over to make patterns on a moist clay form.

A technique traditionally used by many Native Americans is called slip decoration. Liquid clay or slip (see "Making Clay") of a contrasting color is brushed on the moist clay form. It is allowed to dry and is fired. Sgraffito (meaning scratching through) is another method that uses slip and was used with great success by the Greeks. The slip is painted on the leather-hard clay and when the slip and clay is almost dry, a sharp tool is used to scratch a pattern or design through the slip. The underlying color of the clay is allowed to show through the scratches. When the piece is completely dry, it is fired and usually it is sealed with a clear glaze. Engobes are slips with more color and with additives to help them adhere to the clay body.

Polychrome Vase, 8th century Maya. The Mayan Indians of Central America created beautiful and sophisticated ceramics. Indiana University Art Museum, Raymond and Laura Wielgus Collection. Photograph by Michael Cavanagh and Kevin Montague.

An example of decorative ceramics. Lucy M. Lewis "Jar," 1956, earthenware, slipped and painted, 6" x 7¾". Photo courtesy of the U.S. Department of the Interior, Indian Arts and Crafts Board.

Pinch Pot

procedure

1. Knead (wedge) the clay until it is of a workable consistency and the air bubbles have been removed.
2. Roll a ball of pliable clay between the palms of the hands to form a sphere approximately the size of a small orange.
3. Hold the sphere in the fingers of both hands. The thumb should be free to press the clay to form the pot. Keep the thumbs pointed up and form the pot upside down. (See Ill. 1, p. 89).
4. Press the thumbs gently into the center of the sphere and at the same time press with the fingers on the outside while rotating the ball of clay.
5. Continue pressing with both the fingers and thumbs while rotating the clay until the ball is hollowed and the walls are of uniform thickness (approximately ½ inch). Cracks may appear if the clay is too dry or if it is pressed into shape too quickly or forcefully. Repair any such cracks immediately by gently rubbing the fingers over the clay until they disappear.
6. The finished pot, if built correctly, will not have any flat areas. To flatten the bottom of the pot, hold it gently between the fingers with both hands and tap it lightly on a tabletop.
7. Press the end of a key, hairpin, paper clip, etc., into the top edge of the pot, creating a single and interesting decoration.
8. Allow the pinch pot to dry slowly at room temperature.
9. See pages 98 and 99 for firing details.

supplies

Local or commercial water-base clay or self-hardening clay

Variation: Clay Animal Bells

Small clay bells with handles that are animals or animal heads, similar to those crafted by the Mexicans, can be made as a basic pinch pot with some additions. The pot needs to be higher rather than wider and with walls that are of even thickness. The top edge of the pot must be smooth and even. Another piece of clay is used to make the animal, bird, or fish shape for the handle. The bottoms of the handle and the pot should be scored, water or slip applied, and the two blended together. Two holes made with a straw should be put in the bottom of the pot on each side of the handle. Roll a small piece of clay and pierce a hole to make a bead for the clapper. Fire the bell and clapper. Tie a overhand knot in one end of a short piece of jute or string, put it through one of the holes of the bell, and string the bead. Pull the string through the other hole in the bell and tie another knot.

Variation: Connected Pinch Pots

Several pinch pots can be put together by simply scoring or scratching the pots where they are to be joined, applying slip or water to the joints, and smoothing the pots together. If a little space is needed between the pots, buttons of clay can be placed between the pots as long as all surfaces that touch are scored and wet to be blended together.

Variation: Bottle

Two pinch pots can be joined by scoring and putting slip or water on the top edges of both pots. They are then pressed firmly together and then smoothed and sealed with a tool or a finger. It is sometimes helpful to put a coil of fresh clay at the seam to help blend the two pots into a hollow clay ball. With a wire (open paper clip), carefully cut a hole in the top of the ball. This edge should be textured or smoothed as desired if no neck is to be added. It is a good idea to smooth with a tool or finger the inside of the seam where the two parts are joined. A neck for the bottle can be made by rolling a slab of clay and cutting a narrow rectangle with the wire to make a cylinder that will fit the hole in the top of the pot. Remember to score and wet with water or slip the two ends of the rectangle and the edge of the cylinder and the hole. Seal the cylinder to the hole. A small coil of fresh clay at the point where the neck joins the pot is helpful in sealing the two parts.

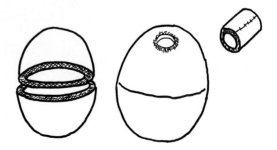

Chapter Five

Coil Pot

procedure

method a

A coil pot consists of coils built on a pinch pot base as done by the Native Americans.

supplies

1. Local or commercial water-base clay
2. Modeling tool
3. Small container for mixing slip

1. Knead (wedge) the clay to a workable consistency.
2. Roll a ball of pliable clay between the palms of the hands to form a sphere approximately the size of a small orange.
3. Hold the sphere in the fingers of both hands. The thumb should be free to press the clay to form the pot. Keep thumbs pointed up and form the pot upside down.
4. Press the thumbs gently into the center of the sphere and at the same time press with the fingers on the outside while rotating the ball of clay (Ill. 1).
5. Continue pressing with both the fingers and the thumbs while rotating the clay until the ball is hollowed and the walls are of uniform thickness (approximately ½ inch). Cracks may appear if the clay is too dry, or if pressed into shape too quickly or forcefully. Repair any such cracks immediately by gently rubbing the fingers over the clay until they disappear.
6. The pot, if built correctly, will not have any flat areas. To flatten the bottom of the pot, hold it gently between the fingers with both hands and tap it lightly on a tabletop.
7. Roll another piece of clay into round strips or coils of approximately ½ inch in diameter, making sure the strip makes a complete turn to ensure its roundness (Ill. 2).
8. Scratch the top edge of the pinch pot base (Ill. 3) and apply a thin coat of slip (liquid clay) over the scratches (Ill. 4). The slip helps the coil adhere to the pinch pot base.
9. Place the coil on the slip-covered edge of the base (Ill. 5). Cut both ends at the same angle so that they fit snugly (Ill. 6). Gently press the coil to the base and fuse the joint both on the outside and inside (Ill. 7).
10. Scratch the top edge of the first coil, apply slip (Ill. 8), and add the second coil (Ill. 9). Remember to fit the ends together tightly. Gently press the second coil to the first coil, and fuse them together.
11. Repeat procedure ten until the coils create a completed form.
12. Allow the pot to dry slowly at room temperature.
13. Check pages 98 and 99 for firing details.

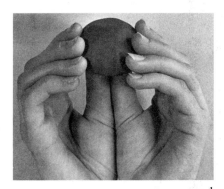

1

2

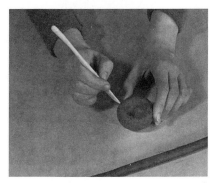

3

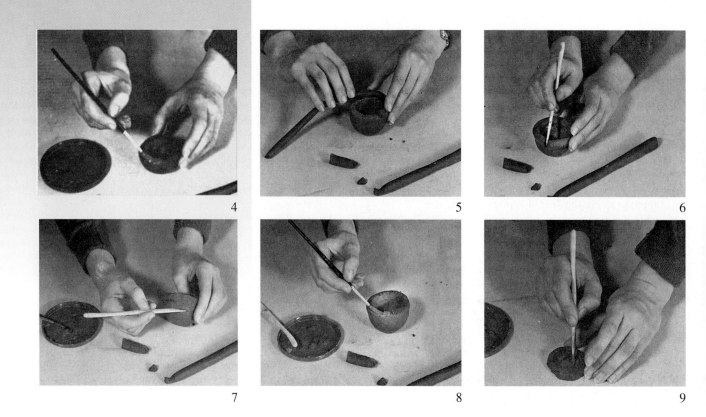

4

5

6

7

8

9

Whether by the use of coils, pinching, or other manipulations, clay ceramic ware has been created for thousands of years. © James L. Shaffer.

method b

1. Knead (wedge) the clay to a workable consistency.
2. Roll the clay into round strips or coils of approximately ½ inch in diameter, making sure the strip makes a complete turn to ensure its roundness (Ill. 2).
3. Wind the strip into a tight coil to the desired size for the base. Fuse the coil together with a small tool or the fingers until all traces of the round strip disappear (Ill. 9). A ball of clay flattened on a damp cloth to approximately ½ inch thickness also makes a good base for a pot when cut to the desired diameter.
4. Scratch the outside top edge of the base, and apply a thin coat of slip (liquid clay) over the scratches. The slip helps the base adhere to the first coil.
5. Place another coil on the slip-covered edge of the base. Cut both ends at the same angle so they fit snugly. Gently press the coil to the base, and fuse the joint both on the outside and inside.
6. Scratch the top edge of the first coil, apply slip, and add the second coil. Remember to fit the ends together tightly. Gently press the second coil to the first coil, and fuse them together.
7. Repeat procedure six until the coils create a complete form.
8. Allow the pot to dry slowly at room temperature.
9. Check pages 98 and 99 for firing details.

Container Coil Pot

A coil pot can be made inside of a plastic bowl so that there is a stable form to hold the coils in place. Make a flat, round slab of clay to put in the bottom of the plastic container. The slab should be large enough to come a little way up the side walls of the container. Gently push the clay slab into the bottom of the bowl with fingertips. Score and wet or apply slip to the top edge of the slab. Roll coils, score, and apply slip or wet and place them on top of the edge of the slab and each other. Patterned flat buttons can be made by pressing a small piece of clay with the palm of the hand and making designs on one side with any tool. Place the button with the pattern toward the plastic bowl and surround with coils and other buttons. Seal the inside of the coils and buttons together by blending them together with the finger or a tool. The clay pot will come out of the plastic bowl when it is partially dry because of the shrinkage of the clay.

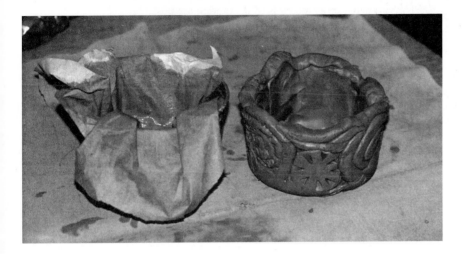

Trivet

Coils can be woven together to make hot pads or trivets from the clay. Wherever the coil touches itself or another coil, it should be scored, slip should be applied on each surface, and then it should be blended together with a tool or finger. Spirals of clay can also be joined in the same manner.

1. Local or commercial water-base clay
2. Rolling pin
3. Two sticks, ½ inch thick
4. Damp cloth
5. Knife, scissors, or wood stick (recommended)
6. Thin paper
7. Sharp pencil

Clay Tiles

procedure

1. Knead (wedge) the clay to a workable consistency.
2. Spread the damp cloth on a smooth tabletop.
3. Place the two sticks on the damp cloth parallel to each other. The space between the sticks will be the width of the finished tile.
4. Roll a ball of clay and place it between the sticks (Ill. 1).
5. Flatten the clay by running the rolling pin along the parallel sticks. The clay will be flattened to the thickness of the sticks (Ill. 2).
6. Cut the slab of clay into tiles, and allow it to become almost dry, or leather-hard (Ill. 3).
7. Plan a design on thin paper, the size of the clay tile.
8. When the clay is almost dry, place the paper design over the tile and transfer the design by retracing the lines with a sharp pencil or instrument.
9. The following three methods of decoration are possible:
   a. Incised—scratch the design into the leather-hard clay with a sharp tool.
   b. Relief—carve away the background areas and allow the design to stand out.
   c. Inlaid—carve out areas of the design and replace with clay of a different color, making sure both clays are of the same consistency.
10. See pages 98 and 99 for firing details.

Variation: Mirror Frames

Make a slab as described under "Clay Tiles." Cut a rectangle or a square from the middle of the slab. Decorate, dry, and fire the frame.

Variation: Coasters

Make a round pattern as large as the top of a glass. Using the pattern, draw and carefully cut out the shapes with a wire. Decorate the disk and gently bend up the edges of the circle. Dry and fire the coaster.

Variation: Cylinder Seal

The cylinder seal was invented by the Sumerian people around 5,000 years ago in the southern Mesopotamian region. With the growth of commerce and trade in this advancing civilization, Sumerians developed the cylinder seal as a way for business people to sign their names to validate business agreements. Individuals created their own unique seals by carving pictures or designs into the surface of a clay or stone cylinder. When the cylinder was rolled across a wet clay surface, these carvings left behind a personalized imprint which served to seal business deals.

To make a cylinder seal, a cardboard can such as that used for frozen juice makes a good form to cast plaster. Follow the directions on mixing plaster (p. 119). After the plaster has been cast in the cylinder form, peel the cardboard can away from the plaster and allow it to dry. Make a design the same size as the cylinder by rolling it on a piece of newsprint to get the necessary dimensions. Follow the directions for carving under "Plaster Block Print" (p. 226). When the carving of the design is completed, roll the cylinder with firm and even pressure over a slab of moist clay. The cylinder seal can also be used in activities involving clay slabs.

Slab Pot

A slab pot is built with flat pieces of clay that are joined together to form a container.

procedure

1. Knead (wedge) the clay to a workable consistency.
2. Spread the damp cloth on a smooth tabletop.
3. Place the two sticks on the damp cloth, parallel to each other. The space between the sticks will be the width of the finished tile.
4. Roll a ball of clay, and place it between the sticks (Ill. 1).
5. Flatten the clay by running the rolling pin along the parallel sticks (Ill. 2). The clay will be flattened to the thickness of the sticks.
6. Place the cardboard pattern over the flattened clay. Using it as a guide, cut around the pattern with a knife (Ill. 3).
7. Using the same cardboard pattern, cut three more slabs and allow them to stiffen to a leather-hard condition.
8. To assemble a pot, score the edge of each slab with a knife (Ill. 4).
9. Put slip on scored edge (Ill. 5), and place two pieced together.
10. Prepare a small roll of clay, and press into the joint of each corner (Ill. 6). Continue this procedure until all four sides are together and smoothed inside and out.
11. Score the edges of a fifth piece, which will be the bottom.
12. Press the four sides on the bottom, and complete (Ill. 7).

supplies

1. Local or commercial water-base clay
2. Rolling pin
3. Two sticks, approximately ½ inch thick and 12–20 inches long
4. Damp cloth
5. Knife, scissors, or wood stick (recommended)
6. Water container for mixing slip
7. Cardboard pattern

 Note: A cylindrical slab pot is made from one slab (Ill. 8) placed on a round base (Ill. 9). Decorations can be done with a syringe filled with slip of a different color. Squeeze syringe, and trail design. Stamp any design in leather-hard clay.

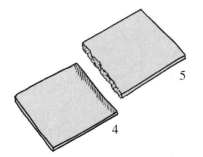

1

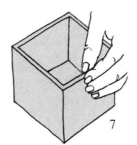

2

3

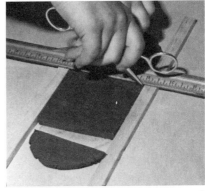

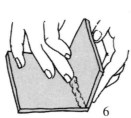

4

5

6

7

8

9

supplies

1. Local or commercial water-base clay
2. Rolling pin
3. Cloth
4. Paper clip
5. Soda straw
6. Two flat sticks, ½ inch thick
7. Pressing tools—spools, forks, nails, screws, etc.
8. Water container
9. Newspaper or paper toweling

Pocket Pot

procedure

1. Knead or wedge clay.
2. Roll out the clay to form a slab, using the rolling pin.
3. Cut one large piece from the slab, using an open paper clip. This is the back of the pot.
4. Cut a second piece from the slab, one-half the size of the first piece. Paper patterns may be used to facilitate this step.
5. Using a soda straw, make a hole close to the top center on the larger slabbed piece. Press and carve designs into the top half of this same piece of clay.
6. Press or carve patterns in the smaller slabbed piece.
7. Wad a tight piece of newspaper or toweling and place it on top of the bottom portion of the larger slab. Score or scratch the bottom face edge of this larger piece of clay.
8. Score or scratch the inside (or underside) edge of the smaller piece of clay.
9. Moisten the fingertips with water or slip and apply to the scratched edges. Now put them together. Seal by pressing both slabs together at the edges.
10. The newspaper wad keeps the shape open while the pot air dries. When the pot is completely dry, remove the paper, and fire in a kiln.

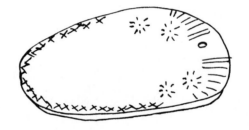

Wind Chimes

procedure

1. Knead or wedge clay.
2. Slab clay. (See "Clay Tiles," p. 92).
3. Cut largest piece, the top of the wind chimes, from the clay slab by using an open paper clip. Any shape may be cut, but be careful of thin projections—they tend to break while drying.
4. The top shape will need one hole for each chime near the lower edge. It will need at least one hole near the upper edge. These holes are made by pushing and turning a large soda straw into the clay. Make sure the holes are far enough away from the edge of the shape so that they will not break. Press and carve designs on both sides of the hanger by using pressing tools.
5. Cut the chimes from the rest of the slab. Put a hole at the top of each. Put patterns on both sides of each chime. Remember different shapes are more interesting.
6. Allow the pieces to dry at room temperature—fire when completely dry.
7. String chimes to hanger by using cords and tying overhand knots.

s u p p l i e s

1. Local or commercial water-base clay or self-hardening clay
2. Rolling pin
3. Cloth
4. Paper clip
5. Two flat sticks, ½ inch thick
6. Pressing tools—spools, forks, nails, screws, etc.
7. Soda straw
8. Fishing line

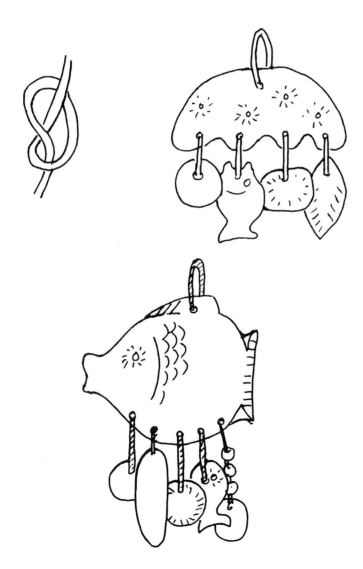

supplies

1. Local or commercial water-base clay (self-hardening clay may be used)
2. Cloth
3. Rolling pin
4. Two flat sticks, ½ inch thick
5. Soda straw
6. Tools for pressing or carving into the clay
7. Empty cardboard cone from inside yarn
8. Paper clip
9. Cord or jute to string bells

Bells and Beads

procedure

1. Knead or wedge clay.
2. Roll out the clay to form a slab, using the rolling pin.
3. Wrap the slab around a cone by laying the cone on the center of the clay, bringing the sides around the cone. Trim away the excess clay with an open paper clip so that the edges overlap. Seal the edges together by pressing with fingers.
4. While the clay is wrapped around the cone, trim the bottom and the top, remembering to keep a small hole in the top of the clay cone. Apply designs and patterns by pressing and carving with any tools (nails, scissors, spools, spoons, forks) available.
5. When finished with patterns, gently remove clay cone from cardboard cone with a twisting motion. Allow to air dry.
6. With the scraps of the slab left, or a new slab, make the clapper for the bell by cutting out a shape with an open paper clip. Make sure the shape will fit inside of the cone. Apply designs or patterns to both sides of clapper and put a hole near the top by using a soda straw.

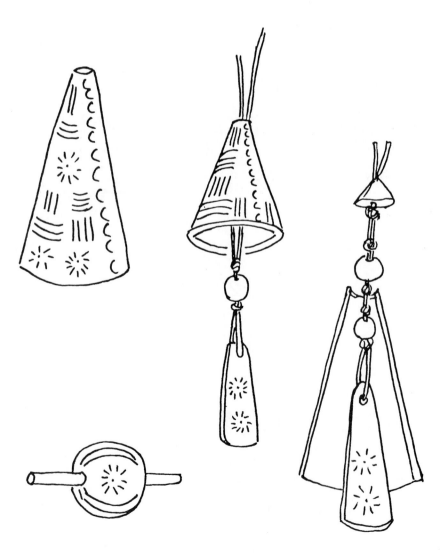

7. Make at least two beads (more are nice) by rolling clay into bead-size balls or other shapes and inserting a soda straw through the shape. Make patterns on the beads and gently remove the straw.

8. Allow all pieces to dry slowly. Fire in a kiln.

9. String bells by putting one end of cord or jute (about 36 to 40 inches) through the hole in the clapper. Bring the ends of the cord together with clapper in the center. Make an overhand knot approximately 2 inches above clapper.

10. Push both cords through the hole in first bead with a twisting motion. Make an overhand knot just above the bead. String cord ends through the top of the cone from the inside.

11. Make an overhand knot in cords, and string a second bead. Make an overhand knot (if additional beads are to be added, always put an overhand knot between the beads). Finish with a final overhand knot at the loose ends of cords.

Special Effects

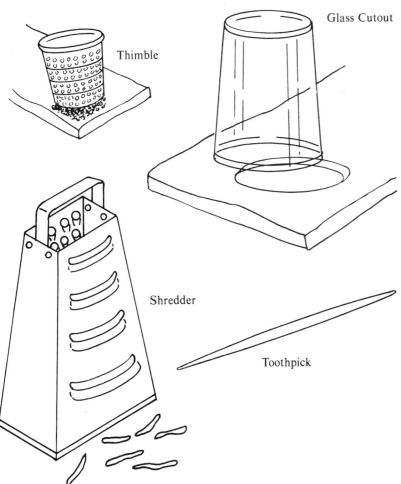

The clay can be manipulated in various ways with common objects or instruments to achieve special effects. Textured objects such as a thimble can be pressed into the clay to produce a textured surface. Glasses, bowls, and the like can be forced through the clay for cut-out shapes. Large pieces of clay can be drawn across a shredder to produce clay slivers to be used in building up or decorating pieces. Toothpicks, nut picks, sticks, and other similar items can be used to manipulate or texture the clay. Glazes can be applied to the clay to provide a watertight glossy or matte coating. They are available in many colors. See "Kilns" in this chapter.

supplies

1. Vented kiln
2. Kiln shelves
3. Shelf supports
4. Kiln furniture (stilts, triangles)
5. Pyrometric cones
6. Kiln wash (Glaze drippings are easily removed from shelves coated with kiln wash.)
7. Kiln cement (for repairing cracks and chips in kiln wall)

Kilns

Clay pieces that have just been completed are called *greenware* and should dry naturally before being fired in a kiln. Artificial heat is likely to cause the piece to crack. All decorations must be completed on the product before the piece is completely dry.

When the clay is completely dry (bone dry), it is ready to be placed in the kiln for firing. Firing will not only vitrify, or fuse, the clay but will burn out any impurities.

There are numerous kilns of all sizes, shapes, and prices, which are fueled with gas, oil, coal, or electricity. Most electric kilns use 220-volt current.

The inside firing chambers of table model kilns have a large range and usually a maximum of 2300° F, which is more than adequate. Several inside firing chamber sizes of electric table model kilns are: (Ill. 1) 14⅜ inch opening, 13½ inches deep, 1.37 cubic feet; (Ill. 2) 17.5 inch opening, 18 inches deep, 2.63 cubic feet; and (Ill. 3) 23⅜ inch opening, 27 inches deep, 7 cubic feet.

 Note: Children should not be near any active kiln.

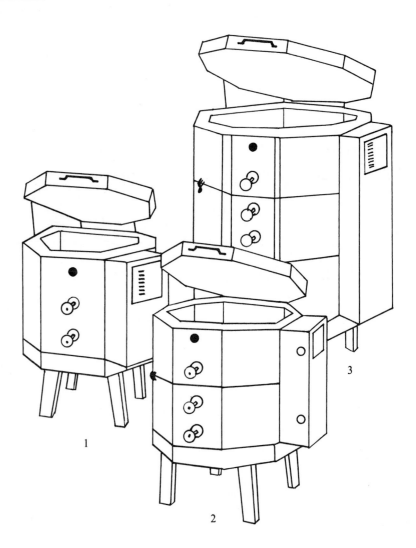

Most kilns will have a switch control for low, medium, and high temperatures. Some will come equipped with a pyrometer, an indicator for reading the kiln temperature. These are ideal, but much cheaper and equally accurate are pyrometric cones (Ill. 4), which are used to indicate fusion.

Three or four of these cones with different fusing points are placed at a slight angle to one of their faces (not on their edge) in a piece of pliable clay (Ill. 4). The clay is allowed to dry, then placed in the kiln so the cones can be seen through the spy hole in the kiln door. A piece of fire brick may be necessary to lift the cones high enough to be seen.

The kiln will heat slowly and a periodic check of the cones through the spy hole will let you know the approximate temperature of the heat as the cones begin to melt. When the last cone (Ill. 5) is beginning to melt, the kiln can be turned off, as the desired temperature has been attained.

A piece fired only once is called *bisque,* or biscuitware, and it can be glazed and fired again. A glaze will give the pieces a glasslike finish. Glazes can be purchased from a commercial company that will give instructions for use and the temperature cone at which the glaze matures. (Avoid any glazes not certified by the manufacturer as being free of lead and nontoxic.) The glaze is applied by spraying, brushing, or dipping. Dipping a piece in and out of a bowl of glaze may be the most practical method. Fingermarks are removed by daubing glaze on the spots with a brush.

Cone Temperature Chart

Pyrometric Cones

	Fahrenheit	Centigrade		Fahrenheit	Centigrade
Cone 018	1328	720	Cone 05	1904	1040
Cone 016	1463	795	Cone 04	1940	1060
Cone 015	1481	805	Cone 03	2039	1115
Cone 014	1526	830	Cone 02	2057	1125
Cone 013	1580	860	Cone 01	2093	1145
Cone 012	1607	875	Cone 1	2120	1160
Cone 011	1643	894	Cone 2	2129	1165
Cone 010	1661	905	Cone 3	2138	1170
Cone 09	1706	930	Cone 4	2174	1190
Cone 08	1742	949	Cone 5	2201	1205
Cone 07	1814	990	Cone 6	2246	1230
Cone 06	1859	1015			

Temperature equivalents figured at firing rate of 300° F or 149° C per hour.

Chalk

Nature of the Medium

Chalk or Pastel

The original chalks for drawing, some still in use today, were pure earth, cut and shaped into implements. The addition of a binder created a fabricated chalk that we know as pastel. Sanguine Conté closely approximates the pure earth material. Chalks used by the early masters were generally limited to reds (sanguine), black, and white. These colors have been greatly increased in number.

Some artists apply chalks in separate strokes, letting the color blending take place in the viewer's eye. Others are not reluctant to blend the colors, and do so successfully, although there is a danger of the colors being muddied. Of course, there is no need to caution children against this; they should be encouraged to explore by rubbing with fingers, stumps, cotton swabs, or anything available. Most children will select and use chalks fearlessly.

Chalk drawing is best done on a paper with "tooth," or a slightly coarse, abrasive surface. This texture helps the paper trap and hold the chalk particles. Many papers have this character, including the inexpensive manila.

Chalks are brittle and easily broken. They are also impermanent, smearing easily. Completed works should be sprayed with a protective fixative; this should be done with optimum ventilation.

Chalks possessing strong color and binding ingredients should not be used on chalkboards—they are nearly indelible.

Chalk strokes can be strengthened and their character altered by wetting the chalk or paper. Various liquids have been used experimentally with interesting results, including dipping the chalk sticks in buttermilk, starch, and sugar water.

Drawing with Chalk

procedure

1. *Light chalks on dark papers*
   This type of drawing is helpful in aiding the child to interpret subjects that are light in value, such as snowscapes, snowmen, polar bears, or spring flowers. The chalk and dark paper produce good contrast in tone and brilliance of color.

supplies

1. Chalks
2. Colored paper
3. Fixative or clear plastic spray
4. Insect sprayer or atomizer for application of fixative over chalk

2. *Chalk on grey paper*
   A middle-tone grey paper allows for good contrasts in both light and dark chalks. This contrast is developed most effectively if some of the paper is allowed to show through.

3. *Chalk on colored paper*
   Subtle and bold contrasts may be achieved, depending on the colors chosen.

4. **Use adequate ventilation when spraying**

Shading with Chalk Dust

s u p p l i e s

1. Chalk
2. Flat, hard tool for scraping
3. Cotton, facial tissue, or chalk applicator

procedure

Scrape the tool along the side of the chalk sticks to produce dust. The dust particles from the chalk may be scraped directly onto areas of drawings done in other media. The cotton can be used to blend the dust in tonal passages that will enrich the original drawing.

 Note: Chalk is easily smeared, thus the completed drawing should have some protection. Commercially manufactured transparent sprays and fixatives are of some help, as is a home recipe to be found on page 341. **Use sprays with optimum ventilation.**

supplies

1. Colored chalks
2. Wet paper

Wet Paper Chalk Drawing

procedure

Draw over the damp paper with the chalk. The colors will generally be brighter and more exciting than those applied to dry paper. It is possible to use wet and dry techniques on one drawing by painting plain water over some areas prior to drawing. If the paper is not of fairly heavy stock, there is a danger of irregular wrinkling and curling.

 Note: Soaking chalk sticks for ten minutes in a strong solution of sugar water before use reduces the tendency to smear. Commercially manufactured transparent sprays and fixatives are of some help, as is a home recipe to be found on page 341. **Use sprays with optimum ventilation.**

Chalk Textures

procedure

1. Hold a thin paper against a surface that has a definite texture and rub the chalk over the paper. The texture will be transferred to the paper by the chalk.
2. Place the paper against another texture and transfer it to another portion of the paper.
3. Textures may be overlapped.

 Note: A number of suggested textural surfaces are shown below. Chalk is easily smeared, thus the completed drawing should have some protection. Commercially manufactured transparent sprays and fixatives are of some help, as is a home recipe to be found on page 341. **Use sprays with optimum ventilation.**

s u p p l i e s

1. Chalk
2. Thin drawing paper
3. Pencil or crayon
4. Textured surfaces

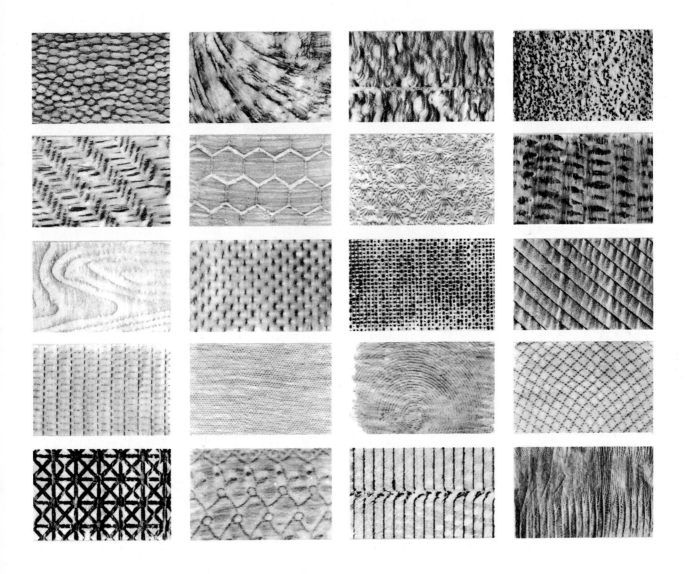

1. Paper
2. Carbon paper
3. Chalk
4. Clear spray

Chalk and Carbon Paper

procedure

1. Draw picture design on paper with colored chalk.
2. Place carbon paper face down on chalk drawing.
3. Run hand over carbon paper to transfer chalk drawing to carbon paper.
4. Remove carbon paper and spray it with clear spray to keep the design from smearing. **Use adequate ventilation when spraying.**

These illustrations are chalk drawings.

These illustrations are carbon paper prints.

Chalk and String Design

supplies

1. String
2. Chalk
3. Soft wooden board
4. Thumbtacks
5. Paper
6. Plastic spray or fixative

procedure

1. Press a tack into the board.
2. Tie a string to the tack.
3. Rub the string with a piece of chalk.
4. Place the string over a sheet of paper, pull the string taut with one hand, and snap the string against the paper with the other hand.
5. Move the paper into different positions and repeat steps three and four after each movement of the paper.

 Note: Assorted colors may be rubbed against the strings. Lines may be intentionally blurred by stroking. Shapes bounded by the lines may be colored in to create a more definite pattern. The chalk should be "fixed" to the paper with a protective coating of clear plastic spray of fixative. **Use adequate ventilation when spraying. Account for all tacks lest they be sat or walked on!**

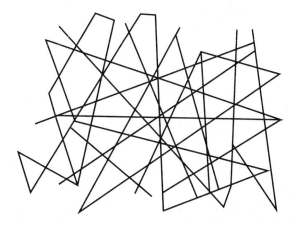

Chalk and Tempera Paint

procedure

1. Make a light pencil outline drawing on paper.
2. Mix tempera or latex paint to the consistency of cream.
3. Dip end of desired colored chalk into chosen color of paint.
4. Apply paint with chalk stick in brushlike strokes.
5. Continue until picture is completed.
6. Detail can be added with plain chalk.
7. Protect the picture with transparent spray. **Use adequate ventilation when spraying.**

Chalk and Tempera Print

procedure

1. Complete a design or drawing with colored chalk on a piece of good quality paper. Be sure to use the chalk heavily.
2. Coat another piece of paper of the same size with white tempera paint. Use a large brush and paint in both directions to smooth the paint over one entire side.
3. While the tempera is still wet, place the chalk drawing face down in the tempera paint.
4. Rub firmly over the paper with fingers and/or the hand.
5. Separate the two papers before they are dry.
6. Two prints will result—the chalk will have merged with the print on both prints (Ills. 1, 2).
7. Experiments with different colors will produce numerous effects.

1

2

Chalk, Tempera, and Starch Print

procedure

1. Mix the liquid starch and tempera paint to produce a dripless paint (Ill. 1).
2. Brush the mixture on a sheet of paper (Ill. 2).
3. Scratch a design in the wet paint (Ill. 3).
4. Coat another sheet of paper with colored chalk (Ill. 4).
5. Place the second sheet, chalk side down, over the wet paint surface (Ill. 5).
6. Lightly rub the back of the top sheet (Ill. 5).
7. Pull off the top sheet (Ill. 6).

supplies

1. Liquid starch
2. Powder tempera
3. Brush
4. A scratching instrument, such as a stick or a spoon
5. Colored chalk
6. Two sheets of paper

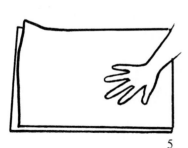

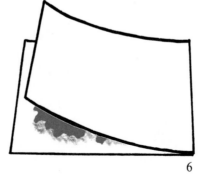

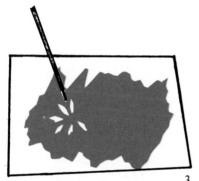

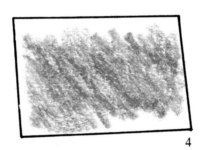

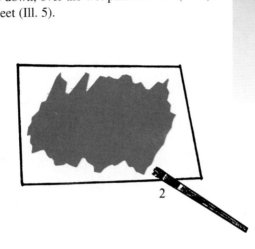

supplies

1. Paper
2. Colored chalk
3. Sugar
4. Water container
5. Water

Chalk Painting

procedure

1. Mix 6 or 8 tablespoons of sugar into a small amount of water until dissolved into a thin solution.
2. Soak the chalk sticks in the sugar water solution for 10 to 15 minutes.
3. Use soaked chalk stick as a paint brush.
4. When chalk strokes become hard and dry, the chalk will not rub off.

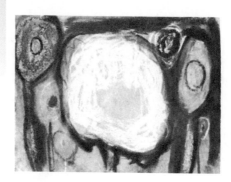
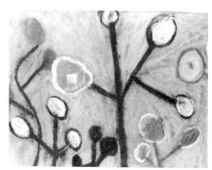

supplies

1. Colored chalk
2. Sandpaper (rough)

 Note: Greater richness of color can be achieved if the sandpaper is moist. It will also attract and hold greater quantities of rich chalk color.

Chalk on Sandpaper

procedure

Draw with the chalk on the sandpaper. The rough surface of the sandpaper will help to achieve rich and vivid textural effects.

Crafts

7

supplies

1. 1 cup cornstarch
2. 2 cups baking soda (1 lb. box)
3. 1¼ cups water
4. Saucepan
5. Stove or hot plate
6. Aluminum foil
7. Food coloring
8. Plastic bag
9. Watercolors or tempera paint
10. Clear commercial spray
11. Ball of clay (not necessary, but good for drying beads)—a piece of styrofoam could serve the same purpose
12. Toothpicks
13. Rolling pin or glass jar

Caution: Some of the activities in this chapter call for the use of X-acto knives. Extreme care and supervision must be utilized whenever X-acto knives are used. Safety instructions should be given before **EVERY** use of the knives. X-acto knives are now sold with safety caps, but separate caps may be purchased for older knives. Heavy corrugated cardboard should always be placed under the paper or material being cut. The X-acto knife is held like a pencil, with the fingers holding the knife on the textured ring. The slanted, sharpened edge should be directly over the line to be cut and the position of the knife or the paper should be changed if the line changes direction. Keep the fingers of the holding hand out of the way of the blade, usually above the cutting area. Remind students often to check themselves and the position of the knife and their hands.

Beads from Soda and Cornstarch Mixture

procedure

1. Combine cornstarch, baking soda, and water in a saucepan. Cook over medium heat, stirring constantly.
2. When the mixture is thickened to doughlike consistency, turn out on a piece of aluminum foil or breadboard.
3. Food coloring may be worked into the clay when it has cooled slightly.
4. Cover the clay with aluminum foil or plastic to keep it pliable when not in use, and store it in the refrigerator.
5. Pinch off a lump of the mixture, and shape into a bead. Spheres and cylinders can be formed easily by rolling the mixture between the palms of the hands.
6. Roll out the mixture flat with a rolling pin or glass jar, and cut flat beads from it.
7. Punch a hole through each bead with a toothpick. Leave the toothpicks in the beads, and stick them into the ball of clay for drying. Turn the toothpicks in the beads occasionally to keep them from sticking.
8. Shellac the beads, and when they are dry, string them.
9. **All cooking should be done by the supervisor. Also, use adequate ventilation when spraying.**

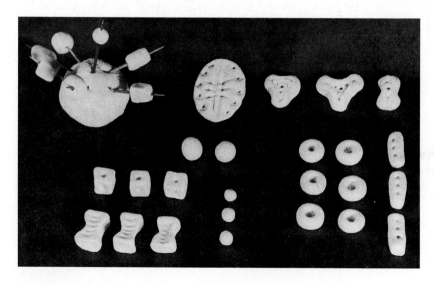

Bleach Painting

procedure

1. Place colored paper on several thicknesses of newspaper.
2. Draw a picture with cotton swab dipped in liquid bleach. Give careful supervision to the use of the bleach.
3. The bleach will lighten the paper in seconds.
4. Allow the colored papers to dry separately from the newspaper.
5. Other media, such as markers, oil pastels, crayons, or ink, may be added to the picture when the bleach is dry.
6. **Be watchful, and provide good ventilation.**

supplies

1. Cotton swabs
2. Plastic container
3. Liquid bleach
4. Colored paper

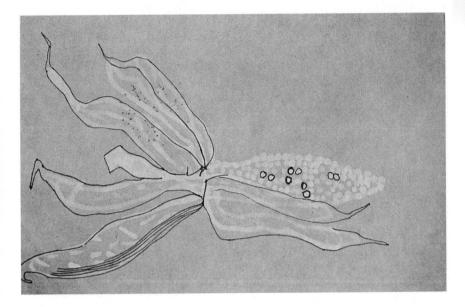

supplies

1. Piece of cardboard
2. A collection of items, most of which might be discarded, such as small scraps of cloth and textured paper, bottle caps, buttons, toothpicks, sand, pebbles, soda straws, string, yarn, rope, or used sandpaper. Use only those items that can be adhered with some permanency to the cardboard.
3. Scissors
4. Paste or glue
5. Use safety scissors and nontoxic glue

Collage

Collage is a French word similar to collé, except that materials of all kinds are admissible to the picture. Painted and drawn passages may be combined with scrap materials to create a desired effect.

procedure

1. Arrange these items into a design or picture.
2. When satisfied with the arrangement, paste or glue the items on the cardboard background.
3. Any necessary details can be added with crayons or paints.

Embossed Metal

procedure

1. Cut the foil to the size of the finished work.
2. Develop a design on paper the same size as the piece of foil.
3. With a pad of newspaper or a cloth under the foil, fasten the design on top of the foil with a piece of tape and draw over the design with a dull pencil.
4. Decide which areas of the design are to be raised (traditionally, the main shapes are raised). Begin tooling with the foil facing down on the pad. Using a suitable tool, make short coloring strokes side by side. Emboss the foil from both sides to avoid wrinkles. Remove the pad, place the foil on a smooth hard surface, and work around the raised portions to flatten the background.
5. India ink, or black acrylic or latex paint, can be wiped over the surface of the foil and quickly wiped off to give the look of oxidation.
6. Colored permanent markers with bullet points can be used to color the foil, particularly if the aluminum side is used as the front.

Variation: Design Coins

Cut 2 circles of the foil. Cut a slightly smaller circle from mat board or cardboard to be the core for the two sides of the tooled coin. Antique the coin surface with the India ink, or black acrylic or latex paint. Glue the sides of the coin to the cardboard core and crimp the edges.

Variation: Egyptian Mask

Using some of the Egyptian masks (such as the gold mask of Tutankhamen) as examples, draw the shape of the mask on the foil. With the gold side as the front, tool lightly on both sides of the foil. Using permanent markers, add color to the headpiece, at the eyes, eyebrows, and the collar piece.

supplies

1. Colored aluminum foil, 38 gauge. Color on one side with bright aluminum on the other.
2. Modeling tool (anything that will not cut or scratch the metal, such as a dull pencil, a sharpened wooden dowel, or a craft stick).
3. Pad of newspaper or towel
4. Pencil and newsprint
5. Acrylic paint, latex paint, India ink, permanent markers
6. Paper towel or piece of cloth

1. Whiting
2. Shellac
3. Powdered tempera
4. Container for mixing the whiting and shellac
5. Containers for storing gesso
6. Brush
7. Carving tools, such as nail, scissors, knife, or hair pin
8. Paper and pencil
9. Wooden box, wooden plaque, or heavy cardboard
10. Paste, wax, and cloth
11. Careful with knives and scissors; safety scissors are best

Gesso Carving

procedure

1. Make a pencil drawing the size of the object to be decorated.
2. Mix the whiting and shellac until it is thick and creamy. Add tempera paint for color.
3. Paint the surface of the box or plaque with gesso until it is approximately ⅛ inch thick.
4. When the gesso is medium dry, transfer the design by laying the drawing over the gesso and retracing it with a pencil. Carve out the necessary areas.
5. When the gesso is thoroughly dry, polish with a paste wax and cloth.

supplies

1. Commercial dry-ground gesso (or see formula on page 339)
2. Hot plate and old double boiler
3. Paper plates
4. Shellac, varnish, or clear plastic spray
5. Brush
6. Tempera paint or enamel paint
7. Careful with knives and scissors; safety scissors are best

Gesso Plate

procedure

1. Mix the gesso according to the directions on the can, or see the formula on page 339.
2. Paint two or three paper plates on both sides with the gesso, which should be the consistency of heavy cream.
3. Press the plates together while still wet, making sure the edges fit tightly. Allow them to dry.
4. Apply as many coats of gesso as are necessary to fill any cracks or nicks, or to produce the desired thickness. Allow this to dry.
5. Sandpaper the plate until smooth.
6. Paint the entire plate with a base color.
7. Decorations can now be added with contrasting colors.
8. Apply a protective coat of varnish, shellac, or plastic spray over the plate if tempera paint is used. **Use sprays with optimum ventilation.**

Linear String

procedure

1. Make a pencil drawing of the desired subject.
2. Cover the pencil drawing with waxed paper, and fasten it in place with tape.
3. Place glue-covered string on waxed paper over the line drawing.
4. When the glue is dry, remove the string construction from the waxed paper.

 Note: If color is wanted, the string can be dyed before or painted after the design is completed. These objects can be incorporated into mobiles.

 supplies

1. Heavy string or cord
2. Waxed paper
3. Glue
4. Pencil
5. Paper
6. Tape

supplies

1. Mailing tube sections (precut by the teacher)
2. Cardboard
3. Colored tissue paper or printed material
4. Large watercolor brushes
5. Polymer or white glue and water (equal proportions)
6. Clear spray

Mailing Tube Containers

This project can be used to make banks, napkins rings, pencil and brush holders, planters, or bracelets.

procedure

1. If a base is needed, place a piece of cardboard under the end of the tube, trace around it, cut it, and affix the base to the mailing tube with the polymer or glue.
2. Paint the surface of the tube with polymer or diluted glue.
3. Tear pieces of the tissue paper and press them on the surface of the tube, or use a printed photo as on page 133.
4. Continue with layers of glue and paper until the desired degree of richness is achieved.
5. Spray surface for protection. **Use adequate ventilation when spraying.**

Notes: If a bank is desired, cut the top as the base, cut in half, cut out the coin slit, then glue together on the top (Ill. 1).
　　If a pencil and brush holder is desired, cut the top, and drill holes in the top before gluing to the tube (Ill. 2).
The object can be further decorated with wrapped string, transfer pictures (see p. 133), or decorative paper strips (Ill. 3). The interior may also be lined with felt.
　　Small rings can be used for napkin rings with decoration added (Ill. 4). If designed as a planter, line the inside with liquid asphaltum to waterproof before use (Ill. 5).

Plaster Mixing

procedure

Mix the plaster as follows:

1. Pour the desired amount of water into the mixing container (Ill. 1).
2. Add the plaster to the water by sifting it through the fingers or gently shaking it from a can or small cup (Ill. 2).
3. Continue adding the sifted plaster to the water until the plaster builds up above the surface. Allow to soak twenty or thirty seconds to thoroughly blend the mixture (Ill. 3).
4. Stir the plaster thoroughly with the hands until it is smooth and creamy, making sure that any lumps of plaster are broken, and stir gently to avoid bubbles (Ill. 4).
5. Once the plaster is mixed, do not add more water to thin, or more plaster to thicken, because the same consistency cannot be regained.
6. Pour the plaster into a container, which can be used for the mold. Gently agitate the mold to bring any bubbles to the surface (Ill. 5).

Note: Begin to clean up immediately after pouring the plaster in the mold, as it will harden rapidly once the chemical reaction takes place. Any remaining plaster should be wiped from the pan immediately and rolled in newspaper so that it might be disposed of more easily. Do not wash plaster down any drain. When cleaning the hands, tools, and mixing pan, be sure the water runs continuously. Teacher should do the bulk of the clean-up.

1. Molding plaster
2. Container for mixing plaster
3. Water
4. Newspaper for cleaning
5. Container to be used as mold

1

2

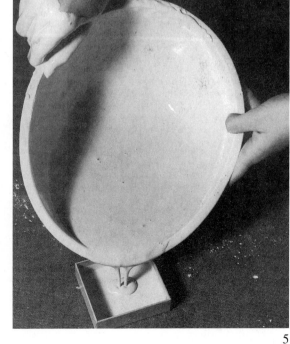

3

4

5

1. Cardboard container to be used as a mold
2. Scraps of thin colored or textured linoleum or thin plastic floor tile
3. Molding plaster
4. Bowl in which to mix plaster
5. Heavy-duty scissors
6. Paste
7. Pliers

 Note: Warming the linoleum will make it easier to cut.

 Note: Begin to clean up immediately after pouring the plaster in the mold, as it will harden rapidly once the chemical reaction takes place. Any excess plaster remaining should be wiped from the pan immediately and rolled in newspaper so that it might be disposed of more easily. Do not wash plaster down any drain. When cleaning the hands, tools, and mixing pan, be sure the water runs continuously.

Mosaic Plaster Plaque

procedure

1. Place the container to be used as a mold on a sheet of paper and trace around it with a pencil. This will provide a pictorial area of the same dimensions as the completed work, on which the preliminary drawing may be done. Divide the subject matter in the drawing into interesting sections that can be easily cut from the linoleum of plastic tile.
2. Transfer the various parts of the design to the linoleum or floor tile of the desired color and cut out with scissors. Break into pieces with the pliers if brittle plastic is used.
3. Place a small spot of paste on the face of each piece and fasten face down in the cardboard mold to form the original design (Ill. 1). Approximately ⅛ inch space should remain between the various sections and the edge of the mold.
4. Mix the plaster (see illustrations, p. 119).
5. Pour the plaster into the mold to the desired thickness (Ill. 2). Gently agitate the box to make sure the plaster completely surrounds the individual pieces of the design and to also bring any bubbles to the surface. If a wall plaque is desired, a wire hook can be placed in the plaster before it hardens completely.
6. Allow the plaster to dry thoroughly before removing the cardboard box mold. If the cardboard adheres to the plaster, wash it off under running water.
7. Smooth any of the sharp edges by scraping with any available tool. Repair any flaws that might appear at this time.
8. The finished plaque can be soaked in a solution of white soap flakes and then wiped dry with a cloth. This will produce a glossy, high-polish finish.

 Note: A plaster relief can be created by carefully lifting out the pieces of plastic tile or linoleum. **It might be best for the supervisor to do the cutting.**

1

2

Plaster Tile Mosaic

procedure

1. Place the wood or masonite to be used as the tile on a sheet of paper and trace around it with a pencil. This will provide a pictorial area the same dimensions as the completed tile.
2. Create a drawing within this area.
3. Transfer the drawing to the wood or masonite.
4. Break the plastic into small pieces with the pliers, and glue in place on the tile. Allow a small space between each piece as it is placed. If pieces are too small they can be picked up with tweezers.
   a. Avoid light-colored tiles, as they will not contrast with the white plaster surrounding each piece.
   b. If the entire tile is not to be covered with mosaic, be sure a border is included.
5. Mix the plaster (see illustrations, p. 119).
6. Pour the plaster over the tile, which has been placed on newspaper, and work it between the mosaic pieces.
7. Level the plaster by pulling the straightedge over the surface. (Thin pieces of mosaic should be used, as thick pieces will be pulled out of place.)
8. Fill in all bubbles and repair any flaws before the plaster becomes too hard.
9. Only a thin film of plaster should appear on the mosaic tiles after scraping with the straightedge.
10. When almost dry, clean film from the tile pieces with fingers, tissue, or rag.

supplies

1. Piece of wood or masonite the size of the mosaic to be made
2. Scraps of thin, colored, plastic floor tile (all must be the same thickness)
3. Molding plaster
4. Bowl in which to mix plaster
5. Pliers
6. Glue
7. Straightedge wider and longer than the tile to be made
8. Tweezers

 Note: Begin to clean up immediately after pouring the plaster into the mold, as it will harden rapidly once the chemical reaction takes place. Any remaining plaster should be wiped from the pan immediately and rolled in newspaper so that it might be disposed of more easily. Do not wash plaster down any drain. When cleaning the hands, tools, and mixing pan, be sure the water runs continuously. Teacher should do the bulk of the clean-up.

Mosaics were widely used in the classical cultures. Floor Mosaic from Antioch, (Roman) 2nd century, A.D. Courtesy of Bowling Green University.

supplies

1. Notepaper or place cards
2. Leaves, delicate flowers, lacy ferns, grasses, and other natural objects
3. Newspapers
4. Glue
5. Clear Contact paper
6. Ruler
7. Scissors

Pressed Nature Notepaper

procedure

1. Collect flowers, ferns, leaves, grasses, and other natural objects, and dry them by pressing between sheets of newspaper weighted with books or other heavy objects. Let them dry about one week, changing newspapers occasionally.
2. Arrange these natural objects where they appear to be most pleasing on the notepaper or place cards.
3. When satisfied with the arrangement, place dots of glue on the backs of the natural objects, just enough to hold them in place until the Contact paper can be applied.
4. Cut a square or rectangle of clear Contact paper large enough to cover and extend a little beyond the design.
5. Peel the backing from the Contact paper and carefully apply it, pressing it firmly to the place card or notepaper. If a bubble forms in the Contact paper, prick it with a pin and press it out.
6. **Use safety scissors if possible.**

Pressed Nature Picture

procedure

1. Collect flowers, leaves, ferns, grasses, and other natural objects and dry them by pressing between sheets of newspaper weighted with books or other heavy objects. Let dry about one week, changing newspapers occasionally.
2. Follow steps one through nine on pages 331 and 332, "Cutting a Mat," to determine the size of the finished picture.
3. White or light plain material may be stretched over the cardboard covering an area an inch larger all around than the opening of the mat.
4. Arrange dry, pressed natural objects into a pleasing design, and when satisfied, glue them into place. (Just dot the backs of the natural objects with glue as they are pressed into place on the picture.)
5. The top mat of the picture may be covered with decorative material if desired. Stretch and turn the under-edge of the material, and hold it in place with double-sided tape. The inside corners of the material will need to be slit in order to turn and tape. Simple, decorative braids, outlining the inside edge of mat, may enhance the picture. It is necessary to experiment to obtain best results.
6. Frame the finished picture. (Frames may be spray painted, stained, or rubbed with gold paint and then buffed.) **Use sprays with optimum ventilation.**
7. **The use of razor blades should be left to the teacher.**

supplies

1. Leaves, delicate flowers, lacy ferns, grasses, and other natural objects
2. Newspapers
3. Matboard and cardboard the same size for backing
4. White or light-colored material (material used for drapery or dress linings is good)
5. Scissors
6. Ruler
7. Pencil
8. Razor blade
9. Glue
10. Decorative braids (optional)
11. Material to cover top mat (tiny checks or prints might enhance picture)
12. Inexpensive picture frame
13. Double-sided tape, if mat is to be covered with material

supplies

1. Cardboard
2. Construction paper
3. White glue
4. Assortment of seeds or natural objects
5. Food coloring
6. Pencil
7. String or yarn
8. Clear spray

Relief Mosaic from Seeds or Beads

procedure

1. Sketch the design on construction paper, carefully defining the areas where seeds are to be placed.
2. Using glue, mount the construction paper on cardboard, the same size as the construction paper.
3. Spread the glue on one area of the design at a time, and press the seeds, beads, or natural objects into place, filling the area. (For a neater appearance in the design, it is best to outline each area, then proceed to fill the rest of the area.)
4. When placing small pieces, it is helpful to put a dab of glue on the end of a toothpick to pick up and place each seed.
5. When the glue is completely dry and excess pieces have been shaken off, spray the design with three thin coats of clear spray. **Use adequate ventilation when spraying.**

 Note: Additional details may be added to the picture with heavy string, yarn, or other decorative materials (for whiskers, stems, and so forth).

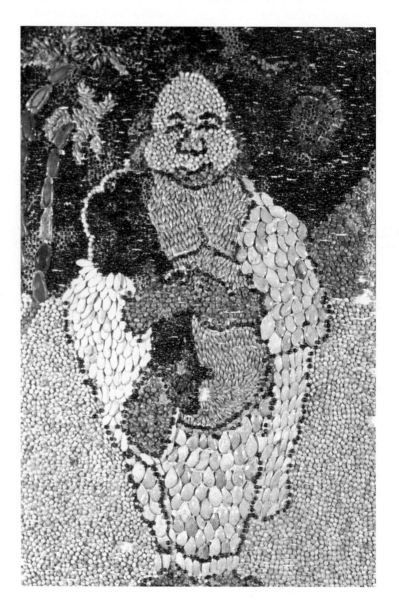

Chapter Seven

Salt and Flour Relief

procedure

1. Cover the cardboard or wood with a thin film of salt and flour mixture.
2. Keeping a design in mind, create a semiround relief, building up masses of the salt and flour mixture to various heights. Additional salt and flour may be added when the first application has dried enough to support another layer.
3. When the modeling is completed, it may be embellished by the addition of color while still moist.
4. Additional interest may be created by pressing objects, textures, and patterns into the wet salt and flour.

 Note: Topographical maps or aerial views are especially suitable for treatment in this manner.

1. Combine three parts salt with one part flour and enough water to bring solution to the consistency of dough. This will create a mass suitable for sculptural modeling; the thickness may be modified for individual needs or desired methods of application by varying the quantity of water.
2. Heavy cardboard or piece of wood
3. Watercolor paints
4. Brush
5. Water container

supplies

1. Wax (old candles work best, but clean and snip off burned wick); paraffin (good and melts rapidly); beeswax (excellent, but too expensive); mutton tallow (good, but becomes rancid too easily). See p. 339.
2. Wicks, cotton twine (old candle wicks)
3. Can or old pan (for melting wax)
4. Colored crayons (for coloring wax)
5. Double boiler
6. Thermometer (candy thermometer)
7. Box or bucket
8. Damp, fine sand
9. Gloves, hot pad, or cloth

Sand Candles

procedure

1. Pack damp sand into a box or bucket (Ill. 1).
2. Hollow the shape of the candle in the damp sand. These shapes can be created with your hands, a bottle, pencils, sticks, or any type of tool that can be pressed into the sand to make a hollow.
3. Place a wick into the mold by tying one end to a stick suspended across the top of the mold (Ill. 2). On the other end, tie a weight and drop it into the hollow. Make sure the wick is centered and stretched tight. A candle itself may be inserted to form the wick.
4. Melt the wax in a double boiler to a temperature of 190° F to 230° F, or 88° C to 110 ° C (standard pouring temperature). Use a thermometer to make sure, for wax reaches a flash point at approximately 400° F, or 204° C.
5. Add colored crayons to the melted wax to reach desired color.
6. Grip the container of melted wax with gloves or hot pad, and pour melted wax into moist sand mold (Ill. 3). Different colored wax poured in layers makes interesting effects.
7. Leave wax in sand until completely hard. Wash off excess sand.
8. If bottom of candle is uneven, it can be leveled on a hot surface.

 Note: In case of fire, cover flame with a lid or baking soda. Never use water to extinguish the flame. Children are merely observers in this activity.

1

2

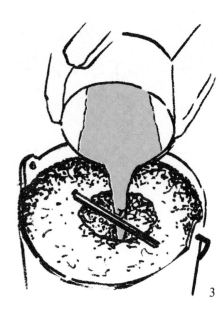

3

Sand Painting

procedure

1. Sketch a design lightly with a pencil on the cardboard or wood.
2. Brush in the background colors in which sand is not desired.
3. Choose the areas to be done in a particular color of sand, and paint a thin coat of shellac, varnish, glue (thin with water), or paste on these parts (paint a small area at a time).
4. Trickle or sprinkle the colored sand from a paper cone or spoon onto the areas that have been covered with paste, varnish, or shellac.
5. Allow the work to dry for a few minutes, then lift the work and tap it lightly so excess sand is removed.
6. Repeat this process for all additional colors.

supplies

1. Fine sand of various colors
2. Jars or bowls (for mixing and storing the sand)
3. Heavy cardboard or piece of wood
4. Paper cone or spoon
5. Varnish, shellac, glue, or paste
6. Watercolor paint
7. Brush

Note: American Indians poured sand from the hand along the second joint of the index finger. The thumb was used to stop the flow of sand.

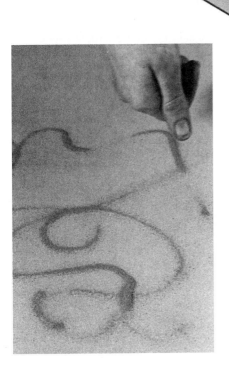

supplies

1. Interesting forms of *flat* plant life, such as leaves, weeds, or grasses
2. Waxed paper
3. Iron

 Notes: Suggested applications for this design are: table runner, bulletin or blackboard frieze, window transparencies, and so forth. Interesting effects using yarn, string, colored paper, and so forth, may also be used.

Sealed Nature Pattern

procedure

1. Cut two sheets of waxed paper that are of equal size.
2. Lay one sheet flat and arrange the plant life on it to create the desired pattern.
3. Place the other waxed sheet over the first, covering the plant life.
4. Iron over the second sheet with a *warm* flat iron. This will seal the waxed sheets together, preserving the plant life.
5. **Teacher should probably handle the iron.**

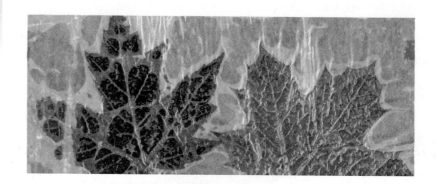

supplies

1. Variety of dried seeds, such as corn, beans, cantaloupe, watermelon, grapefruit, apple, pumpkin, or tree pods
2. Needle
3. Heavy buttonhole cotton thread

 Notes: Ornamental objects may be spaced between the seeds. Cold water will soften the seeds. Shell macaroni can also be used. Dip in hot water to soften.

Sewn Seed Jewelry

procedure

1. After determining the sequence in which the seeds will appear, string the seeds on a predetermined length of thread, making allowance for knots at the ends.
2. Thread the seeds on the thread until there is just room for a triple knot at the end.
3. Tie the knot and, if desired, spray with an acrylic to preserve the seeds. **Use sprays with optimum ventilation.**
4. **Be careful with the needle!**

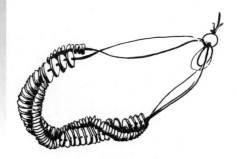 

Stick Construction

procedure

method a

1. First, cut the wooden pieces for the back and front of the structure. (The hole for a wren house should be 1 inch in diameter.)
2. Sticks are then glued to the edges of the front and back pieces to enclose the shape.

method b

1. Various bowls or other constructions can be created by laying sticks on top of one another, much like laying bricks. Place a drop of glue where sticks cross one another.
2. Continue process until bowl is built to desired height.

supplies

1. Popsicle sticks or tongue depressors
2. Fine sandpaper
3. Glue
4. Enamel spray paint or fast-drying clear finish
5. Wooden pieces for back and front of structure

 Note: Various combinations of sticks may be used to create figures, creatures, or objects. **Use adequate ventilation when spraying.**

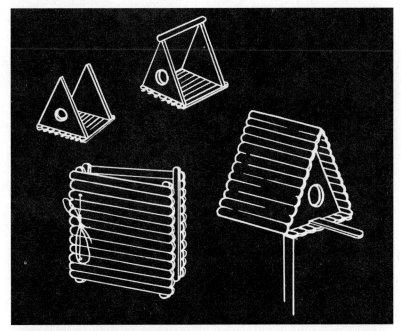

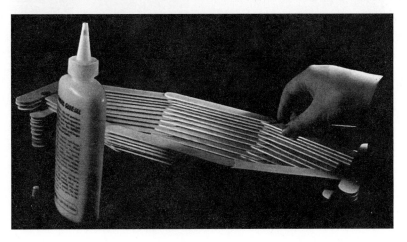

supplies

1. String or yarn
2. Paper
3. Glue

String Picture

procedure

1. Make a light pencil drawing on a sheet of paper. Use colored paper if white string is to be used.
2. Coat the string with glue, then place it over the pencil lines.

 Note: When using yarn, it may be easier to trail the glue on the drawing and place the yarn on the glue.

Chapter Seven

Strata Carving

This project is so named because its nature reminds one of stratified rock. It could easily be correlated with a study of geology.

procedure

1. Mix one part of glue with five parts of whiting and add enough water to produce a consistency that can be painted rather thickly.
2. Divide the mixture into several jars, and add contrasting tempera colors to each jar. Mix well.
3. Brush the surface of the base object with a moderate thickness of the first of the color mixtures (this will be at the bottom). Allow to dry.
4. Continue superimposing color mixture layers until all are used. Allow each layer to dry between each application.
5. Make a drawing on thin paper the size of the item just completed.
6. Transfer the drawing to the top layer. Carbon paper may be used, or the back of the paper can be covered with graphite from a pencil; then the paper is placed on the surface and the drawing is redrawn.
7. Carve through the mixtures to the depth required to expose the desired color. Experiment with carving tools.
8. If desired, the surface may be preserved with the application of a clear spray. **Spray in a well-ventilated area.**

supplies

1. Liquid glue
2. Whiting
3. Container for mixing the paste and several small containers for the separate colors
4. Tempera paint in a number of colors
5. Painting base (block of wood, box, or heavy cardboard)
6. Brush
7. Pencil and paper
8. Carbon paper (optional)
9. Carving and scratching tools, such as nails, knives (with caution), chisels, or hair pins
10. Clear spray (optional)

supplies

1. Upsom board, ½ inch thick
2. Straight pins or finishing nails
3. Assorted colors of thread or string
4. Piece of felt or cloth
5. Tape or glue

Note: Individual creative designs may be produced by experimenting with pin placement.

String and Pin Plaques

procedure

1. Decide on the size and shape of the plaque, and cut it from a piece of Upsom board.
2. Cover the Upsom board with a piece of felt or cloth. Pull the cloth over the edges, and fasten in back with glue or tape. Be sure the cloth is stretched tightly.
3. Push enough straight pins into the cloth-covered Upsom board to form a design. Measure the distance between the pins if the design is to be geometric (Ill. 1).
4. Tie a string or thread to one pin, then wind around other pins to form the design (Ill. 2).
5. Tie the string when one color of the design is completed. Tie another color of string to a pin, and begin to form another part of the design.
6. Place a hook in back so plaque may be hung.

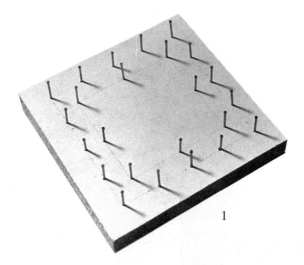

1

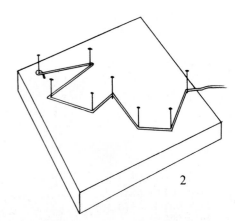

2

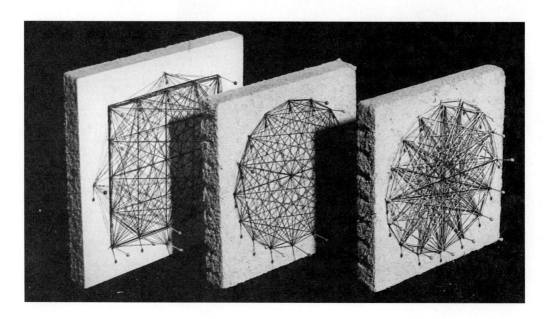

Transfer Picture

procedure

1. Tape the photographic print face up on the waxed paper (Ill. 1).
2. Paint the print with six or seven coats of clear polymer. Alternate the direction of each coat, allowing ten to fifteen minutes drying time between each coat (Ill. 2).
3. Allow one hour for all of the coats to dry.
4. Soak the coated print in warm, sudsy water until all of the paper can be peeled from the back of the picture (Ill. 3). In some cases the paper may have to be rubbed from the back. The soaking time may take an hour, depending on the thickness of the paper. Be careful not to tear or stretch the remaining film of ink and polymer.
5. Allow the print to dry.
6. Apply the print to any surface by first brushing a coat of clear polymer on the surface. Adhere the print while this coating is wet (Ill. 4).
7. Remove any bubbles by pressing out from the center. If any bubbles persist, puncture them with a pin.

supplies

1. Color photograph printed on high-quality glossy paper
2. Clear polymer medium (painting medium for acrylic paint)
3. Paint brush
4. Tape
5. Waxed paper
6. Material or object to which the print is to be transferred
7. Small roller

Note: With proper mounting on clear acetate or plastic, the transfer photographs can serve as slides for projectors (Ill. 5). They are also ideal for mapmaking.

1

2

3

4

5

Stained Glass Windows

procedure

method a

1. Draw a design on paper with pencil. Add lines on the picture surface to divide it to simulate the look of a stained glass window.
2. Draw over all the pencil lines with the black glue.
3. Allow the glue to dry and fill in the areas between the glue with any of the color agents.

method b

1. Fold black construction paper or papers in half, either vertical or horizontal.
2. Cut the outside shape of the window on the open edges of the black paper.
3. Draw shapes on the folded edge, allowing about ¼ inch between each shape and the top and bottom of the paper. Remember it is a folded paper so draw one-half of a symmetrical shape.
4. Open the black paper and carefully fold the right edge of the window to the middle crease. Cut additional shapes on this fold leaving spaces between them. Keep the shapes if they are to be used as patterns for the left side of the window.
5. Open the black paper and repeat step 4 on the left side of the window.
6. Tape or glue pieces of colored cellophane or tissue on the one side of the black paper, usually on the side where the pencil lines appear.

 Note: Two sheets of black paper may be cut at the same time. The cellophane or tissue is sandwiched between the two sheets so that both sides have a clean finish.

s u p p l i e s

1. Black construction paper
2. Scissors
3. Colored cellophane or tissue paper
4. Tape
5. Glue

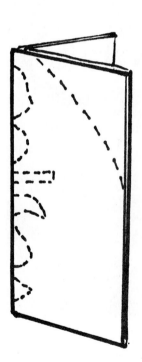
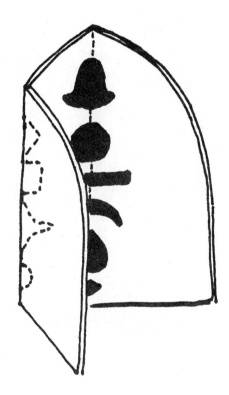

supplies

1. X-acto knives, No. 11 blade
2. Corrugated cardboard
3. Black construction paper
4. Scissors
5. Colored cellophane or
   colored tissue

method c

1. Draw the outside shape of the window and cut with scissors.
2. Within this shape, draw a thick line to make the main shape of the window. Draw connecting lines in the background and within the main design shape to simulate the lead of a stained glass window.
3. Cut carefully with an X-acto knife. **Remember the safety rules.**
4. Carefully cut and fit colored cellophane or colored tissue over the openings.
5. Tape or glue the colored pieces neatly in place.

Chapter Seven

Repoussé

Repoussé is the technique of making patterns in relief on metal usually by hammering. Patterns can also be made by stretching the metal with a simple wooden or plastic tool. Deepest relief is obtained by first tooling all of the metal on one side and then the other side.

procedure

1. Cut the foil to the size of the finished work. Be careful of the sharp edges.
2. Develop a design on newsprint the same size as the piece of foil. Do not make small details.
3. With a pad of newspaper or a cloth under the foil, fasten the design on top of the foil with a piece of tape and draw over the design pressing hard with a pencil.
4. Decide which areas of the design are to be raised (traditionally, the main shapes are raised). Begin tooling with the foil facing down on the pad. Using a suitable tool, make short coloring strokes side by side.
5. When the raised areas are finished, turn the foil over and begin tooling the recessed areas from the front side of the foil.
6. If wrinkles develop, press a flat tool in the direction of the wrinkle with the foil on a flat, hard surface.
7. Copper foil can be oxidized (blackened) by brushing or wiping Liver of Sulphur over the front surface of the foil. When the surface is darkened, wash the foil under running water and allow the foil to dry. Make sure there is adequate ventilation, because Liver of Sulphur smells like rotten eggs.
8. Clean and polish the foil with steel wool. The fine steel wool is good for the final polish. The oxidizing will remain in the low areas.

supplies

1. Copper, aluminum, or brass foil, 36-gauge
2. Modeling tool (anything that will not cut or scratch the metal, such as a sharpened dowel, popsicle stick, tongue depressor, dull pencil, and commercial tools for this technique)
3. No. 000 steel wool, No. 0000 for final polish
4. Pencil and newsprint paper
5. Pad of newspaper or cloth (a Turkish towel is excellent)
6. Oxidizing liquid, Liver of Sulphur (adequate ventilation is a must)

Note: Numerous textures can be embossed to give richness to the modeling. With some foil, it is necessary to polish the foil before the Liver of Sulphur is applied.

Crayons

Nature of the Medium

Crayons

Wax crayons are one of the most familiar art materials. Most of us were introduced to them at a tender age, which may explain why we tend to think that crayons are beneath the dignity of more mature artists. Such is not the case; examples abound of distinguished drawings executed in this humble medium, although few can be dated before the nineteenth century.

Crayons consist of an oily or waxy binder impregnated with pigments. Records exist of a variety of prescriptions for binders, involving soap, salad oil, linseed oil, spermaceti, and beeswax. Crayons are of various types, some soft, some semihard; some are specifically designed for lithographic work, others for general classroom use.

Crayons work well on most papers. They do not blend well; when attempts are made to do this, the wax often "tears." Thus, most drawings are linear in character. Crayons can be scraped thin to produce semitransparent layers of subtle color, and they can be coated with black and scratched through for crayon etchings.

This is an ideal medium for children; it is bold, colorful, clean, and inexpensive.

There are many types of crayons available. They include:

1. Neon or fluorescent
2. Multicultural (include many flesh tones)
3. Glitter crayons
4. Gemtone crayons
5. Metallic crayons
6. Watercolor crayons. This crayon becomes liquid with the addition of water. The crayon can be dipped in water and applied to the paper or the crayon can be colored on the paper and the water brushed on top.

Oil Pastels

Oil pastels combine some of the features of crayon and pastel. The color is brilliant and has the luminosity and depth of oils. The color goes on evenly and covers well. They are softer than crayons and blend easily. There is no dust and no need for a fixative. Oil pastels work very well for resists, rendering, and etching.

s u p p l i e s

1. Wax crayons or oil pastels
2. Dark-colored tempera paint with a few drops of detergent
3. Drawing paper (white or manila)
4. Scraping tool, such as scissors, stick, hairpin, comb, nail, or nail file

Crayon or Oil Pastel Etching

procedure

1. Cover the entire surface of the paper with a heavy coat of brightly colored crayons or oil pastels in either a free or a planned design. Avoid using dark colors. The heavier the colors are applied the better the final result. No definite drawing or design is necessary at this point.
2. Color over the brightly colored crayon or oil pastel surface with black, violet, or any dark color, until no original color shows. Rubbing the crayon-covered surface with a piece of tissue or cloth first will help the dark crayon adhere. Dark-colored tempera paint mixed with detergent can be used in place of the dark-colored crayon or oil pastel. It should be brushed on the colored surface with smooth, even brush strokes and allowed to dry.
3. Having a definite design or drawing in mind, scratch or scrape through the dark surface to the color or colors beneath.

Note: When crayoning over crayon, pat powder or chalk dust over the first layer of crayon before applying the second layer of crayon. The powder or chalk dust aids adhesion of the second layer of crayon.

Crayon or Oil Pastel Doodle Designs

procedure

1. Cover the entire area of the paper with a continuous line drawn with complete spontaneity in light pencil. Make sure this line contains numerous directions made by a variety of straight and curved lines.
2. Look for shapes that are created by the lines and draw them in with a heavy pencil line. Many interesting abstract designs, as well as subject matter, can be found.
3. Color with crayons, oil pastels, or paint.

supplies

1. Paper
2. Pencil
3. Crayons, oil pastels, or paint

 Note: The top doodle was the beginning of each drawing below it. Colored circles indicate the starting points of the doodles.

Original Doodle

Original Doodle

Horizontal Design from Doodle

Design from Doodle

Vertical Design from Same Doodle

supplies

1. Wax crayons
2. Heat lamp or hot iron
3. Cotton fabric, which must be washed thoroughly to cleanse it of all sizing or stiffener

Crayon on Cloth

procedure

1. Draw directly on the cloth with the crayons, using considerable pressure.
2. Melt the crayon into the cloth by placing it under a heat lamp or ironing over it between sheets of paper.

 Note: The color will be semipermanent only if the fabric is washed in *cool* water with a *nondetergent* soap. **Caution should be observed in handling an iron.**

Crayon or Oil Pastel over Tempera Paint

procedure

1. Create the desired painting with tempera paints.
2. Work a contrasting color over each area with crayon or oil pastel, using moderate pressure.
3. Immerse the sponge in water; then "wash" the painting until the underlying tempera paint begins flaking off. The result will be a mottled, textured quality in which the residual crayon or oil pastel will supplement and accent the varied tempera tones that remain. The degree of flaking may be accelerated by brushing or, if it has gone too far, retouching may be done with the crayon or oil pastel.

 Note: This procedure may be modified by applying the crayons more heavily, then holding the drawing under water that is just hot enough to melt them. The use of the hot water necessitates a degree of caution. Perhaps the teacher would elect to perform this phase of the procedure for each child.

 supplies

1. Tempera paints and brush
2. Wax crayons or oil pastels
3. Paper
4. Sponge

supplies

1. Wax crayon or oil pastels
2. Paper
3. Brush
4. Watercolor paints
5. Water container

 Note: If light-colored or white crayons are used, a dark watercolor wash will be most satisfactory.

Crayon or Oil Pastel Resist

procedure

1. Color the drawing or design heavily with crayons or oil pastels, allowing areas of paper to show.
2. Cover the entire surface of the paper with watercolor paint. The paint will be absorbed by the uncolored paper and resisted by the wax crayons or oil pastels.

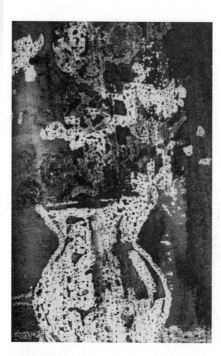

Crayon Resist Batik

procedure

1. Make a light drawing in pencil on manila or heavy wrapping paper.
2. Using the pencil lines as a guide, draw lines and shapes with the crayon, allowing areas of the paper to show through.
3. Soak paper in water and crumple into a ball.
4. Uncrumple the paper, flatten, and blot off excess water.
5. Paint the entire surface with watercolor paint or diluted tempera paint. The paint will be absorbed by the uncolored paper and resisted by the wax crayon, creating a weblike or batik pattern.

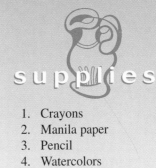

supplies

1. Crayons
2. Manila paper
3. Pencil
4. Watercolors
5. Brush

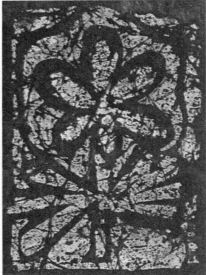

s u p p l i e s

1. Wax crayon or oil pastel
2. Thin drawing paper
3. Pencil
4. Textured surface

Crayon or Oil Pastel Textures Made by Rubbing

procedure

1. Make an outline drawing or design with pencil on thin drawing paper.
2. Hold the drawing against a surface that has a definite texture, and rub the crayon or oil pastel over all areas of the drawing in which the texture will create a pleasing pattern. The texture will be transferred to the paper by the crayon or oil pastel.
3. Place the paper against another texture, and transfer this texture to another portion of the drawing.
4. Textures may be repeated or overlapped.
5. Unusual effects can be obtained by using several colors.

Crayon Shavings

procedure

1. Make a simple rack to hold the electric iron with the ironing surface up.
2. Shave the wax crayons with a knife, catching the shavings on a piece of paper fastened to cardboard. Push the shavings around until the image is created.
3. Pass the paper above the heated iron until the crayon shavings begin to melt. Continue this process with additional crayons until the desired pattern is created.
4. Watercolor, crayons, or tempera paint can be used to add detail to complete the picture.

 Note: **Care should be taken in this activity while handling the iron and knife.** Heat sources other than the iron may be used to melt the shavings. The drawing may be laid in direct sunlight, on a radiator, or over a light bulb. Care should be taken, as too much exposure to heat will make the wax run.

supplies

1. Old electric iron
2. Wax crayons
3. Paper
4. Knife
5. Cardboard

supplies

1. Wax crayons, or see formula for encaustic paint.
2. Old muffin tin
3. A 100 or 150 watt light bulb and extension cord, or an electric skillet.
4. Stiff bristle painting brushes (the use of melted crayon will render the brushes unusable for any other media)
5. Any durable painting surface, such as wood, canvas, board, plaster, masonite, or heavy cardboard
6. Turpentine and soap for cleaning brushes.

 Note: Encaustic painting is also possible by soaking fine crayon shavings in a small amount of turpentine for twelve to fifteen days. The finer the shaving, the quicker it dissolves. The dissolved crayons should be a smooth, creamy medium for painting. With the use of wax or crayons and heat, extreme caution must always be taken. Never melt wax or crayons in direct heat. Baking soda should always be at hand in case of a fire.

Encaustic Painting

Encaustic is a method of painting in which colored waxes are applied to a surface and the color fixed by heat. Encaustic paintings were found in some of the portraits at Pompeii and the Roman portraits found in Fayoum, Egypt.

procedure

1. Sort out the pieces of crayon in a muffin tin according to color.
2. To melt the crayons, float the muffin tin in water in an electric skillet and slowly heat the water. A light bulb placed close to the muffin tin can also be used to melt the crayons. **This step must be closely supervised.**
3. Paint directly on the chosen surface with the hot melted crayons. Many varied effects of luminosity, texture, and tone are unique to encaustic painting.
4. When the painting is finished and cooled it may be polished with a soft cloth.

Fabric Crayons

procedure

1. Draw a design on white paper with a pencil.
2. Color the design with fabric crayons, using considerable pressure.
3. Remove any loose crayon specks and turn the paper design face down on the synthetic cloth, which is on an ironing pad of several layers of paper.
4. Set the iron on the cotton setting and allow it to heat up. Apply the iron to the design, holding it in place for thirty seconds. Lift the iron and move it to the untransferred areas of the design. If the iron is moved excessively, the design may blur.
5. "Sneak a peek" by holding the design and lifting one corner to check the strength of the color and design. Apply the heat until the design is completely transferred.

 Note: As this procedure involves the use of a hot iron, precautions should be observed. Teacher should probably handle the iron. Pillows, wall hangings, table cloths, soft sculptures, banners, and clothing are all possibilities with fabric crayons. Articles can be machine washed using warm water and gentle action. Do not use a bleach or put the work in a dryer. The color can be reapplied, and the design used again.

1. Fabric crayons
2. White paper
3. Synthetic cloth
4. Newspaper
5. Iron (with no steam vents)

supplies

1. Drawing paper
2. Liquid starch
3. Powdered tempera
4. Crayons

Finger Painting over Crayon

procedure

1. Cover the paper with brightly colored crayon.
2. Lay the crayoned paper on a smooth flat surface.
3. Spread liquid starch over the crayon.
4. Sprinkle a small amount of tempera paint on the liquid starch. Be sure that its color contrasts with the crayon color(s).
5. The color will mix as soon as the hand is drawn over the surface.

 Note: See page 171 for finger painting instructions.

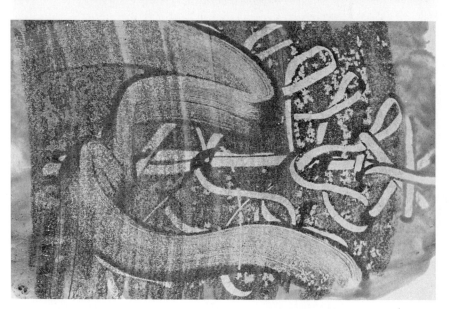

Map Doodle

procedure

1. Cover an area of the road map with a piece of tracing paper.
2. Look for shapes that are created by the roads on the map and draw them in with pencil. Many interesting abstract designs or subject matters can be found.
3. Crayon or paint the finished picture.

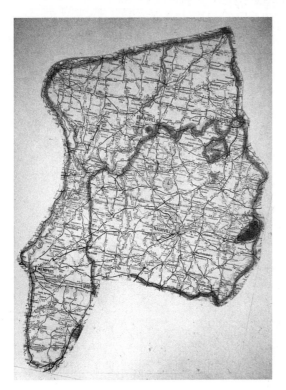

supplies

1. Paper
2. Crayons with paper wrapping removed
3. Candle

Melted Crayon

procedure

1. Hold the crayon briefly over the flame of the candle until it softens, then press, drip, or drag the softened crayon onto the paper. A definite design or drawing can be sketched on the paper beforehand to serve as a guide, or the idea can be created with melted crayon directly.
2. Should the crayon become too short to hold over the flame, a long pin stuck into the crayon will solve this problem.
3. A number of different colors melted on top of one another will not only create an unusual textural effect but will greatly enrich the color.

 Note: Because this procedure involves the use of an open flame, it is suggested that every precaution be observed. White and yellow crayons can be heated but should not be held in the flame for long, as they will carbon.

Pressed Crayon Laminations

procedure

1. Shave the crayons on a piece of wax paper placed on newspaper, creating the image by pushing the shavings around with a small piece of cardboard.
2. Cover the crayon-covered wax paper with another piece of wax paper.
3. Cover both pieces of wax paper with a piece of newspaper and iron with a warm iron.

 Note: Variations are possible by cutting the wax laminations into various shapes and putting them into a design pressed again between two new sheets of wax paper. A string pressed between the wax sheets makes it adaptable for use in a mobile. Teacher should probably handle the iron.

s u p p l i e s

1. Crayons
2. Wax paper
3. Iron
4. Knife or crayon sharpener
5. Newsprint or newspaper

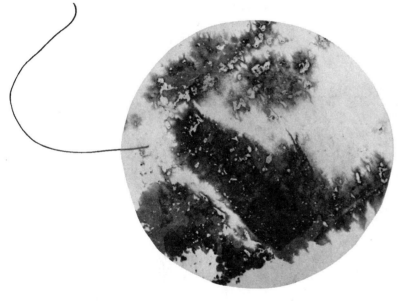

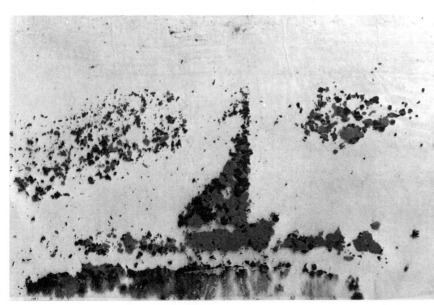

9 Murals

Murals

A mural is a large work of art usually designed for a specific location and intended to be viewed by large numbers of people.

A small mural may be produced by the individual student, whereas a larger work is readily adaptable to classroom work as a group enterprise. As such, and because of its mass audience, it can be developed from a theme of general interest selected from any subject area. Properly handled it can be an effective educational aid.

The quality of artwork in a class-produced mural can be easily diluted by its commitment to subject and audience. (A review of the section on "Basic Concepts of Art Instruction" on pages 2–12 will refresh the reader on the perils inherent in the subjugation of art to other disciplines.) From an art standpoint, little is to be gained from the mural if it is to be confined to a strictly factual presentation. On the other hand, much may be gained if the subject under consideration is studied and researched (on a collective and personal basis) and then submitted to the interpretive abilities of the students. Under such a system of instruction the students could freely debate and vote on the general presentation of the theme and volunteer for selected passages of this theme. The overall plan or layout of the composition could be left in the hands of one student, or it could be produced by the instructor, providing the sketch is not too specific or rigid.

As a public work of art, some consideration should be given to effective placement of the mural in terms of traffic, lighting, and other factors. When the location has been determined, the space available will help to decide the total shape of the mural. Architecture may be a friend or foe; in any case, it must be considered.

Students participating in the design of a mural should be of a narrow age range. When older students are mixed with younger children, there is often an unfortunate tendency to compare. Actually, when ages vary, the products are noncomparable, but this is not always understood, and the general reaction could be frustrating and embarrassing to some students.

When the main composition has been sketched, the surface (wrapping paper is cheap, strong, and quite adequate) may be divided up into a working area for each student. Because of spatial restrictions, it is not always possible to have all artists working simultaneously. Work could proceed on a shift basis, integrating this project with other scheduled activities.

Matisse has designed these figures to work within a specific architectural area. Photograph © 1996 by The Barnes Foundation. All rights reserved.

It is usually advisable to restrict the work on a mural to one or two media. Materials are variable in strength, and the design could be chaotic if all media were used, unless they were subject to some type of coordination. Some media, such as chalk, are perfectly satisfactory but quite impermanent and could be easily smudged during the process of the work. In avoiding this, a fixative or plastic spray could be used to protect the drawing, but this would ruin the surface for further drawing. Crayon is cheap and permanent; poster paint is effective but may flake off if the mural is rolled up or mistreated. Cut paper is a simple and effective medium and is easily combined with other media. Collage techniques may be employed by pasting up fabrics and other textured materials, and papier collé may be used according to the instructions under the activity "Magazine Collé" (see p. 198). A cartoon grid and overhead projector could be useful. If written material is to be included, we refer you to the section on lettering and calligraphy.

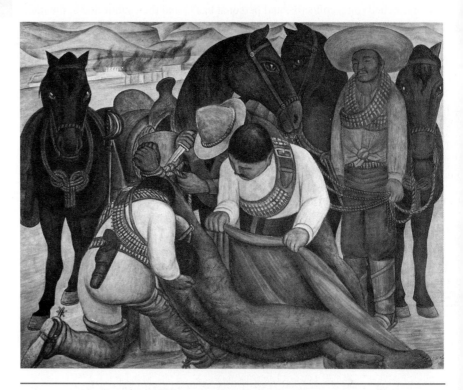

Rivera, a well-known muralist, shows his concern for the underprivileged. Diego Rivera, The Liberation of the Peon, 1931. Fresco, 6 ft 2 in × 7 ft 11 in (1.88 × 2.41 M). Philadelphia Museum of Art: Gift of Mr. & Mrs. Herbert Cameron Morris.

Mural Techniques

procedure

1. Discuss murals past and present, as well as the selected theme.
2. Produce idea sketches.
3. Enlarge selected sketches on wrapping paper (Ill. 1).
4. Cut out the large sketches like paper dolls (Ill. 2).
5. Paint the wall with roller and latex paint.
6. Stretch wrapping paper below the wall. Arrange the cutout shapes on the wrapping paper, using a small loop of masking tape on the back.
7. Make changes by shifting the cutouts on the wrapping paper as necessary.
8. When satisfied with arrangement, draw around cutouts with pencil on the wall (Ill. 3), and return cutouts to wrapping paper (Ill. 4).
9. Paint the wall design with latex paint, giving every child an opportunity to paint.
10. Complete background and details with brush or sponge (see sponge painting, p. 173) (Ill. 5).
11. Black and/or white paint may be used to outline or add detail.

supplies

1. Paper
2. Crayons
3. Wrapping paper
4. Scissors
5. Masking tape
6. Pencils
7. Latex paint (semigloss)
8. Brushes, large and small
9. Rollers
10. Sponges
11. Old shirts (for smocks)
12. Cans with lids, to hold various colored paints

Note: Have a group clean brushes and wipe up any spills. **Use safety scissors if available.**

1

2

© *James L. Shaffer*

3

4

5

Chalk Mural

procedure

1. Discuss murals past and present, as well as the selected theme.
2. Produce idea sketches.
3. Enlarge selected sketches on wrapping paper.
4. Draw with chalks on paper-covered chalkboard or on chalkboard itself.

 Note: A chalkboard mural is suitable only when the chalkboard surface can be spared for a period of time. If adequate chalkboard space is available, chalkboard murals make particularly effective holiday projects.

supplies

1. Colored chalks
2. Wrapping paper or chalkboard

Crayon Mural

procedure

1. Discuss murals past and present, as well as the selected theme.
2. Produce idea sketches.
3. Enlarge selected sketches on wrapping paper (Ills. 1, 2, and 3; see pp. 157–158). Crayons are not suitable for use on walls or chalkboard.
4. Older children possessed of patience may like to do parts of the mural in the crayon etching technique (see p. 140).

supplies

1. Crayons
2. Wrapping paper

Cut Paper Mural

procedure

1. Discuss murals past and present, as well as the selected theme.
2. Produce idea sketches.
3. Enlarge selected sketches on wrapping paper (Ills. 1, 2, and 3; see pp. 157–158).
4. Cut out the subjects and pin or paste them to the bulletin board or paper background.

supplies

1. Drawing paper
2. Painting or drawing materials for any technique chosen
3. Paper or bulletin board background
4. Pins, paste, or glue
5. Scissors

supplies

1. Tempera paints
2. Brushes
3. Wrapping paper or chalkboard

Note: A painted chalkboard mural is easily washed off because tempera paint is not waterproof.

Tempera Mural

procedure

1. Discuss murals past and present, as well as the selected theme.
2. Produce idea sketches.
3. Enlarge selected sketches on wrapping paper (Ills. 1, 2, and 3; see pp. 157–158).
4. Paint the mural on the paper or on the chalkboard.

Paint and Ink

Nature of the Medium

Watercolor

Watercolor is a brilliant, transparent, water-soluble painting medium. The pigment is available as color blocks in pans or in the more expensive and professional tubes.

The distinguishing property of watercolor is the sparkling quality resulting from its transparency. Most painters strive for a spontaneous effect by utilizing the whiteness of the paper and the fluid blending of the colors. Watercolor requires planning, as does any art form, but there can be a good deal of improvisation. Unlike oil paintings, watercolors are worked up quickly and rarely reworked.

The prerequisite to the successful use of watercolor is familiarity with its effects, achieved only through experimentation. Prior to painting, the paper should be dampened; then use bold, wet washes, with intermingled colors. Bold and fine strokes should be attempted, both wet and dry. In addition, try wet-on-dry techniques, blotting, tilting the paper to control the flow of color, various resists, and combinations of watercolor with other media. For serious efforts, the paper should be fastened to a board with paper tape after soaking, to allow the painting to dry without distorting the paper.

Three types of professional paper are available for watercolor painting:

Hot-pressed: a smooth paper, for detailed work
Cold-pressed: moderate texture, and the most common
Rough: highly textured surface, producing clear, sharp effects

These professional papers are, however, beyond the needs and means of most children. A paper of fairly heavy weight such as manila (or its equivalent) is a satisfactory, inexpensive paper for general classroom use.

Brushes used for watercolor painting should be washed frequently, and the cleaning water should be replaced often. Smocks or aprons are useful, as are newspapers and paper towels. Expect a mess; it's the only way to learn.

Tempera Paint

Tempera is a water-soluble paint that is available as a liquid or a dry powder. It is an extremely versatile medium for classroom experiences in art and works well on a variety of surfaces. (When painted on nonporous materials, a small amount of liquid detergent should be added.)

Tempera may be spread by brush, roller, sponge, stick, or, if slightly reduced with water, it can be sprayed. Lights and darks are controlled by additions of white or black.

Unlike watercolor, tempera is an opaque medium; the appearance of the paper is not such a factor, nor does it have to be stretched. The paint may be mixed semi-dry and built up to create a textured surface. The other possibilities are too numerous to list here but include screen printing, block printing, finger painting, and lettering.

Young children using a potentially messy medium such as tempera should wear smocks if possible. Clear water should be kept handy for keeping brushes clean. Small plastic or paper cups can be provided for the various colors.

Inks

A liquid vehicle and a soluble pigment are required for making ink, and this is satisfactory only if it can flow evenly and has good tinting strength. The earliest ink known, black carbon, was prepared by the early Egyptians and Chinese. This was followed by iron-gall (from growths on trees), bistre (burnt wood), and sepia (a secretion from cuttlefish). Today, there is a wide variety of inks, transparent and opaque, water-soluble and waterproof. Perhaps the type best known to the art student is India ink, which is really a waterproof carbon black. All of these inks serve effectively for *line* drawings; drawing *washes* are usually produced with ink sticks or watercolors. A tremendous number of inks can be made with fruit and vegetable juices, aniline, or coal dyes.

Pen and ink drawings are generally characterized by their clarity and precision. This, of course, can be modified by choice of instrument or method of control. It takes a great many strokes to produce an area of tone, which is the principal reason why pen and ink drawings are best created on a fairly small scale.

Pens

Those of us who take the familiar metal pen point for granted may not realize that it is a fairly new invention, which had not been successfully developed until the last century. The reed pen had been the pen of the ancients, and the quill pen the principal writing instrument from the medieval period to modern times. Most of us probably remember the use of quill pens in the drawings of Rembrandt and in the historical documents drawn up by the founders of our republic.

Today, the advent of ball, felt, and plastic tip pens have revolutionized the writing industry, as well as providing artists with yet another drawing tool. Artists, however, still make use of the earlier pen types on occasion, and even resort, at times, to matchsticks and other unlikely things for making ink marks on paper. Each drawing instrument leaves its own distinctive mark and helps to develop special interests and disciplines for the artist. In the hands of children, the mechanical metal points and felt and plastic tips are generally more suitable, but other kinds of pens might provide some exciting moments for the older child.

Brushes*

Brush making as a craft originated in France, later spreading into Germany. It became identified, quite naturally, with the carpenter, who turned brush maker by tying bristle to his finished handle and was known as "carpenter-brush maker."

The art student learned from his Master how to make brushes in the most elementary way—hair or bristle would be primitively washed and straightened, then tied onto a wooden handle or stick with string or cord. Modern brush making had its beginning as an industry in the early part of the nineteenth century.

Bristle is obtained from the body of hogs and boars found in Russia, Japan, Formosa, Korea, France, and Central and Eastern Europe. While all animal hair has "points," bristle has "flags" (the individual bristle splits into two or three tiny forks on the end). Only pure natural white and black bristle with their original flags preserved are used in Liquitex® brushes.

Brown Squirrel Hair, known as Kazan, is generally found in the Kazan Region of Russia. It has finer points and is more elastic than other squirrel hair, making it ideal for camel hair watercolor brushes.

Camel Hair is the trade name for squirrel hair and pony hair. Squirrel hair is obtained from the tails of various types of Russian squirrels (Scuirus Vulgaris Calotus).

*Courtesy Consumer Products Division of Binney and Smith Inc.

Ox Hair—The best grades are selected and prepared from ox ear hair found in Central Europe and certain parts of North and South America. Ox ear hair with its strong body and fine tapered points is especially suited for brushes used in oil or heavier colors, since it will hold plenty of color, retain its elasticity, and perform smoothly. It will also perform well for show card and watercolor brushes, though here again the special qualities of red sable hair cannot be equaled.

Pony Hair is obtained from pony hides. It ranges in color from light or dark brown and is straight and soft but does not have the fine points that distinguish squirrel hair.

Red Sable Hair—The most valuable hair used in artist brushes is obtained from the tail of the kolinsky (Mustela Sibirica) found in the Amur Region of Siberia, and in The Republic of Korea. Red sable hair, pale red in color with darker tips, has special qualities unmatched by any other hair—strength along with slim body, extremely fine points, and great resiliency. Not only will it come to a needle-fine point or knife-like edge, but will retain its full elasticity, making it virtually irreplaceable for the best brushes used in any watercolor medium.

Sabeline Hair is specially treated silken ox hair, light in color with exceptional points, and lots of snap.

The Care and Use of Brushes

1. Use watercolor brushes for watercolor and oil brushes for oil. Do not mix.
2. Clean brushes after each use. Neglect will cause the brush to lose its shape.
3. Never rest a brush vertically on its hairs. Suspend it, if possible; if not, rest it on its side.

Water color	Wash	Easel	Tempera and poster lettering	Oil red sable
	Round Oval	Flat Round	Round Flat	Flat
Water color Wash, rendering ceramics, textile, leathercraft etc.	**Water color** Wash, sky rendering and tempera painting.	**Flat** Easel painting and oil painting. **Flat Chiseled** Easel painting in powdered tempera and other mediums. **Round** Camel hair for easel painting bristle for oil and easel painting.	**Round** Lettering and poster. **Flat** Lettering, posters, water color, ceramic glazing, varnishing, etc.	**Round** Fine detail in oil, ceramics, textile, etc. **Flat** Smooth textural effects on oil, ceramics, textiles, etc.

cleaning procedures

1. Water-based brush media:
   a. Repeatedly wash in cold water.
   b. Straighten the hairs to their natural shape before drying.
   c. Rinse repeatedly in clean water while in use.
2. Oil-based brush media:
   a. Squeeze paint from the brush with waste paper or rags.
   b. Lather on the palm of the hand with soap and water.
   c. Rinse repeatedly until all paint is removed.
   d. Restore the original shape of the bristles.
3. Acrylic and polymer brush media:
   a. Clean in cold water immediately after use.
   b. Clean in warm water if the paint has hardened.

Notes: Clean house paint, oil stain, enamel, or varnish with turpentine, proprietary brush cleaner, or paint thinner.

Clean shellac or alcohol stain with alcohol.

For lacquer, use lacquer thinner.

Detergent soaps are effective for cleaning oil, acrylic, and watercolor brushes.

Oil bristle	Acrylic and oil	Utility, lacquering and paste	Stencil
Short Flat	Flat Flat Chiseled	Artist Style Painter's Style	
Short Flat Textured brush effects in oil painting, ceramics, textile. **Long Flat** Flexible brush stroke technique in oil painting.	**Flat** For advanced work. **Flat Chiseled** For all acrylic and oil techniques.	**Artist Style** Lacquering, enameling, paste, glue, varnish, ceramics and utility. **Painter Style** Enameling, varnish, house paint, paste and utility.	Stencilling on paper, wood, metal, textile, and stippling on ceramics.

supplies

1. Pen
2. Brush
3. Soft wood sticks of various types, such as matchsticks or popsicle sticks
4. Ink
5. Paper

Drawing with Ink

procedure

1. Pen and ink drawing is capable of arousing great interest if approached in an experimental manner. For instance, pen points of different types create varied lines, and these lines in turn may be combined with each other to create stippled, crosshatched, scumbled, and other textural effects.

2. Brush and ink drawing is a highly expressive medium due to the flexibility of the brush line. The quality of line may be controlled by the type of brush (bristle or sable), wide or narrow, fully or sparsely haired; the hand pressure applied; the quantity of ink carried by the brush; and the calculating or spontaneous attitude of the artist.

   As in most drawing, greater freedom is obtained from the brush by avoiding the grip used in writing. Instead, hold the brush between the thumb and forefingers while supporting the hand on the other three fingers. The movement of the brush should be initiated with the body ("body English") and directed through the arm. Drawing done with the fingers or wrists is more suited to the development of surface details.

3. Stick and ink is a lesser-known drawing procedure, but one that has enough individuality to justify its frequent use. In technique it is very simple—merely dip an absorbent piece of wood into the ink, allow it to become semisaturated, and draw as you would with a pen. Interesting effects may be obtained by using sticks with frayed, sharp, broad, and smooth ends.

 Note: Ink is very effective when used with other media. It may be added to watercolor, tempera, and crayon to enhance the brilliance of colors or provide accents and outline. The above may, in turn, be used over ink. When ink is used on wet paper, the results are unexpected and interesting.

Rembrandt used both pen and brush in this drawing. The Metropolitan Museum of Art, New York, The H. O. Havemeyer Collection. Bequest of Mrs. H. O. Havemeyer, 1929. (29.100.934)

Ink Dots

procedure

1. Draw the design lightly on the piece of white paper.
2. Begin to place dots of ink by touching the marker point to the paper, lifting it and putting it down again. It is easiest to begin with the outline of the main shape.
3. By placing the dots very close together with little space between them, the area will be shaded and dark. By allowing more space between the dots the value will be lighter.

supplies

1. Marker; Sharpie black works well.
2. White drawing paper

1. Paper, paper-covered object, or cloth
2. Multicolored plastic or felt tip pens or markers
3. Pencil
4. Clear spray. Use adequate ventilation when spraying.

 Note: Experimenting with the different kinds of markers is very exciting. They can be used with any subject, the results are immediate, and the colors are wonderful.

Plastic or Felt Tip Pen or Marker Drawing

Many different kinds of markers are available and all can be useful for different projects. Permanent markers are markers that will not smear or dissolve if water or anything moist is put on top or near the marker line or area. Permanent markers come in many different colors and the points or tips may be extra fine, fine, chisel point, wedge point, or broad point. Permanent markers sometimes have an unpleasant odor and clean up is a little more difficult.

There are even more types of watercolor markers or pens on the market. The watercolor marker or pen will smear or diffuse if water or a moist material is placed near them. These pens have different types of tips and many different colors.

Classic colors usually refer to the primary and secondary colors with the addition of black and brown.

Tropical colors are pastels and include gray.

Bold colors are intermediate colors.

Fluorescent colors are very bright.

Multicultural colors include all different flesh tones.

Crazy tips are markers with split nibs.

Changeables use a color changer that looks white but when it is drawn over the other colors in the package it will turn that color into a new one. Yellow turns to fuchsia and so on. This type of marker is wonderful to use to make patterns.

Overwriters come with two different kinds of markers in the package. Under colors are used on the paper first and Over colors are used on top of the first color.

procedure

1. Use preliminary light outline drawing in pencil on the paper.
2. Draw over the pencil lines with marker or pen and fill in with color.
3. When the project is finished the picture can be sprayed to fix it but this is not usually necessary.

Pulled String Design

procedure

1. Place a sheet of paper on a flat surface.
2. Coat the string thoroughly with paint or ink. If tempera paint is used, be sure it is thin.
3. Arrange the paint-soaked string on the paper. Twisted loops in the string will make interesting effects. Allow one or two ends to extend beyond the same edge of the paper.
4. Place another piece of paper over this string arrangement.
5. Cover this paper with a firm piece of cardboard, wood, masonite, or magazine, and hold it in place lightly with one hand. With the other hand, grasp the ends of the string and pull it gently from between the papers.
6. Carefully peel the two papers apart. The design will be duplicated on the second sheet of paper.

supplies

1. String
2. Paper
3. Paint or ink
4. Board, heavy cardboard, masonite, or a magazine
5. Brush or sponge

1. Paper
2. Watercolor or thin tempera paint
3. Scissors
4. Paste

Notes: After experimenting, it will be possible to control the results by placing the paint according to a predetermined pattern.

Don't overlook the possibility of using several colors in one blotto or adding details with other media. **Use safety scissors if available.**

Blottos

procedure

1. Cut a number of paper squares and rectangles of various sizes.
2. Crease each paper square in the middle so that later it can be folded easily.
3. Sprinkle a few drops of paint on one side of the crease.
4. Fold the paper on the creased line with the paint inside and press—this causes the paint to be squeezed into various and interesting shapes.
5. When the paper is opened, the result will be surprising—it might resemble an insect, a flower, a butterfly, or any number of items.
6. After a number of blottos are made, cut them out and arrange them into a picture or pattern. When satisfied with the arrangement, paste them in place on a piece of paper of desired size.

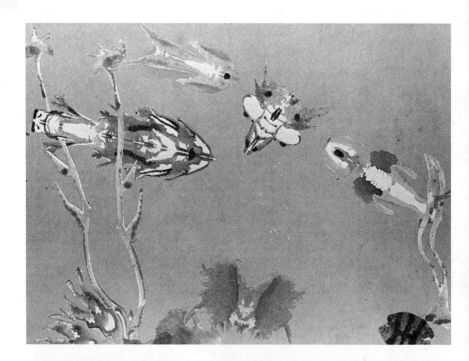

Finger Painting

procedure

1. Soak the paper in water in any of the following ways, making sure both sides are thoroughly wet.
   a. Put the paper under the faucet in a sink, or
   b. Roll the paper into a tube and submerge it in a container of water, or
   c. Spread the paper on a table and soak it with sponge and water. The paper adheres more firmly to a surface if wet on both sides.
2. Place the wet paper on a smooth and flat surface. Do not place it too close to the edge of the tabletop, as the paint may drip over. Make sure the glossy side of the paper is up and all wrinkles and air bubbles are smoothed out. Satisfactory finger paintings cannot be made on an uneven or unsteady surface.
3. Place approximately 1 tablespoonful of finger paint on the wet paper. If powdered finger paint is used, sift it lightly over the entire paper; more can be applied later if necessary. Paint applied too heavily will crack or chip off when dry.
4. Spread the paint evenly over the entire surface of paper with the palm of the hand or the forearm to create the background of the finger painting.
5. Varied movements of the hands and forearms in various positions will create interesting effects. The side of the hand, when held rigid and pulled over paper, makes long and delicate leaves. This same hand position moved in a zig-zag motion creates an altogether different effect. Experiment with a variety of hand and arm movements and positions. An infinite number of effects are possible by using the closed fist, bent fingers, open palm, heel of the hand, wrist, etc. Other various effects can be obtained by using a comb, a small notched piece of cardboard, etc. Areas of color can also be cleaned away with a sponge.
6. New beginnings can be made until the paper loses its gloss. If the finger paint becomes too sticky, sprinkle a few drops of water on the paper to allow the hand or arm to slide easily over the paper.
7. Spread the paper or newspaper on the floor in a seldom-used area. Lift the finger painting by two corners and lay it on some newspapers.
8. Allow the painting to dry. Press it on the unpainted side with a hot iron. **The iron should be left in the hands of the teacher.**

 Notes: It is suggested that only a few children work at one time unless a large room with adequate table space is available. Finger paintings can be used to decorate items of many kinds, including knitting boxes, wastebaskets, book jackets, or portfolio covers.

Colored paper cut to particular shapes and pasted in place on finger paintings adds further detail.

A stencil cut from paper and pasted over a finger painting is another variation. If finger painting is used as a decorative covering, it should be sprayed with clear plastic spray or painted with shellac for permanence. **Use adequate ventilation when spraying.**

A comb or piece of notched paper will give good results if it is drawn through the wet paint.

supplies

1. Finger paint (recipe on p. 341)
2. Glossy or glazed paper
3. Sponge
4. Iron
5. Plastic spray or white shellac
6. Water must be available in a sink or large container, to soak the paper

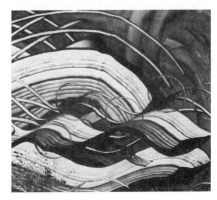

supplies

1. Drawing paper
2. Liquid starch
3. Powdered tempera
4. Crayons

 Note: See page 171 for finger painting instructions.

Finger Painting over Crayon

procedure

1. Cover the paper with brightly colored crayon.
2. Lay the crayoned paper on a smooth flat surface.
3. Spread liquid starch over the crayon.
4. Sprinkle a small amount of tempera paint in the liquid starch. Be sure that its color contrasts with the crayon color(s).
5. The color will mix as soon as the hand is drawn over the surface.

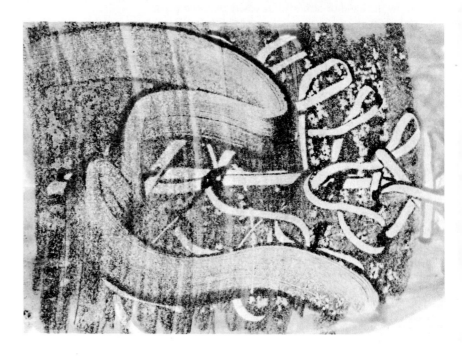

Soda Straw Painting

procedure

1. Place several little pools of variously colored paint on the paper with a brush.
2. Point the end of the straw at the pools of paint and blow in the direction the paint is meant to move.
3. Overlapping of colors creates numerous effects in blending colors.
4. Add details when dry.

supplies

1. Sponge or cellulose sponge cut into a variety of sizes and shapes
2. Scissors
3. Watercolor or liquid tempera paint
4. Paper
5. Brush

 Note: Experiment by trying this on both wet and dry paper. Also allow the color to mix and blend. **Use safety scissors if available.**

Sponge Painting

procedure

1. Soak the paper thoroughly in water.
2. Lay the wet paper on a smooth surface and remove all the wrinkles and excess water.
3. Use small pieces of moist sponge as a brush by dipping them into the tempera paint.
4. Apply the paint to moist paper that may have general areas of a design marked with a pencil.
5. Details and accents can be added with a brush when the painting is dry.

Tempera Painting on Damp Paper

procedure

1. Soak the paper thoroughly in water.
2. Lay the wet paper on a desk top or drawing board and smooth out all the wrinkles.
3. Blot up any pools of water with the blotting material.
4. Paint directly on the damp paper. Make sure to use more pigment than water, for the colors tend to lose their brilliance when dry. Paint the light colors first, and add second and third colors before the paper dries, so colors will mingle and blend into spontaneous and soft shapes. After the paint is applied, avoid reworking.
5. Leave some areas unpainted to add sparkle.
6. Details, if necessary, can be painted in when the painting is dry.

supplies

1. Dry or liquid tempera paint
2. Brush
3. Paper
4. Water container
5. Blotting material, such as a rag, sponge, or paper towel

 Note: Damp paper tempera painting must be done hurriedly to be lively. Don't expect complete success on the first try, for only experience will tell just how wet the paper must be and how much paint should be used. Clean the brush and the water in the container often.

1. White paper, the softer the better. Paper toweling works well
2. Container for the dye or color
3. Food coloring or watered down watercolor or tempera paint

Fold and Dye

procedure

1. Fold the paper in different patterns.
2. Dip the corner of the folded shape into the dye and lift immediately.
3. When the corners have been dipped, allow the paper to dry before unfolding. Unfold very carefully.

 Note: This is a great way to introduce Tie and Dye. It is also a good way to investigate color mixing.

Accordion pleating and folding that shape in half and in half again.

Fold into triangles.

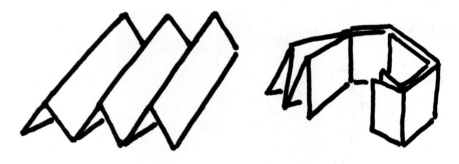

Fold into squares.

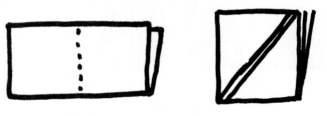

Make up folds so that the corners can be dipped into the dye.

Tempera Resist

procedure

1. Paint some areas of the paper with tempera as necessary to suggest the design. By all means, leave much of the paper unpainted to allow the ink to be absorbed by these areas. The paint used should be of a fairly heavy body.
2. When the paint is completely dry, paint over everything—tempera and paper—with India ink.
3. When the ink is dry, hold the drawing under running water, allowing the force of the water to dislodge the ink. Should this ink prove stubborn, its removal may be accelerated by light strokes of the finger. A certain amount of caution should be exercised in removing the ink. Excessive washing could remove too much of the paint and ink. However, many seeming disasters have turned out beautifully at second glance. Furthermore, any lost color can be replaced with watercolor, ink, crayon, or tempera.

 Note: If the color is to remain, it must be painted on the paper, not over another color.

supplies

1. Tempera paints
2. Brush
3. Paper
4. Higgins India ink

supplies

1. Watercolor paint
2. Paper
3. Rubber cement
4. Brush
5. Eraser

Note: Rubber cement can be painted over the areas previously painted with watercolor and repeated as often as desired. Make sure each is dry before applying the other. **Guard against the inhalation of any rubber cement fumes.**

Watercolor and Rubber Cement Resist

procedure

1. Paint a picture on the paper with rubber cement. Use the brush attached to the rubber cement jar or apply with a finger.
2. Allow the rubber cement to dry.
3. Paint over the rubber cement picture with watercolor paint. Several colors can be mingled together. The rubber cement will resist the paint.
4. Allow the paint to dry.
5. Clean away the rubber cement with an eraser, and expose the paper and original drawing.

John Marin. Phippsburg, Maine. 1932, watercolor, h. 15 1/4 w. 19 7/8 in. Marin let the white paper show through, as does the rubber cement. The Metropolitan Museum of Art, Alfred Stieglitz Collection, 1949. (49.70.145)

Watercolor Painting on Damp Paper

procedure

1. Soak the paper thoroughly in water.
2. Lay the wet paper on a desk top or drawing board and smooth out all the wrinkles.
3. Blot up any pools of water with the blotting material.
4. Paint directly on the damp paper. Make sure to use more pigment than water, for the colors tend to lose their brilliance when dry. Paint the light colors first, and add second and third colors before the paper dries, so colors will mingle and blend into spontaneous and soft shapes. After the paint is applied, avoid reworking.
5. Leave some areas unpainted to add sparkle.
6. Details, if necessary, can be painted in when the painting is dry.

supplies

1. Transparent watercolors
2. Brush
3. Drawing paper
4. Water container
5. Blotting material such as a rag, sponge, or paper towel

Note: Damp paper watercolors must be painted hurriedly to be lively. Don't expect complete success on the first try, for only experience will tell just how wet the paper must be and how much paint should be used. Clean the brush and the water in the container often.

Watercolor Wax Resist

procedure

1. Place wax paper over the drawing paper.
2. Draw heavily on the wax paper with a pencil or the wooden end of a brush. The pressure will transfer the wax to the drawing paper.
3. Remove the wax paper and paint over the drawing with transparent watercolor. The lines drawn with the pencil will remain white.

supplies

1. Wax paper or wax stencil paper
2. Paper
3. Pencil
4. Transparent watercolors
5. Brush
6. Water container

Note: Drawing with paraffin or a wax candle will achieve the same result as the wax paper.

1. Watercolors, tempera, or acrylic
2. Cotton swabs
3. White paper

Pointillism

The Impressionists' theories on light and color led to a more scientific approach to painting. Georges Seurat and Paul Signac divided all colors into their primary parts and then applied small dots or dabs of pure colors to the canvas to build up variations of shade without losing the brightness of the colors. This technique, called Divisionism at first but now called Pointillism, relied upon the viewer's eye to mix the color. For instance, if yellow dots are placed next to blue dots, the color area will look like green from a distance and the value and intensity of that green will vary depending upon the number and color of dots used.

procedure

1. Draw a design lightly on white paper.
2. Fill in the main objects with color by touching the cotton swab first into color and then touching it down on the paper within the pencil lines. Continue to print the dots close together but with a bit of white paper between them.
3. The dots will dry quickly, particularly with watercolor, and dots of another color can be put in between and overlapping the original color.
4. More than two colors can be used but the original form should still be visible.
5. The background space around the main objects should also be filled in with dots of color to finish the painting.

Small colored dots were excitingly juxtaposed, with our vision sometimes blending them together. Georges Seurat, Study for Le Chahut, *1889—oil on canvas 21–7/8 ×18–3/8". Albright-Knox Art Gallery, Buffalo, New York, General Purchase Fund, 1943.*

Gouache

Gouache is a technique that mixes watercolor with another material, usually gum arabic, to make it opaque. In this case, white powdered tempera is mixed with the color to make it opaque and a tint of that color.

supplies

1. Watercolors
2. Brush
3. White powdered tempera
4. Dark colored construction paper

procedure

1. Draw lightly on the colored construction paper.
2. Dip the brush in water and in paint and finally touch the brush into the powdered white tempera.
3. Paint.
4. Paint will dry quickly and additional details can be added to enrich the painting.

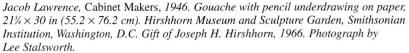

Jacob Lawrence, Cabinet Makers, *1946. Gouache with pencil underdrawing on paper, 21¾ × 30 in (55.2 × 76.2 cm). Hirshhorn Museum and Sculpture Garden, Smithsonian Institution, Washington, D.C. Gift of Joseph H. Hirshhorn, 1966. Photograph by Lee Stalsworth.*

11 Paper and Cardboard

Caution: Some of the activities in this chapter call for the use of X-acto knives. Extreme care and supervision must be utilized whenever X-acto knives are used. Safety instructions should be given before **EVERY** use of the knives. X-acto knives are now sold with safety caps, but separate caps may be purchased for older knives. Heavy corrugated cardboard should always be placed under the paper or material being cut. The X-acto knife is held like a pencil, with the fingers holding the knife on the textured ring. The slanted, sharpened edge should be directly over the line to be cut and the position of the knife or the paper should be changed if the line changes direction. Keep the fingers of the holding hand out of the way of the blade, usually above the cutting area. Remind students often to check themselves and the position of the knife and their hands.

Paper Textures

The flat surface of a piece of paper can be changed into a textured surface by many methods, five of which are suggested below. Also see "Paper Sculpture," pages 254–257.

procedure

method a

Cut or slit a paper with a cutting instrument, and push the shapes out from the back. **Safety precautions and supervision are necessary when X-acto knives are used.** Be sure to place a piece of cardboard under the work when cutting.

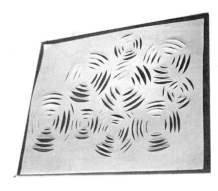

method b

Form numerous small three-dimensional paper shapes of various colors, and fasten to a piece of paper in a contrasting color to form a texture picture. **Adequate ventilation is required if rubber cement is used.**

A

Enlargement of A

Paper and Cardboard

method c

Curled paper strips, fastened close together on a piece of paper, will also create an interesting texture.

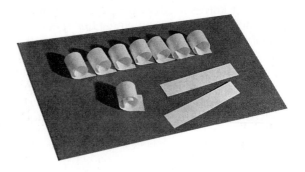

method d

Strips of paper with one edge cut in a decorative manner and the other edge folded to a right angle, and then fastened close together on a base paper, create interesting textures.

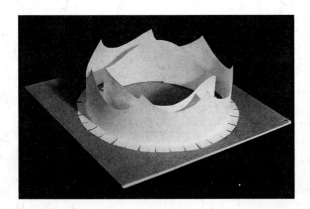 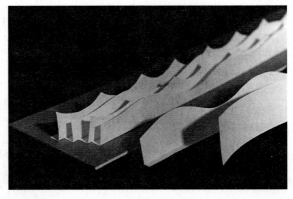

method e

Scoring and folding a flat sheet of paper will create numerous three-dimensional textures. Scoring is achieved by pressure with a comparatively dull, smooth instrument, such as a closed scissors or metal file, drawn across the paper in order to dent the paper so it can be folded more easily. After folding and creasing the paper on the scored lines, it can be opened and forced into lowered and raised creases.

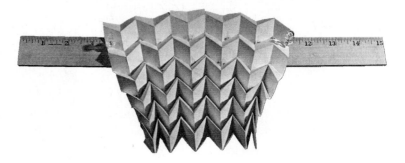

Chapter Eleven

Three-Dimensional Picture or Poster

procedure

1. Cut the subjects from a drawing or painting. **Use safety scissors if available.**
2. Make a number of small cardboard stilts of various sizes, and paste them on the back of each cutout. A narrow strip of cardboard folded into a square shape and fastened with a piece of tape makes an ideal stilt.
3. Paste each cutout on background paper, making sure that any subject that is meant to appear close to the viewer projects higher from the paper than those meant to be in the distance.

 Note: With a little experimentation, many other methods of creating a three-dimensional effect in paper can be achieved.

s u p p l i e s

1. Colored construction paper
2. Pencil
3. Scissors
4. Paste, glue, or tape

Pierced Paper

procedure

1. Lightly draw the design on the paper. Decide what should be pierced. Smaller shapes in a definite pattern are much more interesting.
2. With a cardboard under the paper, cut the sides of the pattern shapes leaving one edge to be the hinge. **X-acto knives must be used with caution.**
3. Lift the pattern shapes to make them 3-D.
4. The ends of the sheet of paper may be joined together to make a cylinder or a contrasting color may be mounted on the back. Dual-tone paper is a very nice alternative.

Stabile

procedure

1. Draw a frame around the edge of the paper to insure a solid base.
2. Draw the picture lightly, keeping the shapes from overlapping except when it is necessary to support the weight of the shape. Don't allow the shapes to be too tall.
3. Add color to the shapes. Color around the shapes on the base is optional.
4. Cut the sides and tops of the shapes, leaving the bottom edge as a hinge to fold up and support the shape. **Scissors or X-acto knives may be used but remember to use caution.**

Cardboard Relief

procedure

1. Cut a cardboard base on which to build a design.
2. Cut a second piece of cardboard into shapes of different sizes and glue to the cardboard base.
3. Cut a third piece of cardboard into shapes smaller in size than the previous pieces and glue in place.
4. Continue to cut and glue smaller and smaller pieces until a design of different levels results.
5. Cut and add details, if necessary.
6. **Use safety scissors if available.**

supplies

1. Soft cardboard, such as tablet backing or shirt boards
2. Glue
3. Scissors
4. Paint
5. Brush

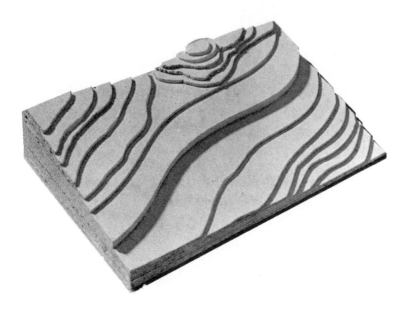

supplies

1. X-acto knife
2. Colored mat board

Mat Board—Cut and Peel

procedure

1. Cut lightly into the surface and around each shape that has been previously drawn on colored mat board. **X-acto knives must be used with safety precautions and supervision.**
2. Peel out each area after it has been cut.
3. Contrasting color areas can be added with colored paper, paint, crayons, or colored pencils.

Colored Tissue Paper

procedure

method a

1. Fold and cut (or sketch, then cut) simple, bold shapes from colored tissue. **Use safety scissors if available.**
2. Arrange these shapes on a white mounting board, overlapping to achieve the most pleasing design and color effects.
3. Cover the tissue paper shapes with rubber cement and gently adhere them to the mounting board. **Adequate ventilation is required with the use of rubber cement.**

 Note: Boxes, jars, bottles, and trays may be sprayed with white enamel and then decorated in the above manner. Articles to be decorated must be clean and sprayed according to the directions on the can of enamel. Apply tissue shapes that have been coated with rubber cement to the article, spreading smooth so that there are no wrinkles. Remove excess rubber cement with a ball of dried rubber cement, using care, as the tissue tears easily. If desired, additional decorative effects may be added with gold paint and brush to highlight tissue designs. When the paint is dry, spray the entire article with clear enamel to protect designs. Several thin coats, allowed to dry between applications, are necessary. **Use spray with optimum ventilation.**

method b

1. Cover the board with a thin solution of the glue and water.
2. Cut or tear pieces of colored tissue; press these in place on the glue-covered board while glue is wet. **Use safety scissors if available.**
3. Add additional layers of the paper with glue solution between each layer, until the desired richness of color is achieved.
4. Apply clear spray to protect the design. **Adequate ventilation is necessary when spray is used.**

Variation: Use black crayon or permanent marker to draw on the mounting board before applying the tissue and glue. Drawing can also be done after the tissue dries and before it is sprayed.

 Note: Colored tissue paper may be used to decorate a wide variety of items in the home, such as mirrors, wastebaskets, planters, or recipe boxes. Tissue blends with glue; work light to dark.

supplies

1. Corrugated cardboard
2. Scissors
3. Colored paper
4. Paste or rubber cement
5. Ink, paint, or crayon

Corrugated Cardboard

procedure

method a

1. Cut out pieces of colored construction paper, corrugated cardboard, or both. **Use safety scissors if available.**
2. Paste these pieces on a piece of corrugated cardboard to form the desired pattern. **Adequate ventilation is required if rubber cement is used.**
3. Accents can be added with ink, tempera paint, or crayon.

supplies

1. Corrugated cardboard box
2. X-acto knife
3. Paint, ink, or crayons

method b

1. Cut through the paper surface of a corrugated cardboard box with a *sharp knife* and peel out areas to expose the corrugations. **Use X-acto knife with caution.**
2. Color can be added with paints or crayons when the picture is complete.

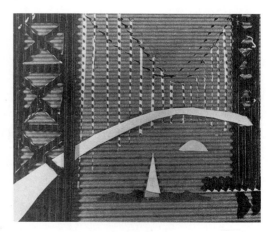

method c

Interesting effects are created by painting directly on the corrugated cardboard. Try painting in the ridges, on top of the ridges, or across the ridges. Further interest may be obtained by using one color inside the ridges and another one on top of the ridges.

s u p p l i e s

1. Corrugated cardboard
2. Tempera paint
3. Brush
4. Water container

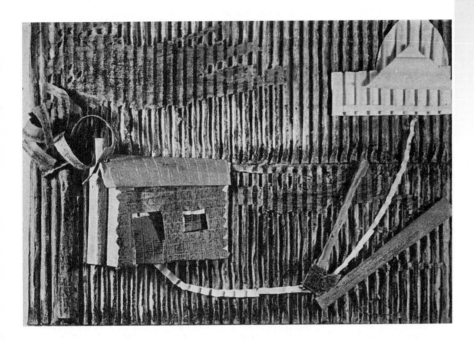

Cut Paper Design

procedure

1. Fold the paper into eighths as in illustration 1.
2. Cut numerous small shapes out of the paper until there is more paper cut away than there is remaining (Ill. 2). **Use safety scissors if available.**
3. Carefully unfold the paper so as not to tear it when opening.
4. The design can be mounted on a contrasting colored paper. Numerous designs can be created through an inventive approach using variously colored, shaped pieces under the cut design (Ill. 3). **Adequate ventilation is necessary when rubber cement is used.**

1

2

3

Cut Paper Rubbings

procedure

1. Cut related shapes from pieces of construction paper (Ill. 1). **Use safety scissors if available.**
2. Arrange the shapes on another piece of paper; if desired, the pieces may overlap (Ill. 2).
3. Fix the pieces in place with rubber cement. **Adequate ventilation is necessary when rubber cement is used.**
4. Place another piece of paper over the affixed shapes (Ill. 3).
5. Rub crayons over the paper, using overlapping strokes. The images of the cut shapes will appear (Ill. 4).

Note: Textures may be rubbed onto a piece of paper from any rough surface by laying the paper over the object and rubbing the paper with graphite pencil, crayon, oil pastel, or colored pencils.

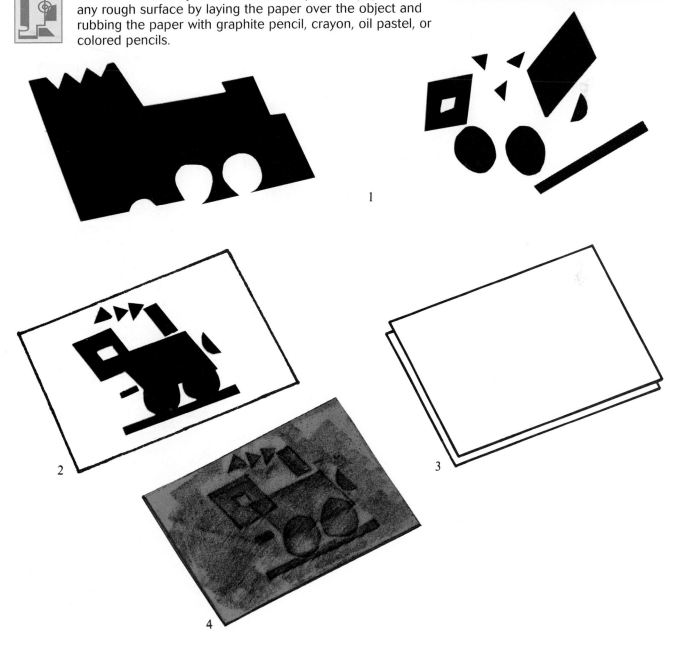

1

2

3

4

s u p p l i e s

1. Colored paper
2. Scissors
3. Translucent paper, such as tracing paper, onion skin paper, or tissue paper
4. Rubber cement

Note: As long as the first silhouette is visible through the translucent paper, the procedure can be continued. Translucent paper that is too heavy reduces the number of silhouettes. Designs cut from colored cellophane and placed between translucent paper make interesting transparent window decorations.

Distance Silhouette

procedure

1. Make an outline drawing on paper with pencil.
2. Cut out the shapes to appear in the background **(use safety scissors if available),** and rubber cement them to a sheet of white paper (Ill. 1). Adequate ventilation necessary when rubber cement is used.
3. Place a piece of the translucent paper over the cutout shapes, and hold in place by folding over the gluing to the back (Ill. 2).
4. Cut out shapes, and rubber cement these for the middle ground of the original drawing on the above translucent paper (Ill. 3).
5. Cover this with another translucent paper, and hold it in place by folding over and gluing to the back (Ill. 4).
6. Complete the picture by rubber cementing objects on the top of the translucent paper (Ill. 5).

1

2

3

4

5

Geometric Design

procedure

1. Cut geometric shapes that are varied in size and color. **Use safety scissors if available.** Cutting some of these shapes into halves or quarters not only offers more variety of shapes but also correlates well with the teaching of fractions.
2. Group a number of geometric shapes together until they form a picture.
3. When satisfied with the arrangement, paste the shapes in place on background paper.

s u p p l i e s

1. Colored paper
2. Scissors
3. Paste or glue stick

Fernand Leger, Three Women *(Le Grand dejeuner). 1921. Oil on canvas, 6′1¼″ × 8′3″ (183.5 × 251.5 cm). The Museum of Modern Art, New York. Mrs. Simon Guggenheim Fund. Photograph © 1996 The Museum of Modern Art, New York.*

1. Tissue paper in many bright colors
2. Fine and medium basket reed
3. Masking tape
4. Rubber cement or white glue
5. Sharp scissors

Note: Above all, for the best results, work neatly. Draw the circles with a compass and handle the tissue gently when applying rubber cement. The decorative discs may be used as units in a mobile, to decorate windows, plastic bottles, glass panels, or put on straight reed stems and arranged in a container as a bouquet. They will resemble decorated lollipops.

Colored Tissue Transparent Discs

procedure

1. Soak the larger reed in water until it can be bent into circles without breaking. (A fine reed may bend without being soaked.)
2. Cut to make the size circle desired, using the fine reed for the small circles and the medium reed for the larger ones. **Use safety scissors if available.**
3. Overlap the ends of the reed at least ½ inch on the small circles and more on the larger ones, then fasten with small strips of masking tape. Allow the reed to dry thoroughly. (It may be easier to allow the reed to dry partially before fastening with masking tape, as the tape will hold better.)
4. Cut a circle out of tissue paper a little larger than the reed frame.
5. Apply white glue or rubber cement to the reed and press onto the tissue circle. **Adequate ventilation is required if rubber cement is used.**
6. Cut tissue designs in various colors.
7. Cover the design with rubber cement and place on tissue circle. Two, three, or more tissue designs may be placed one on top of another to achieve a really beautiful effect. These may be of the same color or different colors. Only by experimenting can the possibilities be realized.
8. Trim away the tissue extending beyond the frame.

Letter Collé

Collé is a technique invented by the early cubists in which scraps of papers are pasted to the canvas to provide decorative and tactile embellishments. This is in contrast to another French word, "collage," which pertains to the use of various scrap materials.

procedure

1. Select a number of magazine letters of various sizes and colors.
2. Cut out selected letters. **Use safety scissors if available.**
3. Combine two or more letters to create figures, scenes, or a design.
4. Arrange this group of letters on a piece of background paper.
5. Paste the letters in place when satisfied.

1. Colored magazine pictures to be used as texture
2. Scissors
3. Paste or glue stick
4. Sheet of white or colored paper for background

Magazine Collé

Collé is a technique invented by the early cubists in which scraps of paper are pasted to the canvas to provide decorative and tactile embellishments.

procedure

1. Select a number of magazine pictures containing areas that may be used for textural effects.
2. Cut these areas into shapes that, when combined, will create a scene or design. **Use safety scissors if available.**
3. Arrange these paper shapes on background paper.
4. Paste the paper shapes in place when satisfied.

Note: Do not use the texture to create the subject matter from which it came—instead adapt it to other uses (that is, an illustration of cornflakes could be cut to represent a plowed field, haystack, rumpled hair, and so on).

Torn Paper Picture

procedure

1. Determine the subject to be treated, and tear the paper into shapes adaptable to the subject.
2. Arrange these torn shapes on a piece of paper that will serve as a background.
3. Paste each piece in place to complete the picture.

Note: Drawing can be added to provide detail.

supplies

1. Scissors
2. Paper
3. Paste or glue stick
4. Crayon

Paper Script Design

procedure

1. Fold the paper in half.
2. Write a word or name in script with a crayon along the creased edge. The crayon is used to ensure enough thickness of line to permit the cutting of letters on both sides.
3. Cut on both sides of the crayoned line, making sure each letter is held together by the fold. **Use safety scissors if available.**
4. Paste the cutout letters on contrasting colored paper. Additional cut paper may be added to develop a suggested image.

 Note: A word containing a letter that extends below the line (such as f, g, j, p, q, y) must be written above the fold so that only the extension of that letter reaches the fold. View the accompanying illustrations from the side in order to see the original name from which the design was created.

Variation: A three-dimensional form can be created by gluing the design so that parts are lifted above the mounting surface.

Paper Quilling

procedure

method a

Two-Dimensional

1. Draw design on paper.
2. Tape design to hard surface with wax paper taped over design.
3. Roll piece of strip (approximately 3 inches long) around corsage pin or toothpick. Glue end to coil or quill to keep it from unrolling.
4. Make additional quills, shaping them as desired.
5. Place quills on wax paper over design and begin gluing quills together, using a toothpick or pin to apply glue. Do not glue to wax paper.
6. Glue from the center of the design out to the edges of the design (Ill. 1).
7. When complete, seal the finished quilling shape with clear acrylic spray or acrylic media. **Use spray with optimum ventilation.**

method b

Three-Dimensional

1. Follow steps 1 through 4 in method a.
2. Glue quills to a solid three-dimensional armature or shape, such as a blown egg, box, or Paris Craft object (Ill. 2).
3. Seal with acrylic spray or acrylic media. **Use spray with optimum ventilation.**

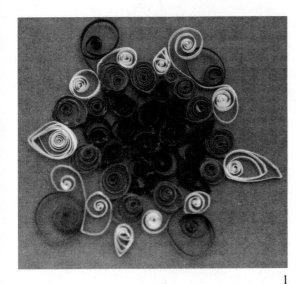

1

2

supplies

1. Corsage pin or round toothpick
2. Paper, cut into 1/4 inch wide strips, or commercial quilling strips may be used
3. White craft glue
4. Clear acrylic spray or acrylic media
5. Wax paper

Basic Rolls

 Loose Roll

 Tight Roll

 Eye Roll

 Rain Drop

 Square

 Triangle

 Heart

Scrolls

 Scroll

 "S" Shape

 Heart

 "V" Shape

 Decorative Scroll

supplies

1. Scissors
2. Colored paper scraps or colored magazine pictures
3. Paste or rubber cement
4. Corsage or hat pin (for lifting pieces of paper)
5. Pencil
6. Background paper

Paper Mosaic

A mosaic is a design made by the close placement of small pieces of colored material. Historically, mosaics can be traced back to classical antiquity. They were composed of small pieces of colored glass or stones imbedded in a binding agent.

procedure

1. Make a light pencil drawing on the background paper.
2. Cut the colored paper into small fairly uniform sizes. **Use safety scissors if available.** (Try to keep the pieces sorted by color to save time later when pasting.)
3. Apply the paste or rubber cement to the individual pieces, and place them on the drawing. **Adequate ventilation is required if rubber cement is used.** Leave a narrow space of background color between the pieces of paper. A corsage pin will help in picking up the bits of paper.
4. Continue pasting until the design is completed.

Note: Other interesting mosaics can be made with confetti, seeds, grain, punched paper bits, and so on.

Positive and Negative Design

procedure

method a

This is the simpler procedure of the two and the one most appropriate for young children.

1. Select one sheet of colored paper (Ill. 1) and one-half sheet of a contrasting color (Ill. 2).

2. Fold the small sheet in half (Ill. 3).
3. Cut a design directly out of the folded side (Ill. 4). **Use safety scissors if available.** (A pencil drawing may be helpful in cutting out the design.) The cutout section is the positive part (Ill. 6) and the section containing the opening is the negative part (Ill. 5) of the design.

4. Unfold both parts, laying the negative section (Ill. 7) on the uncut sheet of contrasting color paper, squaring it up on one end. Paste in place. **Adequate ventilation is required if rubber cement is used.**
5. Place the positive section (Ill. 8) on the other half of the uncut sheet and paste it in place.

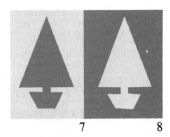

6. To carry a design further, cut both the positive (Ill. 9) and negative (Ill. 10) pieces on the fold.
7. Alternate the positive and negative pieces, and paste on contrasting colored paper (Ill. 11).

1. Colored paper
2. Paste or rubber cement
3. Scissors

Note: Many variations and allover patterns can be created by changing designs and color. In a pure positive-negative design, no scraps will be left over.

supplies

1. Colored paper
2. Paste or rubber cement
3. Scissors

 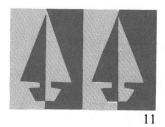

9   10   11

method b

An allover pattern.

1. Select one sheet of colored paper (Ill. 1) and one-half sheet of a contrasting color (Ill. 2).

1   2

2. Cut the smaller sheet into four or eight equal parts (Ill. 3). **Use safety scissors if available.**

3   4   5

3. Fold one part in half, and cut a design directly from the folded edge (Ill. 4) (a pencil drawing may be helpful in cutting out the design). The cutout section is the positive; the section containing the opening is the negative part of the design.

   If the allover pattern is to be repeated in every respect (color and design), fold the remaining parts in half and lay the negative piece over each part in turn. Trace the design with a pencil, then cut out each part along the pencil line.
4. Unfold all of the positive and negative sections and cut along each fold so that each section is divided into two parts.
5. Paste one-half of the negative part in the upper left-hand corner of the full sheet (Ill. 5). **Adequate ventilation is required if rubber cement is used.**
6. Paste one-half of the positive part so the original design is completed.
7. The allover pattern can be completed by alternating the positive and negative sections until all the sections are used and the paper is filled.

Paper Mola

procedure

1. With light pencil lines, draw a simple silhouette of a bird, simple animal, lizard, reptile, or insect.
2. Cut out the shape and erase the pencil lines. **Use safety scissors if available.**
3. Draw the second silhouette, on a contrasting color, 1/4 inch away from the edge of the smaller shape being used as a pattern.
4. Cut out the second shape and use it as a pattern on a third piece of contrasting color. Draw around it and cut it out. (There should be three pieces of different colors and sizes.)
5. With the scraps left from the colored sheets, cut out designs to be used with the creature. Make the shapes in the same color order as the creatures, so that the smallest shape is cut from the first color used.
6. Cut three sets of color and size for each design.
7. Carefully arrange the design around the creature in the same order of size and color.
8. Mount the largest color creature on a fourth sheet of paper after trying out different arrangements. Glue the largest shapes first, medium shapes next, and finally the smallest shapes.

supplies

1. Variety of colored construction paper
2. Scissors
3. Pencil
4. Glue or glue stick

supplies

1. Powder paint or oil paint
2. Large vessel containing water (a wide shallow container such as a photographic tray is best)
3. Paper
4. Small vessels for color mixing
5. Turpentine or liquid starch
6. Soap or detergent
7. Paper towels or cloths

Swirl Paper

procedure

1. Pour a small quantity of turpentine or starch on the surface of the water in the mixing vessel, and add enough powder paint or oil paint to bring it to the desired color strength.
2. Stir the water, thereby exciting the turpentine or starch into interesting patterns.
3. Pick up the color patterns with the paper. In doing this the paper may be dropped on, or dragged across, the surface of the water. A little experimentation will demonstrate that various methods of color pickup may be used in obtaining the desired effects.
4. Cleanse the containers, using soap or detergent and cloths or paper towels.

 Note: If multicolored designs are desired, they may be created by adding more than one color to the water and the container or by dipping one color at a time until several are combined. Although spontaneity is the most interesting feature of swirl paper, it should be pointed out that it is possible to achieve a degree of control over the patterns. Portions of the patterns may be placed where desired by simply touching certain areas of the paper to the water.

Swirl papers are a great stimulant for the imagination. Many things may be read into the pattern, and these may be made more visible by adding chalk, crayon, or ink.

Swirl papers may be used decoratively as a covering for such objects as notebooks, wastebaskets, or boxes.

Papier-Mâché

12

Caution: Some activities in this chapter call for the use of X-acto knives. Extreme care and supervision must be utilized whenever X-acto knives are used. Safety instructions should be given before **EVERY** use of the knives. X-acto knives are now sold with safety caps, but separate caps may be purchased for older knives. Heavy corrugated cardboard should always be placed under the paper or material being cut. The X-acto knife is held like a pencil, with the fingers holding the knife on the textured ring. The slanted, sharpened edge should be directly over the line to be cut and the position of the knife or the paper should be changed if the line changes direction. Keep the fingers of the holding hand out of the way of the blade, usually above the cutting area. Remind students often to check themselves and the position of the knife and their hands.

Nature of the Medium

Papier-Mâché

Papier-mâché is repulped paper mixed with glue or paste. It was first used in the Orient where it was covered with lacquer. France adopted it in the early 18th century and it migrated to England and Germany. Various papier-mâché products were made in the late 18th and well into the 19th century. These included toys, picture frames, figurines, and ornamental moldings.

Paris Craft

Paris Craft is often used to make sculptural items. It is sold commercially as a fabric, in a roll, with a preapplied coating of plaster. It is immersed in warm water and then applied to some supporting structure (an armature) and modeled to create the desired forms.

Papier-Mâché Bowl

procedure

1. Cover the outside surface of the bowl with a film of cream, Vaseline, or grease. This will keep the papier-mâché from sticking to the bowl.
2. Place the bowl upside down on newspaper or cardboard.
3. Cut newspaper or paper toweling into strips, approximately ½ inch wide. **Use safety scissors if available.**
4. Mix the paste in a bowl or pan to the consistency of cream.
5. Place a strip of paper into the paste until it is saturated. Remove the strip from the bowl, and wipe off the excess paste by pulling it between the fingers.
6. Apply the paste-saturated strips directly on the oiled surface of the bowl. One or two layers of strips of just wet paper applied directly to the bowl before applying the paste-saturated strips will serve the same purpose as greasing the bowl.
7. Continue to apply strips until the entire bowl is covered. Repeat until at least six layers of paper strips are applied. The number of layers can be readily counted if a different kind or color of paper is used for each layer. The strength of the finished bowl will be much greater if each layer of strips is applied in a different direction. Also, make sure that all wrinkles and bubbles are removed after each strip is added.
8. Allow the papier-mâché to dry thoroughly before removing the bowl.
9. Trim the edges of the papier-mâché bowl and apply additional strips to strengthen and smooth the edges. Other imperfections can be repaired at this time.
10. When the repairs are thoroughly dry, sandpaper the surface until smooth and then decorate.
11. If tempera paint is used for decoration, the surface should be sprayed with clear plastic or painted with shellac or varnish for permanence. **Use adequate ventilation when spraying.**
12. Asphaltum painted on the inside of the bowl will waterproof the container.

Note: If wallpaper paste is used, it may contain an insecticide; check this for safety. Some instant papier-mâché contains asbestos. Paper cutter should be employed by the teacher.

1. Newspapers, paper toweling, or any absorbent paper
2. Scissors or paper cutter
3. Paste thinned to the consistency of cream, such as wheat paste, library paste, or modeling paste; methylan paste is widely used
4. Container for mixing paste
5. A smooth bowl to be used as a mold. The bowl should also have a small base and a wide mouth with no undercuts.
6. Vaseline, grease, or cream
7. Sandpaper
8. Paint, such as tempera, enamel, oil paint, acrylic
9. Brush
10. Clear plastic spray, shellac, or varnish for protective finish if tempera paint is used
11. Asphaltum to waterproof bowl

s u p p l i e s

1. Small pieces of styrofoam
2. Newspapers, paper toweling, or any absorbent paper
3. Scissors or paper cutter
4. Paste thinned to consistency of cream, such as wheat paste, modeling paste, or library paste; methylan paste is widely used
5. Container for mixing paste
6. Sandpaper
7. Paint, such as tempera, enamel, latex, or acrylic
8. Brush
9. Clear plastic spray, shellac, or varnish for protecting finish, if tempera paint is used
10. Glue
11. Jewelry findings, for example, pin and/or earring backs

Papier-Mâché Jewelry

procedure

1. Shape a piece of styrofoam to correspond identically to the desired piece of jewelry.
2. Cut newspaper or paper toweling into strips, approximately ¼ inch wide. **Use safety scissors if available.**
3. Mix the paste in a bowl or pan to the consistency of cream.
4. Immerse a strip of paper into the paste until it is saturated. Remove the strip from the bowl, and wipe off the excess paste by pulling it between the fingers.
5. Apply the strips directly to the styrofoam.
6. Continue to apply strips until the entire piece of jewelry is covered. Repeat until several layers of paper strips are applied. The number of layers can be readily counted if a different kind or color of paper is used for each layer. Make sure that all wrinkles and bubbles are removed after each strip is added.
7. Add any desired particular features. This can be done either with papier-mâché or by adding other materials.
8. Allow the papier-mâché to dry thoroughly.
9. Sandpaper the surface until smooth and then decorate.
10. If tempera paint is used for decoration, the surface should be sprayed with clear plastic or painted with shellac or varnish for permanence. **Use adequate ventilation when spraying.**
11. Fasten earring or pin to the back of dry papier-mâché jewelry using glue mixed with a small piece of cotton.

 Note: Paper cutter should be employed by the teacher.

Papier-Mâché Maraca

procedure

1. Cover the surface of the light bulb with a film of cream, Vaseline, or grease. This will keep the papier-mâché from sticking to the bulb.
2. Cut newspaper or paper toweling into strips, approximately ½ inch wide. **Use safety scissors if available.**
3. Mix the paste in a bowl or pan to the consistency of cream.
4. Place a strip of paper into the paste until it is saturated. Remove the strip from the bowl, and wipe off the excess paste by pulling it between the fingers.
5. Apply the paste-saturated strip directly to the oiled surface of the light bulb.
6. Continue to apply strips until the entire bulb is covered. Repeat until at least six layers of paper strips are applied. The number of layers can be readily counted if a different kind or color of paper is used for each layer. The strength of the finished maraca will be much greater if each strip is applied in a different direction. Also, make sure that all wrinkles and bubbles are removed after each strip is added.
7. Place the maraca on a crumpled piece of newspaper and allow to dry thoroughly. The crumpled paper allows the air to circulate around the maraca.
8. When the papier-mâché is completely dry, rap the maraca sharply against the floor, wall, or radiator to break the bulb inside the paper covering. The broken pieces of glass provide the sound when shaken. If a hole is punctured, it is easily repaired with the addition of more strips.
9. Sandpaper the surface until smooth, and then decorate.
10. If tempera paint is used for decoration, the surface should then be sprayed with clear plastic or painted with shellac or varnish for permanence. **Use adequate ventilation when spraying.**

 Note: Paper cutter should be employed by the teacher.

supplies

1. Newspapers, paper toweling, or any absorbent paper
2. Scissors or paper cutter
3. Paste thinned to the consistency of cream, such as wheat paste, library paste, or modeling paste; methylan paste is widely used
4. Container for mixing paste
5. Large, burned-out electric light bulb
6. Vaseline, grease, or cream
7. Sandpaper
8. Paint, such as tempera, latex, enamel, or acrylic
9. Brush
10. Clear plastic spray, shellac, or varnish for protecting finish if tempera paint is used

1. Newspapers, paper toweling, or any absorbent paper
2. Scissors or paper cutter
3. Paste thinned to the consistency of cream, such as wheat paste, library paste, or modeling paste; methylan paste is widely used
4. Container for mixing paste
5. Balloon
6. Sandpaper
7. Paint, such as tempera, enamel, oil paint, or acrylic
8. Brush
9. Clear plastic spray, shellac, or varnish for protective finish if tempera paint is used

Note: Paper cutter should be employed by the teacher.

Papier-Mâché over Balloon

procedure

1. Cut newspaper or paper toweling into strips, approximately ½ inch wide. **Use safety scissors if available.**
2. Mix the paste in a bowl or pan to the consistency of cream.
3. Inflate the balloon to the desired size and tie it closed.
4. Place a strip of paper in the paste until it is saturated. Remove the strip from the bowl and wipe off the excess paste by pulling it between the fingers.
5. Apply the paste-saturated strip directly to the balloon.
6. Continue to apply strips until the entire balloon is covered. Repeat until at least six layers of paper strips are applied. The number of layers can be readily counted if a different kind or color of paper is used for each layer. The strength of the finished object will be much greater if each strip is applied in a different direction. Also, make sure that all wrinkles and bubbles are removed after each strip is added.
7. Allow the papier-mâché to dry thoroughly.
8. A number of different and interesting objects can be created at this point.
   a. An opening can be cut into an egg shape, and an Easter egg crèche can be built inside.
   b. A perfect sphere can be used as a globe for the geography class. The continents can be painted, built up with papier-mâché, or built in relief with a salt and flour mixture (see p. 344).
   c. When cut in half, the balloon shape can be used as a foundation for two masks, two bowls, or one of each. If a mask is desired, openings can be cut for the eyes, and features added with either papier-mâché or by fastening other materials in place, such as yarn for hair, kernels of corn for teeth, or cut paper for ears.

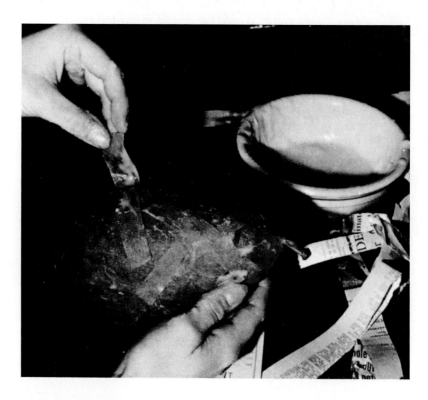

d. The shape of the papier-mâché balloon might suggest an animal, bird, or fish. Its particular features can be applied with papier-mâché or by fastening other material to the form.

9. Sandpaper the surface of any of the above objects before decorating.

10. If tempera paint is used for decoration, the surface should be sprayed with clear plastic or painted with shellac or varnish for permanence. **Use sprays with optimum ventilation.**

supplies

1. Newspapers, paper toweling, or any absorbent paper
2. Scissors or paper cutter
3. Paste thinned to consistency of cream, such as wheat paste, library paste, or modeling paste; methylan paste is widely used
4. Container for mixing paste
5. Bottle on which to build form
6. Sandpaper
7. Paint, such as tempera, latex, enamel, or acrylic
8. Brush
9. Clear plastic spray, shellac, or varnish for protecting finish if tempera paint is used

Papier-Mâché over Bottle

procedure

1. Cut newspaper or paper toweling into strips, approximately 1/2 inch wide. **Use safety scissors if available.**
2. Mix the paste in a bowl or pan to the consistency of cream.
3. Submerge a strip of paper in the paste until it is saturated. Remove the strip from the bowl, and wipe off the excess paste by pulling the strip between the fingers.
4. Apply the paste-saturated strip directly to the bottle.
5. Continue to apply strips until the entire bottle is covered. Repeat until at least six layers of paper strips are applied. The number of layers can be readily counted if a different kind or color of paper is used for each layer. The strength of the finished piece will be much greater if each strip is applied in a different direction. Also, make sure that all wrinkles and bubbles are removed after each strip is added.
6. Place the bottle on a crumpled piece of paper and allow it to dry thoroughly. The crumpled paper allows the air to circulate around the piece.
7. When the papier-mâché over the bottle is dry, sandpaper the surface until smooth. The surface can then be decorated with a choice of three-dimensional materials that are held in position with paste-covered strips.
8. If tempera paint is used for decoration, the surface should be sprayed with clear plastic or painted with shellac or varnish for permanence. **Use sprays with optimum ventilation.**

 Note: Paper cutter should be employed by the teacher.

© James L. Shaffer

Papier-Mâché Pulp Objects

procedure

1. Tear (do not cut with cutter or scissors) paper into small pieces no bigger than ½ inch square. Be sure edges of pieces are ragged.
2. Place the torn paper in a container, cover with water, and at the same time, stir to make sure all the paper becomes wet.
3. Add a teaspoonful of salt for each quart of mixture to prevent spoilage. Allow to soak for at least 36 hours.
4. Mix and squeeze the mixture until it becomes pulp.
5. Mix in wallpaper paste in small amounts as needed.
6. Model the forms with the mixture.
7. Allow the pulp to dry thoroughly.
8. Sandpaper the surface of the pulp object until smooth, and then decorate.
9. If tempera paint is used for decoration, the surface should be sprayed with clear plastic or painted with shellac or varnish for permanence. **Use sprays with optimum ventilation.**

Note: Papier-Mâché pulp can be used for dishes, plaques, ornaments, puppets, marionettes, maps, and so on.

1. Newspaper, tissue, or paper towels
2. Wallpaper paste or modeling paste; methylan paste is widely used
3. Table salt
4. Container

supplies

1. Window screen, chicken wire, wire, paper, mailing tubes, sticks, rolled and taped newspaper, and so on (to be used individually or collectively to form the general shape of the object to be covered with papier-mâché)
2. Wire, nails, gummed paper, glue, and so on, for use in fastening the frame together
3. Newspaper, paper toweling, or any absorbent paper
4. Scissors or paper cutter
5. Paste thinned to the consistency of cream, such as wheat paste, library paste, or modeling paste; methylan paste is widely used
6. Container for mixing paste
7. Sandpaper
8. Paint, such as tempera, enamel, oil paint, or acrylic
9. Brush
10. Clear plastic spray, shellac, or varnish for protecting finish if tempera paint is used

 Note: Paper cutter should be employed by the teacher.

Papier-Mâché or Paris Craft over Frame

procedure for Papier-Mâché

1. Build a frame or armature to the general shape of the chosen subject. Fasten the various parts of the skeleton together securely, using the wire, nails, tape, or appropriate material.
2. Cut newspaper or paper toweling into strips, approximately ½ inch wide. **Use safety scissors if available.**
3. Mix the paste in a bowl or pan to the consistency of cream.
4. Place a strip of paper in the paste until it is saturated. Remove the strip from the bowl and wipe off the excess paste by pulling the strip between the fingers.
5. Apply the strips directly over the frame.
6. Continue to apply strips until the entire frame is covered. Repeat until at least six layers of paper strips are applied. The number of layers can be readily counted if a different kind or color of paper is used for each layer. The strength of the finished frame will be much greater if each strip is applied in a different direction. Also, make sure that all wrinkles and bubbles are removed after each strip is added.
7. Add any particular features not incorporated in the original skeleton. This can be done either with papier-mâché or by adding other materials.
8. Allow the papier-mâché to dry thoroughly.
9. Sandpaper the surface until smooth, and then decorate.
10. If tempera paint is used for decoration, the surface should be sprayed with clear plastic or painted with shellac or varnish for permanence. **Use sprays with optimum ventilation.**
11. Additional materials such as yarn for hair, buttons for eyes, etc., can be added to further enhance the finished product.

procedure for Paris Craft

1. Cut the Paris Craft into appropriate sized strips and pieces.
2. Dip the strips into warm water and lay them in different directions over the base form. Smooth each strip before putting on the next strip. Three or four layers would be sufficient but always check for holes. Check edges to make sure they are smooth.
3. Finish form as you would papier-mâché.

Printing

Caution: Some of the activities in this chapter call for the use of X-acto knives. Extreme care and supervision must be utilized whenever X-acto knives are used. Safety instructions should be given before **EVERY** use of the knives. X-acto knives are now sold with safety caps, but separate caps may be purchased for older knives. Heavy corrugated cardboard should always be placed under the paper or material being cut. The X-acto knife is held like a pencil, with the fingers holding the knife on the textured ring. The slanted, sharpened edge should be directly over the line to be cut and the position of the knife or the paper should be changed if the line changes direction. Keep the fingers of the holding hand out of the way of the blade, usually above the cutting area. Remind students often to check themselves and the position of the knife and their hands.

Printmaking—Basic Processes

There are four fundamental techniques of printmaking utilized by the artist: screen process (silk screen, serigraphy), intaglio, relief, and lithography. In *screen printing,* ink is forced through a screen onto the printing paper by pressure applied to a squeegee. The preparation of the screen determines the ink pattern. *Intaglio printing* usually involves a metal plate that the artist has cut into or etched using acid. Ink is rubbed into the crevices of the plate and then wiped so that only those crevices contain the ink. Under the pressure of a press, the ink is then forced out of the plate onto the printing paper. *Lithography* makes use of stones or metal plates that are treated so that ink will be retained by certain areas. The printing is accomplished by using a press with a scraper bar. The pressure of the bar forces the ink to cling to the paper. *Relief printing* utilizes the concept of the venerable woodcut; wood (or linoleum or a commercial block) is cut away, the remaining surface rolled up with some form of ink, and the block pressed against the paper with a smooth-surfaced instrument. Many prints have used combinations of these techniques.

In intaglio printing, the ink is drawn out of the areas that have been bitten (with acid) or cut out of the plate. From John Ross and Clare Romano, The Complete Intaglio Print. *© 1974, The Free Press.*

In lithography, ink will be accepted by the sensitized areas and rejected by the others. From John Ross and Clare Romano, The Complete Screen Print and Lithograph, *© 1974, The Free Press.*

In relief printmaking, the nonprinting area is removed as in this case with a wood gouge. From John Ross and Clare Romano, The Complete Relief Print, *© 1974, The Free Press.*

Crayon Transfer Print

procedure

1. Completely cover a sheet of white paper with a heavy coating of light-colored chalk.
2. Cover the coating of chalk with a very heavy layer of darker-colored crayon.
3. Place a piece of white paper containing a drawing (Ill. 1) over the crayon- and chalk-colored paper.
4. Using a dull pencil or ball-point pen, and using pressure, trace over the drawing (Ill. 2).
5. The pressure causes the crayon to adhere to the underside of the drawing (Ill. 3) and creates a separate drawing on the crayon- and chalk-covered paper (Ill. 4).

supplies

1. Paper
2. Colored chalk
3. Crayons
4. Pencil or ball-point pen

Completed drawing   1

2

Print made on back of drawing (this will reverse the image).   3

Print made on underlying sheet as crayon is removed.   4

supplies

1. Medium to coarse grades of sandpaper of small dimensions
2. Wax crayon
3. Paper
4. Water-soluble or oil-base printers' ink (Water-soluble printers' ink is much easier to clean)
5. Brayer (roller)
6. Ink slab (9 inch × 9 inch floor tile, or a piece of glass with taped edges to prevent cut fingers)
7. Mineral spirits for cleaning the brayer and ink slab, if oil-base printers' ink is used
8. Newspapers

 Note: The frame in the illustration is made according to the instructions contained in "Three-Dimensional Picture Frame," on page 336.

Sandpaper Print

procedure

1. Draw directly on the sandpaper with the crayon. Areas or lines that are drawn with crayon will be the parts that will be reproduced—make sure they are crayoned heavily. It is not necessary to use more than one color crayon, since the prints will be reproduced in the color of the ink that is used.
2. Squeeze some printers' ink from the tube onto the inking slab.
3. Roll the ink with the brayer until it is spread smoothly. Make the roller rotate several times until it is completely covered with ink.
4. Roll the inked brayer over the crayon drawing on the sandpaper until it is evenly covered with ink.
5. Place the printing paper on top of a pad of newspapers.
6. Lift the inked sandpaper, and place the inked side down on a piece of the printing paper.
7. Hold the sandpaper in place with one hand, and with the other hand rub over the back of the inked sandpaper with a smooth instrument. (A small glass jar with a smooth bottom works well.)
8. Rub until the original drawing has been reproduced. It would be wise to peel back the corner of the sandpaper occasionally to determine whether further rubbing is necessary for a strong print.
9. Reink the sandpaper for subsequent prints.

Nature Print

procedure

1. Place the natural object on the scrap paper (a leaf should have the veined side up).
2. Brush or roll over the object with ink.
3. Place the printing paper over the object.
4. Hold the top paper securely with one hand, and press and brush the paper with the other hand.
5. Lift off the printed paper, turn it face up, and allow to dry.
6. Clean up oil-base ink with mineral spirits; water-soluble with water.

Note: Assorted colors may be used and multiple prints may be taken on the same sheet of paper.

1. Natural objects that can be flattened with relative ease, such as leaves, grasses, ferns, or blossoms
2. Oil-base or water-soluble printers' ink (Water-soluble printers' ink is much easier to clean)
3. Fairly stiff brush
4. Scrap paper (newspaper will be satisfactory)
5. Printing paper

supplies

1. Piece of cardboard (if thick, edges should be beveled)
2. Polymer—acrylic medium (or gesso) for plate saturation
3. Assorted flat textures
4. Polymer modeling paste (dries slowly)
5. Polymer medium—gel form
6. Old toothbrush
7. Oil paints, colored printing inks, or tempera paint
8. Scrap piece of mat board for spreading ink
9. Mat knife or X-acto knife. Knives must be used with caution.

 Notes: Excessively thick, hard, and/or sharp materials will cut the paper; check your surfaces!

Tempera paint dries quickly; inking and printing must be hurried!

Teacher should probably cut the cardboard in preparation for this project.

Collagraph

procedure

Pieces of cardboard must be given two or three coats of polymer acrylic medium; following that, the following list indicates *some* of the things that may be done.

1. Modeling with paste on board
2. Modeling with gel
3. Embedding of textures; seal with polymer medium or gel
4. Engraving or scratching with any firm point
5. Sprinkle with grits or seal sandpaper
6. Always allow to dry completely

Printing

1. As relief—use roller or brayer to apply color
2. As intaglio—work color into depressions with toothbrush, wipe surface clean with old newspaper
3. Both—apply intaglio ink first (as in #2, above), then apply relief ink
4. Print by using printing press, clothes wringer, or rub vigorously with large spoon or some smooth hard object

Materials may be applied or pressed, and gesso and other substances may be modeled to make a printing surface. From John Ross and Clare Romano, The Complete Collagraph, © 1980, The Free Press.

Cork Print

procedure

1. Use the cutting tool to cut a design around the edge and/or the middle of the cork.
2. Place a pad of newspapers under the paper to be printed. Have a scrap paper or paper towel available on which to try the design to determine whether too much paint is being used.
3. Cover the surface of the cork with paint, and print on a scrap of paper to eliminate any excess paint. One or two prints may be tried on the scrap paper so that too much paint is not being used. Printing may now begin. A single application of paint will serve for three or four printings, which may be combined to make an overall pattern.
4. Several different colors may be applied. If these are also applied to different areas of the cork, interesting prints may result.

supplies

1. Cork
2. X-acto knife or penknife
3. Paper
4. Tempera paint
5. Brush

Note: As this procedure involves sharp-edged instruments, precautions should be observed.

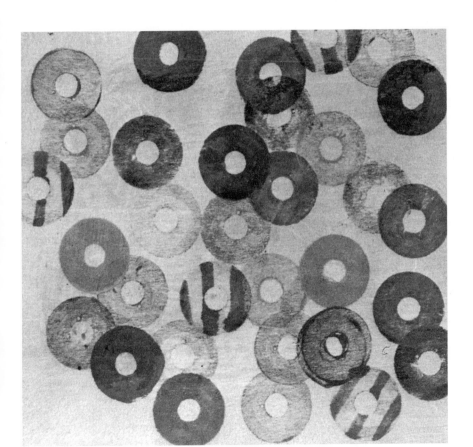

supplies

1. A piece of inner tube or cardboard
2. Scissors
3. Paste or glue
4. Heavy cardboard, floor tile, or a piece of wood
5. Water-soluble or oil-base printers' ink (Water-soluble printers' ink is much easier to clean)
6. Brayer (roller)
7. Ink slab (9 inch × 9 inch floor tile, or a piece of glass with taped edges to prevent cut fingers)
8. Paper
9. Newspaper
10. Turpentine or kerosene for cleaning the brayer, inking slab, and printing block, if oil-base printers' ink is used

Cardboard or Rubber Block Print

procedure

1. Cut shapes from pieces of cardboard or inner tubes, and glue them to a cardboard background for printing. **Use safety scissors if available.**
2. Squeeze a small amount of ink from the tube onto the piece of glass or floor tile.
3. Roll the ink with a brayer until it is spread smoothly on the inking slab (Ill. 1).
4. Roll the inked brayer over the mounted design from side to side and top to bottom to ensure an even distribution over the entire surface.
5. Place a piece of paper over the inked design, and rub gently and evenly with the fingers, or with a smooth bottom of a small jar until the entire design is reproduced. It would be wise to peel back a corner of the paper to determine whether further rubbing is necessary for a strong print (Ill. 2).
6. Reink the design for subsequent prints.

1

2

Paraffin or Soap Block Print

procedure

1. Smooth one side of the block with a straight-edge scraper. Make sure any design is removed and the surface if flat. If paraffin is used, the surface can be smoothed by using a cloth saturated with turpentine.
2. Plan a design on paper the size of the block.
3. Place the design over the block and retrace the lines with a pencil to inscribe the design on the block.
4. Carve the design in the block with any suitable tool. Cut away all areas that are not to be printed.
5. To check the design, place a thin piece of paper over the carving and rub the surface with a crayon or soft pencil.
6. Squeeze a small amount of ink from the tube onto the inking slab, and roll with the brayer until ink is spread smoothly.
7. Roll the inked roller over the carved design. Ink from side to side and top to bottom to insure an even distribution of the ink over the entire surface.
8. Place a piece of paper over the inked surface, and rub gently and evenly with the fingers until entire design has been covered. It would be wise to peel back a corner of the paper to determine whether further rubbing is necessary.
9. Reink the block for each subsequent print.
10. If a commercial piece of paraffin is not available, make your own block as follows:
    a. Melt pieces of paraffin in an old double boiler over a low fire. Heat slowly to avoid bubbles. An electric heat lamp is also suitable for melting paraffin.
    b. Pour the melted paraffin into a small cardboard box to a thickness of approximately ¾ inch.
    c. When paraffin is cool and hard, remove it from the container.
    d. Smooth the surface of the block of paraffin with a straight-edge scraper. A cloth saturated with turpentine will further smooth the surface.

supplies

1. Paraffin or large bar of soap
2. Carving tool, such as nail, scissors, knife, or orange stick
3. Straight-edge scraper for smoothing surface of the soap (table knife)
4. Water-soluble or oil-base printers' ink (Water-soluble printers' ink is much easier to clean.)
5. Brayer (roller)
6. Ink slab (9 inch × 9 inch floor tile, or a piece of glass with taped edges to prevent cut fingers)
7. Paper
8. Mineral spirits for cleaning brayer, ink slab, and block design, if oil-base printers' ink is used

 Note: To prevent distortion of the printing surface, avoid too much pressure when printing.

supplies

1. Modeling plaster
2. Ink slab (9 inch × 9 inch floor tile, or a piece of glass with taped edges to prevent cut fingers)
3. Plastic clay (plastilene)
4. Shellac and brush
5. Carving tools, such as V- or U-shaped gouges set in wooden handles, penknife, nail, hairpin, or orange stick
6. Thin paper
7. Water-soluble or oil-base printers' ink (Water-soluble printers' ink is much easier to clean.)
8. Brayer (roller)
9. Mineral spirits for cleaning brayer, ink slab, and plaster block, if oil-base ink is used
10. A second piece of glass is advised (it will provide a perfectly smooth surface on which to pour the plaster)

 Note: If oil-base ink is used, the quality of the print may be improved by soaking the paper briefly in water and blotting the surface prior to printing.

Plaster Block Print

procedure

1. Mix the plaster. (See p. 119)
2. Pour the plaster into the mold, and allow it to dry. A small, lightweight cardboard box, such as a jewelry box, can be used as a mold. If one is not available, make a mold by building the wall with plastic clay on a piece of glass.
3. Remove the mold by peeling the cardboard away or removing the clay wall and sliding the plaster block from the glass.
4. Allow the plaster to harden further.
5. Brush the surface of the plaster with shellac to give it a surface color through which the cuts can be seen.
6. Plan a design to fit the cast plaster shape.
7. Transfer the design to the plaster shape with carbon paper by retracing the lines with pencil.
8. Carve the design in the plaster shape with any suitable tool. **Use carving tools with caution.** Cut away all areas or lines that are not to be printed. Brush away all plaster crumbs.
9. Squeeze a small amount of ink from the tube onto the piece of glass or floor tile.
10. Roll the ink with a brayer until it is spread smoothly on the inking slab.
11. Roll the inked brayer over the carved plaster design from side to side and top to bottom to ensure an even distribution over the entire surface.
12. Place a piece of paper over the inked design, and rub it gently and evenly with the fingers or the smooth bottom of a small jar until the entire design is reproduced. It will be wise to peel back a corner of the paper to determine whether further rubbing is necessary for a strong print.
13. Reink the plaster design for subsequent prints. Two or three dozen impressions can be made if the plaster shape is handled carefully.

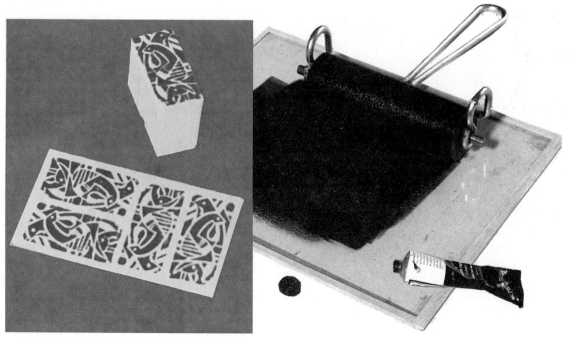

Chapter Thirteen

Stick Print

procedure

1. Make a light pencil drawing on paper.
2. Cut a number of sticks of different sizes and shapes, 2 or 3 inches long, making sure the ends are cut square.
3. Mix a small amount of paint on a piece of nonabsorbent scrap paper, and smooth it with a brush to an even consistency.
4. Dip the stick in the film of paint.
5. Press the stick to a scrap of paper, and print one or two images to remove any excess paint.
6. Now, press the stick to the drawing that has been placed on a pad of newspaper, and repeat until the image becomes too light.
7. Repeat steps 4–6 until design is completed.
8. A mosaic effect is obtainable by leaving a narrow space of background paper between each individual print; overlapping individual prints and colors also creates interesting effects, as does twisting the stick when printing.

supplies

1. Small sticks, 2 to 3 inches long, of various sizes and shapes
2. Tempera or latex paint
3. Brush
4. Paper
5. Pad of newspaper

 Note: Angle irons, jar lids, matchbox folders, and so on, are also possible printing tools. Unusual patterns may be created by dipping the edges of any of the above in paint.

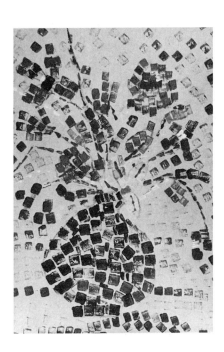

supplies

1. Heavy cardboard
2. Insulation foam tape (comes in rolls of various widths and thicknesses)
3. Scissors
4. Watercolor or tempera paint
5. Brush
6. Water container
7. Paper

Insulation Foam Print

procedure

1. Draw a design on cardboard with pencil. Remember to reverse the design, especially letters.
2. Cover pencil lines with foam insulation tape. Cut foam to fit. **Use safety scissors if available.** Do not overlap. Remove the paper back from the foam strip, and place sticky side down on top of the pencil lines.
3. Brush paint on foam.
4. Print by pressing, foam side down, on a piece of paper.

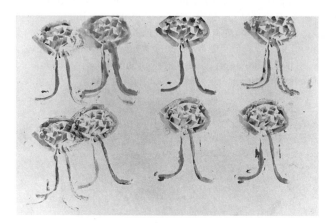

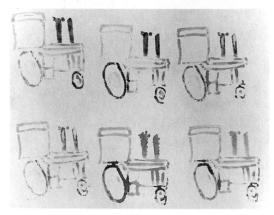

Potato Print

procedure

1. Cut the potato in half so that each surface is *flat*. If a large potato is used, it may be cut into several pieces, but each piece must be large, so that it will not break in printing.
2. Young children may incise or scratch the design into the surface of the potato with a nail file, pencil, or other tools.
3. Cut around the edge of the design to approximately ⅛ inch in depth, then remove the background by cutting to the design from the outer edge of the potato.
4. Place a pad of newspapers under the paper to be printed. Have a scrap paper or paper towel available on which to try the design and to determine whether too much paint is being used.
5. Cover the surface of the design with paint and print on a scrap of paper to eliminate any excess paint. One or two prints may be tried on the scrap paper so that too much paint is not being used. The texture of the potato should be transferred for more interesting prints. Printing may now be continued. A single application of paint will serve for three or four printings, which may be combined to make an overall pattern.
6. Several different colors may be applied. If these are also applied to different areas of the potato, interesting prints will result. The water contained in the potato will make the colors blend and run, producing more colorful designs.

 Note: Carrots, turnips, cabbage, and so on, also may be used for successful printing. This process may be employed to make attractive wrapping paper, Christmas cards, program covers, decorations, place cards and so on.

supplies

1. Solid potato (see note)
2. A scratching tool, such as pencil, nail file, comb, nail, scissors, or orange stick. Small children may work satisfactorily with these tools without the dangers involved in the use of sharp-edged tools.
3. A sharp-edged cutting tool, such as a paring knife or pocketknife
4. Colored construction paper, drawing paper, tissue paper, brown wrapping paper, manila paper, or newsprint
5. Paint brush
6. Water jar
7. Watercolors, tempera paint, or finger paint
8. Tray for mixing colors
9. Absorbent cloth

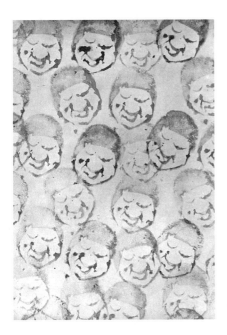

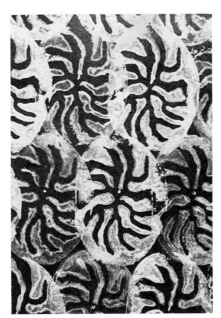

© James L. Shaffer

supplies

1. String
2. Glue
3. Block of wood
4. Paper
5. Tempera paint, watercolor, or water-soluble block-printing ink
6. Brush

 Note: Instead of painting the design, a print may also be obtained by stamping on an ink pad.

Stamps for Printing

procedure

1. Cover one side of the block with a thin coating of glue.
2. Deposit a small amount of glue on a piece of cardboard, and pull the string through the glue, using the fingers to give the string an even coating of glue.
3. Place the string in the glue on the block so it forms a design. Allow to dry thoroughly. Make sure the string does not overlap.
4. Paint the string on the block. (If tempera paint is used, make sure it is thin.)
5. Print:
   a. Lay the printing paper over several thicknesses of newspaper.
   b. Press the block on a scrap of paper to eliminate any excess paint.
   c. Several prints can be made from the printing paper before applying more paint.

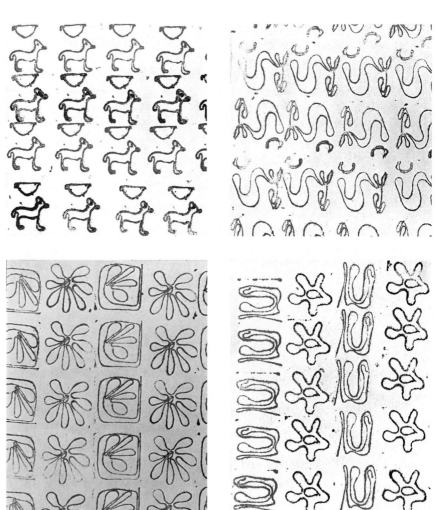

Finger Paint Monoprint

procedure

1. Do a finger painting directly on the tabletop or other smooth flat surface.
2. Lay a piece of paper directly on the wet painting and rub with the hand until the painting is transferred to the paper.
3. Lift the painting, and place on the newspaper to dry.
4. When the print has dried, place it face down on a flat surface and press with a warm iron. **Teacher should probably manipulate the iron.**

supplies

1. Finger paints
2. Smooth flat surface, such as a piece of glass with edges taped to prevent cut fingers or tabletop
3. Paper
4. Newspaper
5. Iron

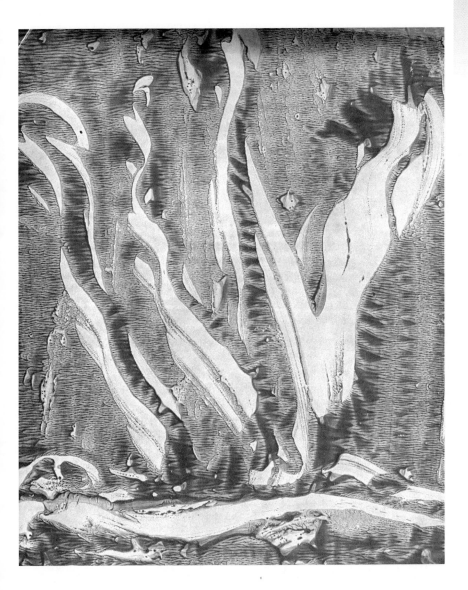

supplies

1. Smooth, nonabsorbent hard surface, such as glass, plastic, or tabletop
2. Drawing paper
3. Tempera paint
4. Brush
5. Water container

Paint Monoprint

procedure

1. Paint a design directly on a nonabsorbent surface. Keep the design simple with large colored areas. Allow to dry (Ill. 1).
2. Thoroughly dampen a sheet of drawing paper.
3. Press the dampened paper firmly and evenly over the painted design with the palm of the hand.
4. Carefully peel the paper from the design (Ill. 2).
5. A single impression printing will appear on the paper as a mirror image (Ill. 3).

1

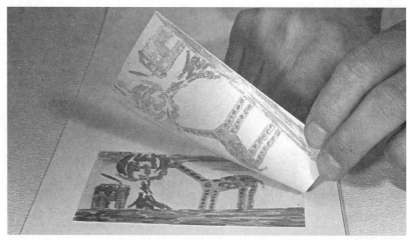

2

3

Chapter Thirteen

Glue Print

procedure

1. Create an image on the paper with a pencil.
2. Transfer the drawing to the cardboard. Carbon paper can be used, or the back of the paper can be covered with graphite from a pencil, the paper placed over the cardboard, and the image redrawn.
3. Squeeze the glue along the lines of the pencil design. Do not overlap the lines. Leave the cap off the squeeze container overnight if the glue is too thin.
4. Allow the glue to dry throughout (Ill. 1).
5. Roll out the ink, using a brayer as in the other printing processes.
6. Use the ink-loaded brayer to roll out the ink on the standing glue surfaces. If only the glue is to print, light pressure is recommended. If portions of the background cardboard are to print, greater pressure may be applied (Ill. 2).
7. Print by placing a piece of paper over the inked image, then press, rub, or roll a hand, spoon, rolling pin, or any smooth, hard object on the paper (Ill. 3).

supplies

1. White glue in a squeeze bottle
2. Piece of cardboard
3. Paper, for printing. Soft paper will probably work best
4. Pencil
5. Brayer (roller)
6. Oil- or water-base relief printing ink, or tempera paint mixed rather thick, with a few drops of liquid detergent added. (Water-soluble printers' ink is much easier to clean)
7. Carbon paper (optional)
8. Spoon (or some smooth, hard-surfaced object) or rolling pin

1

2

3

1. Paper
2. Ink pad
3. Newspapers

Ink Pad Print

procedure

1. Place a pad of newspapers under the paper to be printed.
2. Press a finger, heel of hand, side of hand, or any item to be printed on the ink pad.
3. Press the inked area to the printing paper. One application of ink should serve for several impressions, which can be combined to make an overall pattern.

Note: Sticks, jar lids, pencil erasers, or any small flat item may make an interesting printing tool.

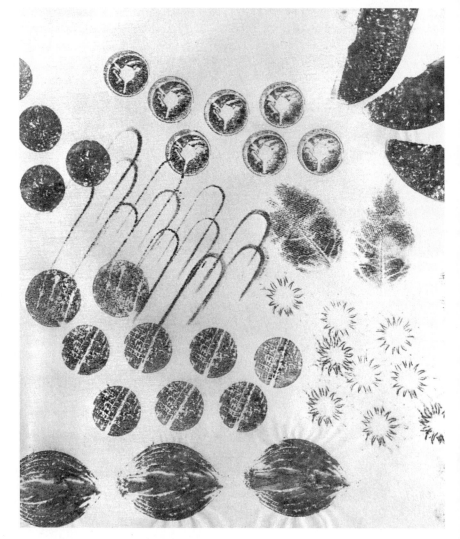

Screen Print

procedure

1. Using two or three layers, stretch the material tightly between the embroidery hoops. If a wooden frame is used, tightly stretch the material, and staple it in place.
2. Cut the design from the stencil paper (Ill. 1), using paper that is a bit larger than the surface of the stretched material. The cut design must fit within the area of the stretched material. The stencil should be cut following the directions on pages 276 and 277.
3. Place a piece of paper on a flat and smooth surface.
4. Place the stencil on the paper (Ill. 2).
5. Place the screen on top of the stencil (Ill. 3). Make sure the material is in contact with the stencil to prevent the paint from running under the stencil.
6. Place some commercial screening paint, or finger paint of toothpaste consistency, in the frame or hoop (Ill. 4).
7. Hold the frame with one hand and scrape the paint across the stencil with a squeegee. In this process, the paint or ink is forced through the cloth and adheres the stencil to the screen, except where the design was cut out, and these areas will be reproduced (Ill. 5).
8. Gently lift the stencil and frame, making sure the stencil remains adhered to the material (Ill. 6).
9. Place the frame and stencil on another paper and repeat steps six and seven for additional prints. Work rapidly to prevent paint from drying and clogging the material.

Note: Lines and shapes may be created in this print by using crayon as a resist. The drawing should be done with the crayon directly on the material in the screen.

1. Embroidery hoop, or small wooden picture frame
2. A piece of material large enough to cover the hoop or frame, such as dotted swiss or cheese cloth
3. Stapler
4. Stencil paper (the back of typewriter stencil serves as a most satisfactory and inexpensive paper)
5. Squeegee, such as a tongue depressor, small piece of linoleum with a straight edge, small plastic windshield scraper, or felt dauber
6. Paper
7. Cutting tool (scissors, knife, or single-edge razor blade)
8. Finger paint or commercial screen process ink (other paints clog the pores of the cloth). A good, inexpensive silk screen paint can be made by mixing liquid or instant powder tempera with a stiff mixture of soap flakes (not detergent) and warm water, or with a media mixer.
9. Beware of commercial solvents when using oil-based silk screen products.

1

2

3

4

5

6

supplies

1. Art gum eraser
2. X-acto knife
3. Pencil
4. Paper
5. Stamp pad

Eraser Stamp

procedure

1. Draw around the eraser on a piece of newsprint and make a design in that space. Remember your design will print backwards so any letters will need to be reversed and words would also need to be backwards.
2. Draw the design on the eraser.
3. Carefully cut the eraser on the lines with an X-acto knife. **Use extreme care and close supervision.** It is not necessary to cut deeply. Make sure the knife is slightly slanted away from the design.
4. After the design has been outlined with the knife, carefully break out the spaces that are not going to be printed. Brush away all crumbs.
5. Press the eraser firmly down on the stamp pad and then on the paper to make the print. The eraser can be printed several times before it needs to be reinked.
6. Another color ink pad can be used, but it is necessary to "stamp out" all of the previous color on a piece of scrap paper.

supplies

1. Styrofoam pieces, cut smaller than stamp pad
2. Masking tape
3. Pencil
4. Paper
5. Stamp pad

Styrofoam Stamp

procedure

1. Draw around the piece of styrofoam on a piece of paper. Make a design, remembering that the design needs to be reversed.
2. Draw design on styrofoam with pencil with enough pressure to make a good impression.
3. Using masking tape, make a handle on the back of styrofoam stamp. Press the end of a short piece of masking tape to the styrofoam with the other end pressed down next to the first end. The middle of the tape should stick together to make a short handle.
4. Press styrofoam stamp on ink pad, pressing carefully with fingertips.
5. Press stamp on paper, using fingertips to make sure there is pressure on all parts of the foam. Stamp may be printed at least 2 times before reinking.

Styrofoam Print

procedure

1. Cut the styrofoam in various shapes, making sure each printing surface is flat. **Be careful with cutting tools.**
2. Designs may be incised (scratched) into the surface of the styrofoam with a pencil, nail file, scissors, or other similar tool.
3. Place a pad of newspapers under the paper to be printed. Have a scrap paper or paper towel available on which to try the design and to determine whether too much paint is being used.
4. Cover the surface of the design with paint, and print on a scrap of paper to eliminate any excess paint. One or two prints may be tried on the scrap paper so that too much paint is not being used. The texture of the styrofoam should be transferred for more interesting prints. A single application of paint will serve for three or four printings, which may be combined to make an overall pattern.
5. Several different colors may be applied. If these are also applied to different areas of the styrofoam, interesting prints will result.

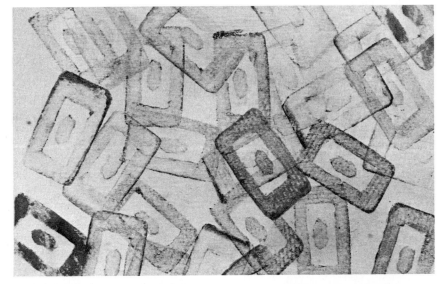

© James L. Shaffer

1. Safety-Kut or Soft-Kut print blocks are preferred but battleship linoleum may be used with caution and with supervision.
2. Carving tools, such as V- or U-shaped gouges set in wooden handles or penknife. Cutting tools are available that are drawn toward you. These reduce the risk of children cutting themselves.
3. Paper
4. Carbon paper
5. Water-soluble or oil-base printers' ink (Water-soluble printers' ink is much easier to clean.)
6. Brayer (roller)
7. Ink slab (9 inch × 9 inch floor tile or piece of glass with taped edges to prevent cut fingers)
8. Newspapers
9. Turpentine or kerosene for cleaning glass, brayer, and linoleum block, if oil-base printers' ink is used

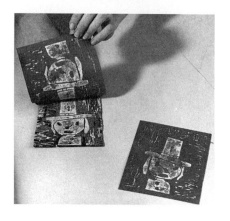

Printing Blocks

Linoleum has a long history in its use as a print medium. However, it tends to be hard and has a slick surface which makes it a resistant material for children to use. It also tends to get brittle as it gets older. It is always necessary to have a way to hold the linoleum in place while cutting. Even with close supervision and caution the cutting of a linoleum block can be dangerous. There are new products on the market that give the student the same experience and that are much safer. These products are soft, pliable, and will grip the table while they are being cut. The same tools and the same printers' ink are used. The products are about 3/8 inch thick and can be cut on both sides which makes them more economical.

procedure

1. Cut the block to the desired size and plan the design on a sheet of paper of equal dimensions.
2. Transfer the design from the paper to the block with carbon paper and sharp pencil. If lettering is incorporated in the design, it must be drawn and carved in reverse. Do not press too firmly with the pencil.
3. Carve the design in the block by cutting all lines or areas that are not to be printed. If linoleum is used, warm it for easier cutting. **Keep the holding hand out of the path of the cutting tool.** (See supply list for safe tools.)
4. Check the design from time to time by placing a thin piece of paper over the carving and rubbing over the surface with a crayon or pencil.
5. Squeeze a small amount of ink from the tube onto the ink slab.
6. Roll the ink with the brayer until it is spread smoothly on the inking slab.
7. Roll the inked brayer over the carved block design until it is completely and evenly covered. Include the corners.
8. Print.
   a. Lay a piece of paper on which the printing is to be done over several thicknesses of newspaper. Place the inked block design face down on the paper and cover with another piece of paper to keep the block clean, and print by pressing down firmly with the hand or foot. Tapping with a mallet is also a good method.
   b. Place a piece of paper over the inked block design, and rub gently and evenly with the fingers or the edge of the hand when it is in a fist position. It is wise to check the print by peeling back one corner at a time to determine whether further rubbing is necessary for a strong print.
9. Reink the block for subsequent prints.

Note: If oil-base ink is used, the quality of the print may be improved by soaking the paper briefly in water and blotting the surface prior to printing.

Variation: Cut only the outlines of the design and print with desired color ink. Clean the block and allow the print to dry. Cut additional areas and reink the block with a different color ink. Print on top of the original print. The first color ink will show only where there was additional cutting. These steps can be continued until there is very little left of the original block. This technique of printing a multicolored print was perfected by Pablo Picasso and is known as a reduction block.

Wood-Block Print

procedure

1. Plan a design on paper to fit the wood-block size, deciding on which areas are to be cut away or left in relief.
2. Transfer the design from the paper to the wooden block with carbon paper and a sharp pencil. If lettering is to be incorporated in the design, it must be carved in reverse.
3. Carve the design in the wood block. Cut away all the lines or areas that are not to be printed. In carving the wood, all cuts should be made in the direction of the grain. Cross-grain cuts will bind the tool and splinter the wood. **Keep the hand that holds the wooden block out of the path of the cutting tool.** (See supply list for safe tools.)
4. Check the design from time to time by placing a thin piece of paper over the carving and rubbing over the surface with a crayon or pencil.
5. Squeeze a small amount of ink from the tube onto the piece of glass or floor tile.
6. Roll the ink with the brayer until it is spread smoothly on the inking slab.
7. Roll the ink brayer over the carved wood-block design until it is completely and evenly covered.

supplies

1. Soft piece of pine wood
2. Carving tools, such as V- or U-shaped gouges set in wooden handles or penknife. Tools are available that can be drawn toward you. These eliminate the possibility of cut fingers.
3. Paper
4. Carbon paper
5. Water-soluble or oil-base printers' ink (Water-soluble printers' ink is much easier to clean.)
6. Brayer (roller)
7. Ink slab (9 inch × 9 inch floor tile, or a piece of glass with taped edges to prevent cut fingers)
8. Newspapers
9. Mineral spirits for cleaning brayer, ink slab, and wood block, if oil-base printers' ink is used

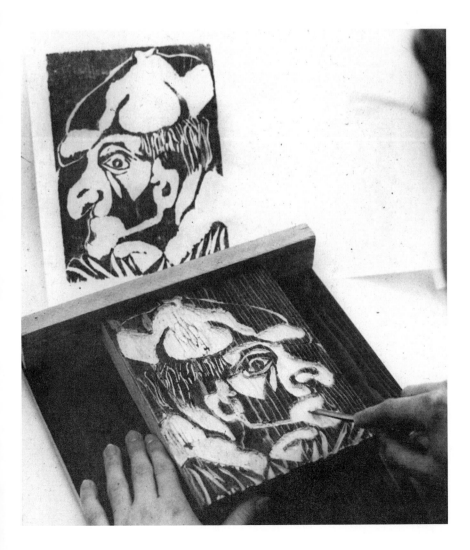

8. Print.
    a. Lay a piece of paper on which the printing is to be done over several thicknesses of newspaper. Place the inked block design face down on the paper, cover with a piece of paper to keep the block clean, and print by pressing down firmly with the hand or foot. Tapping with a mallet is also a good method.
    b. Place a piece of paper over the inked block design, and rub gently and evenly with the fingers, a spoon, or the smooth bottom of a small jar until entire design is reproduced. It would be wise to peel back a corner of the paper to determine whether further rubbing is necessary for a strong print.
9. Reink the block for subsequent prints.

 Note: To make use of the decorative advantages of the wood's grain, soak the wood in water so that the grain stands out in relief. If only certain areas of the grain are to be used, the remainder of the block may be sealed with shellac and the exposed area soaked with water. Too much soaking, however, will cause the block to warp or buckle. Brushing with a stiff wire brush will also expose the grain. The block may also be given textures by scratching the surface with various types of abrasives or tools, or by striking patterns with chisels, screwdrivers, etc. If oil-base ink is used, the quality of the print may be improved by soaking the paper briefly in water and blotting the surface prior to printing.

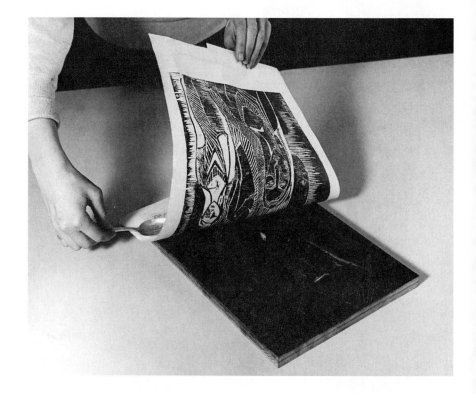

Sculpture

14

Sculpture—A Brief Review

Sculpture is created by manipulation (example: clay modeling), subtraction (carving), substitution (plaster or bronze casting), and addition (welding). On occasion these may intermix (more clay added to a clay piece) or be combined. It is quite possible that this is the earliest form of "art" because stone pieces are the oldest artifacts extant. It might be argued that these are not art in the sense that we know it because they may have been primarily utilitarian, or for religion or magic. Perhaps it all began with stone flaking for weapons and stone forming for mortars and pestles used in grinding grain.

The historical sequence of sculpture seems to be carving, modeling (often followed by firing), and casting. These techniques persist to the present with some cultures favoring certain of them. The early Greeks, for example, specialized in carving.

New approaches have proliferated in the twentieth century. Plastics, welding, holography, fluorescent and other light forms, and synthetic metals and media have been utilized by contemporary artists. Some are aided by computers in the planning and execution of their works.

Sculpture pieces may be mammoth or minuscule and massive (tectonic) or open (atectonic). Open sculpture may feature voids (passages through the work) or large open spaces between attenuated forms. A significant advance in this direction was made by Alexander Calder with his "mobiles" that not only utilized space but were constructed to move with air currents so that they presented constantly changing views.

A number of artists, Picasso included, have made sculpture works with "found" objects, usually discarded items that could be found in junk yards. These were then assembled to form the sculpture. This concept is represented in several of these activities. Analogies from the art world can be found for all of these activities.

Caution: Some activities in this chapter call for the use of X-acto knives. Extreme care and supervision must be utilized whenever X-acto knives are used. Safety instructions should be given before **EVERY** use of the knives. X-acto knives are now sold with safety caps, but separate caps may be purchased for older knives. Heavy corrugated cardboard should always be placed under the paper or material being cut. The X-acto knife is held like a pencil, with the fingers holding the knife on the textured ring. The slanted, sharpened edge should be directly over the line to be cut and the position of the knife or the paper should be changed if the line changes direction. Keep the fingers of the holding hand out of the way of the blade, usually above the cutting area. Remind students often to check themselves and the position of the knife and their hands.

A great variety of materials were used to construct life-size animals. Artist: Nancy Graves (1940–1995). American. Camel VI, VII & VIII, 1968–1969. National Gallery of Canada, Ottawa. Camels VII & VIII (camels on left and right): Gift of Allan Bronfman, Montreal, 1969. © 1996 Estate of Nancy Graves/Licensed by VAGA, New York, NY.

Box Sculpture

procedure

Containers such as those suggested under "supplies," when combined with miscellaneous materials, lend themselves to the construction of animals, figures, totem poles, hats, percussion instruments, and so on.

Bread Dough Sculpture

procedure

1. Remove the crusts from four slices of bread.
2. Tear the bread into small pieces, mixing them thoroughly with three tablespoons of white glue and 1 or 2 drops of lemon juice.
3. Model or cut as desired, allowing 1 to 2 days for complete drying.
4. Pieces may be painted with watercolor, tempera, or acrylic paints.
5. The clay can be preserved for modeling by wrapping in plastic and placing in a refrigerator.

1. Cardboard container to be used as a mold (paper plate, lid or bottom of a box, and so on)
2. Molding plaster
3. Container for mixing plaster
4. Carving tool, such as scissors, knife, chisel, or nail
5. Pencil and paper
6. See procedure seven for supplies used in finishes

 Note: Begin to clean up immediately after pouring the plaster in the mold—it will harden rapidly once the chemical reaction takes place. Any remaining plaster should be wiped from the pan immediately and rolled in newspaper so that it might be disposed of more easily. Do not wash plaster down any drain. When cleaning the hands, tools, and mixing pan, be sure the water runs continuously.

Carved Plaster Bas-Relief

procedure

1. Mix the plaster (see page 119).
2. Allow the plaster to harden and dry thoroughly before removing the cardboard mold. Should some of the cardboard adhere to the plaster, wash it off under running water. A thin coating of Vaseline will prevent the plaster from sticking to the box.
3. Smooth the sharp edges by scraping with any available tool.
4. Prepare a drawing to be transferred to the plaster.
5. Transfer the drawing to the plaster.
6. Carve the design into the plaster, using any suitable carving tool. **Use carving tools with care.** Soaking the plaster in water will facilitate its carving. As plaster is very brittle, it is suggested that it be placed on a soft pad to avoid breakage.
7. Any of the following finishes can be applied to the carved plaster.
   a. If tempera paint decorations are applied to the plaster, clear plastic spray, shellac, or varnish can be painted over the surface for permanency. **Use spray with optimum ventilation.**
   b. A pure white glossy finish can be achieved by soaking the plaster relief for approximately 30 minutes in a solution of dissolved white soap flakes, and then wiping dry with a cloth.
   c. An antique finish can be obtained by soaking the plaster cast in linseed oil. The cast should then be removed from the bath and, while still wet, dusted with dry yellow ochre or umber. Wipe off any excess coloring with a cloth until the antique finish is suitable.
   d. The plaster plaque, when decorated with enamel or oil-base paint, needs no protective finish.

Cast Plaster Bas-Relief

procedure

supplies

1. Cardboard container (lid or bottom of a box, paper plate, and so on)
2. Modeling clay (either water- or oil-base clay)
3. Modeling tool, such as an orange stick, nail file, or knife
4. Modeling plaster
5. Container for mixing plaster
6. Separating agent, such as salad oil, green soap, or Vaseline
7. Brush
8. See procedure nine for supplies used in finishing

1. The container is to be used as a mold. Place it on a sheet of paper, and trace around it with a pencil. This will provide a pictorial area of the same dimensions as the completed work. The preliminary drawing may be done in this area.
2. Fill the bottom half of the container with plastic clay.
3. Place the drawing over the clay in the container, and transfer the drawing to the clay by tracing over the lines with a sharp pencil, pressing only heavily enough to make an impression in the clay.
4. Model or carve the design in the clay, making sure that none of the edges have undercuts. **Use carving tools with caution.**
5. Brush a thin film of oil on the clay to serve as a separating agent.
6. Mix the plaster (see illustrations on page 119).
7. Pour the plaster into the mold over the clay relief to the desired thickness. Agitate the container gently to bring any bubbles to the surface. A wire hook can be placed in the plaster before it hardens completely (Ill. 1).
8. Allow the plaster to harden before removing the cardboard mold. Then, remove the clay from the plaster. Apply the final finish after repairing any flaws that may appear in the plaster. Wash off any water-base clay that adheres to the plaster (Ill. 2).
9. Any of the following type finishes can be applied to the plaster.
   a. If tempera paint decorations are applied to the plaster, clear plastic spray, shellac, or varnish can be painted over the surface for permanency. **Use spray with optimum ventilation.**
   b. A pure white glossy finish can be achieved by soaking the plaster relief for approximately 30 minutes in a solution of dissolved white soap flakes and then wiping dry with a cloth.
   c. An antique finish can be obtained by soaking the plaster cast in linseed oil. The cast should then be removed from the bath, and while still wet, dusted with dry yellow ochre or umber. Wipe off any excess coloring with a cloth until the antique finish is suitable.
   d. The plaster plaque, when decorated with enamel or oil-base paint, needs protective finish.

 Note: Begin to clean up immediately after pouring the plaster in the mold, as it will harden rapidly once the chemical reaction takes place. Any excess plaster remaining should be wiped from the pan immediately and rolled in newspaper so that it might be disposed of more easily. Do not wash plaster down any drain. When cleaning the hands, tools, and mixing pan, be sure the water runs continuously.

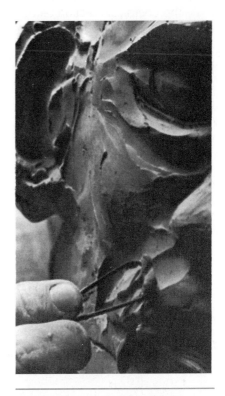

Clay may be formed with the hands, blocks, or modeling tools.

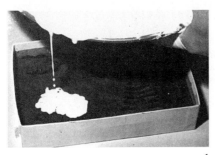

1

2

supplies

1. Empty milk cartons or plastic containers
2. Knife, single-edged razor blade, or scissors
3. Masking tape or glue
4. Tempera paint
5. Brush
6. Small amount of liquid detergent

Container Sculpture

procedure

1. Make a decision as to the kind of sculpture desired (people, animals, machinery, buildings, cars, trucks, and so on).
2. Make the necessary cuts or cutouts with a cutting tool. (**Take care with cutting tools.**)
3. Fasten the parts together with tape or glue.
4. Paint, if necessary. A few drops of liquid detergent added to tempera paint will allow paint to adhere to waxy surfaces.

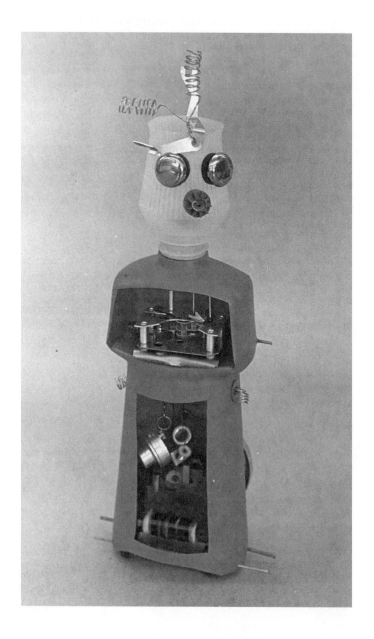

Foil Sculpture

procedure

1. Crumple the foil into individual forms that, when assembled, will create a piece of sculpture.
2. Join these forms together with tape or straight pins.
3. Color can be added to the surface by painting with a drop or two of liquid detergent mixed in the tempera paint.

Paper Sculpture with Foil Sculpture

The combination of paper sculpture and foil sculpture lends itself to the creation of fascinating three-dimensional work. This is best discovered through experimentation with the two materials. See pages 254–257 ("Paper Sculpture") and page 247 ("Foil Sculpture") for suggestions.

Folded Three-Dimensional Animals

supplies

1. Tag board
2. Scissors
3. Glue or glue stick
4. Crayons, markers, or oil pastels

procedure

1. Fold tag board in half to form a tent shape.
2. Draw and cut a rounded shape on the open edges to form the four legs. **Use safety scissors if available.**
3. Color the outside of the body and legs.
4. Cut and color additional pieces of tag board to add necks, heads, ears, tails and anything else to make the chosen animal.
5. Glue in place. Cut pieces of tag board may need to be used to hold some things in place.
6. If necessary, use glue tabs to hold legs in position so that the animal will stand.

supplies

1. Natural material (seeds, twigs, pine cones, seed pods, stones, driftwood, and so on)
2. Quick-drying glue
3. Clear, quick-drying spray
4. Paint
5. Construction paper
6. Felt

Natural Object Sculpture

procedure

1. Collect a number of natural objects of various sizes and colors.
2. Arrange several of these items to create a small piece of sculpture.
3. When satisfied with the creation, glue it together.
4. Paint or colored paper can be added to enhance the sculpture.
5. Spray with clear spray to preserve the finish. **Spray with optimum ventilation.**
6. Glue a piece of felt to the bottom to prevent scratching.

Liquid Solder Ornaments

procedure

1. Draw design with felt tip pen on breakable hollow shape. If balloon is used, inflate to desired size and tie the end.
2. With a firm pressure on the tube of liquid solder, follow felt tip pen lines.
3. Stop squeezing tube just before crossing or meeting another line. Solder tends to spread when two wet lines meet.
4. When design is completely covered with liquid solder, allow to dry. Repeat the same process over the first design at least two more times. Continue to use the same precautions.
5. When completely dry, break the hollow form over a paper bag or wastebasket to catch the numerous chips that result.
6. Gently smooth any rough edges with tweezers.
7. Spray ornament with desired color. **Use spray with adequate ventilation.**

Note: Flat designs, as in the following illustrations, can be created on wax paper with liquid solder. Peel away the wax paper when the design is hard. Turn the design over and draw a line of solder over the first design.

A handle can be made by either covering the lower half of the shape with a design and adding several lines of solder over the top that are connected to each side of the design, or by drawing several straight lines of solder on wax paper that can be peeled off when hard and attached to the sides of the basket with a dab of solder.

supplies

1. Thin, breakable, hollow glass Christmas ornament; small balloon, or egg shell (blown) (See page 338.)
2. Liquid solder
3. Felt tip pen
4. Wax paper
5. Tweezers
6. Spray paint

supplies

1. Thread
2. Supports, such as heavy stove pipe wire, small welding rods, strips of wood, or dowels
3. Wire cutters
4. Glue
5. Materials for making objects to be suspended (paper, wire, plastics, cardboard, soda straws, plaster, clay, and so on)

 Note: A wire stretched in a seldom-used corner of the room will enable the children to hang their mobiles while working on them. There is no limit to the ways a mobile can be constructed, once the principle of movement and balance is understood.

Mobiles

Mobiles have been in existence for centuries in many countries. The Chinese glass windbells are probably the best known. A mobile is created to produce movement with changing patterns. In addition, a mobile is a problem in balance, design, sculpture, form, space, and color. Mobiles, like many other projects in this book, when simplified, are most successful in the primary grades. This form of sculpture was further developed by the American sculptor, Alexander Calder.

procedure

1. Decide the number of units to be used in the mobile and their method of construction. These objects can be made from paper, wire, papier-mâché, salt and flour, wood, and so on, or a combination of any of these materials. Remember that an effective mobile should contain objects that have some kind of relationship to each other.
2. Attach a thread to each object so that it hangs evenly. This would make a finished mobile for the child in the primary grades.
3. Cut a support (a piece of wire or small wood dowel) and suspend an object from each end, making sure that the separation is great enough to prevent the parts from touching. **Use wire cutter with caution.**
4. Place a spot of glue on the very ends of the wire or dowel to help hold the thread of each object when tied in place. The threads supporting the objects should be comparatively short but of different lengths.
5. Tie another thread to the wire or dowel supporting the mobile by the thread. Slide the thread back and forth on the wire or dowel until it finds a point of balance. Secure it with a spot of glue. This would be a complete mobile for older children. A mobile is built from the bottom up, so that this part will be the bottom if more pieces are to be added and the mobile is to become more complex.
6. The thread holding the section just completed should be tied to the end of another wire or dowel and held in place with glue. Suspend an object from the other end of the wire or dowel.
7. Balance both sections on a single thread.
8. Any number of sections can be added as long as balance is maintained.

Alexander Calder, Antennae with Red and Blue Dots, *1960. Metal kinetic sculpture, 3 ft 7¾ in × 4 ft 2½ in × 4 ft 2½ in (1.11 × 1.28 × 1.28m). Tate Gallery, London/Art Resource, NY. © 1996 Artists Rights Society (ARS), New York/ADAGP, Paris.*

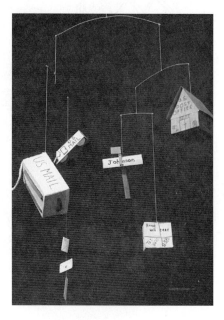

1

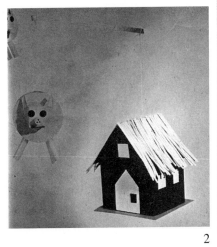

2

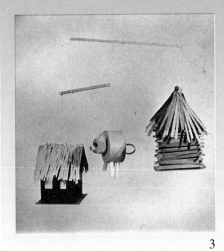

3

Development of mobile by adding and balancing related units from numbers 1 through 7.

4

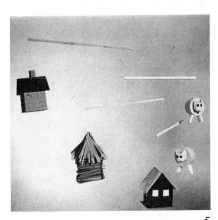

5

6

7

supplies

1. Paper (There are many kinds of paper suitable for paper sculpture—rough, smooth, thick, thin, heavy, fragile, transparent, translucent, opaque and so on; each has its own particular quality.)
2. Scissors, sharply pointed knife, or single-edged razor blade (be careful with the cutting tools)
3. Adhesive material (transparent tape, masking tape, rubber cement, library paste, and so on)
4. Fasteners (small staples, pins, paper clips, and so on)
5. A ruler, compass, or paper punch will be helpful

Paper Sculpture

procedure

Experiment with the numerous possibilities of shaping the paper into three-dimensional forms. Several such forms fastened together may result in fascinating figures, animals, or birds. A textured surface can be accomplished by punching a series of holes in the paper or by cutting a series of small slits in the paper and then bending them either inward or outward to enrich the surface.

 Note: There are a number of books in publication that deal exclusively with the three-dimensional possibilities of paper.

Paper generally is thought of in terms of two dimensions, such as flat cutout paper shapes fastened to a contrasting color sheet of paper. However, paper can be modeled into numerous three-dimensional forms after some experimentation. Any one or any combination of the following methods can be employed to produce fascinating paper sculpture.

Bending	Illusion of a solid	Rolling
Curling	Joining	Scoring
Cutting	Perforating	Slitting
Folding	Pinking	Twisting
Fringing	Pleating	Weaving

The following are examples of basic techniques that can be given many variations to suit the needs of the artist. Also see "Paper Textures," pages 183–184.

Bending—a combination of curling and fringing. The fringes of any inside curves must be notched to eliminate overcrowding. The edges may then be fastened to other pieces.

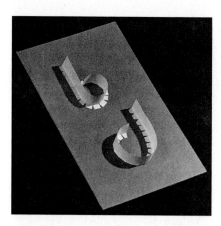

Curling. A strip of paper pulled lightly across the dull edge of a scissors blade or over the edge of a table will curl the paper.

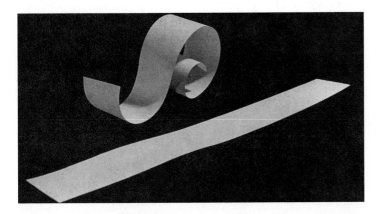

Cutting. Cut a slit into a folded section, and insert another piece of paper.

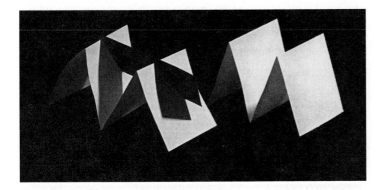

Folding. Cut along the solid lines of the folded paper, and push into fold on the dotted lines.

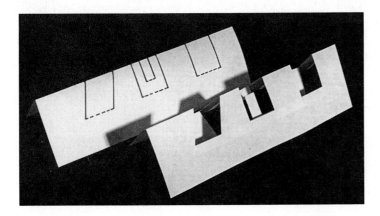

Fringing. A piece of paper folded on the dotted line and cut (fringed) along the solid lines will enable the paper to be formed into numerous shapes with an edge to fasten to other pieces.

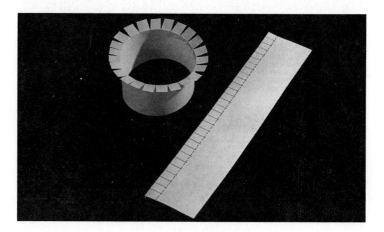

Illusion of a solid. Any formal image (both sides the same) can take on the illusion of a three-dimensional form. Cut a number of desired shapes, fold them in half, and cement them together.

Joining. Cut along the lines indicated, and join the two ends to produce a three-dimensional form.

Rolling. Using a thin piece of paper, begin at one corner and roll paper as tightly as possible.

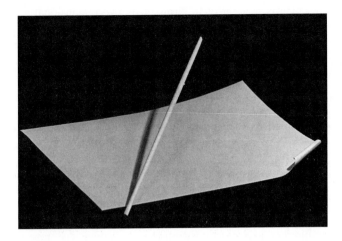

Scoring. In order to fold paper along a curve, it is necessary to apply pressure with a comparatively dull instrument (closed scissors or metal nail file) along the length of the curve.

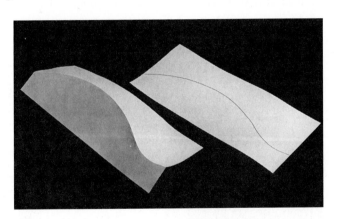

1. Roll of gummed paper tape (the tape, when moistened, will adhere to itself)
2. Scissors (use safety scissors if available)
3. Masking or transparent tape
4. Small sponge
5. Dish for water

Paper Tape Sculpture

Gummed paper tape is thought of in terms of its two-dimensional applications, such as taping shut a box for mailing. However, gummed paper tape can be modeled into numerous three-dimensional forms after some experimentation. Any one of the following methods can be employed to produce a fascinating piece of tape sculpture.

Bending	Joining (several pieces together)
Curling	Perforating
Cutting	Pinking
Fluting	Scoring
Folding	Twisting
Fringing	

procedure

Experiment with the numerous possibilities of shaping the tape into three-dimensional forms. Several such forms fastened together may result in fascinating figures, animals, or birds. A textured surface can be accomplished by punching a series of holes in the tape or by cutting a series of small slits in the tape and then bending them either inward or outward to enrich the surface.

Chapter Fourteen

Paris Craft Figures

procedure

1. Roll up the cardboard to produce a cone. Staple or glue the ends together. Cut off the point.
2. Tear off a piece of cotton the size desired for the head.
3. Cut Paris Craft into small strips, which can be dampened and wrapped around the cotton ball.
4. When dry, glue the head on the narrow end of the cone.
5. Cut fairly long strips of Paris Craft to a width suitable for arms. Roll them up until the desired arm thickness is achieved. Cut the roll in half and dampen.
6. Glue the arms to the cone (body).
7. Glue the pieces of yarn to the head, building it up to simulate hair. If desired, the yarn may first be dipped in wheat paste, in which case the glue is unnecessary.
8. Paint the face, its features, and the arms.
9. Produce the desired clothed effect by painting and/or gluing material to the body.

supplies

1. A piece of cardboard, to be used as a body, cut according to the desired size (a tube may be used)
2. Yarn, to be used as hair
3. Assorted fabrics
4. Glue
5. Cotton
6. Paints (acrylic is recommended, tempera is suitable)
7. Wheat paste (optional)
8. Paris Craft (fabric, in roll, with preapplied coating of plaster)

 Note: This procedure describes a method of making small figures; experimentation will reveal many other possibilities.

1. Cardboard box (shoe box, hat box, and so on)
2. Scissors
3. Rubber cement, paste, glue, or stapler (Avoid inhaling rubber cement.)
4. Tempera paint, watercolors, crayons, colored chalks, or color inks
5. Paint brush and water jar, if paints are used
6. Assorted papers
7. A variety of materials to be used for decorative purposes: cloth, felt, ribbon, yarn, dried coffee grounds, buttons, clay, salt and flour mixture, twigs, pebbles, and so on. These materials can be determined more easily after deciding on the subject for the peep box.

Peep Box

procedure

As in the shadow box (p. 265), the procedure for this project will vary somewhat, depending upon the type of peep box to be made. Scenes from children's stories, poems, or songs may be depicted in the peep boxes. It is possible, too, to create make-believe aquariums (suspend the fish and other aquarium animals and objects from strings and use colored cellophane over the top and face of the box to give the illusion of water). Peep boxes can also be very effective as Christmas crèches and puppet theaters.

1. Cut a small spy hole opening in one end of a box. In some cases an opening at each end is advisable. **Use safety scissors if available.**
2. Cut a number of openings or doors in the lid in order to allow light in the box. These openings can be placed strategically to allow spotlighting. Light can be controlled in the box by opening or closing the "doors" in the lid.
3. Design the sides of the box. Any one of a number of techniques may be used for this: potato print, crayon engraving, chalk stencil, colored paper, finger paint, watercolor, and so on. A combination of several of these techniques will make an interesting peep box.
4. Many methods are available for making trees, houses, barns, figures, etc. Cleansing tissue can be modeled as the foliage for trees. It may be tinted with colored inks or tempera paint. Twigs, match sticks, and paper cylinders can serve as the trunks of the tree. Bits of sponges also make suitable foliage when painted. One may choose to use paper sculpture as a method of making trees, shrubs, and so on.

   Houses, barns, and other buildings can be made from tiny boxes, corrugated cardboard, or paper sculpture. These, too, may be painted with colored inks or tempera paints.

   Figures and animals can be made from wire, pipe cleaners, clay, salt and flour mixture, papier-mâché, clothespins, and so on.

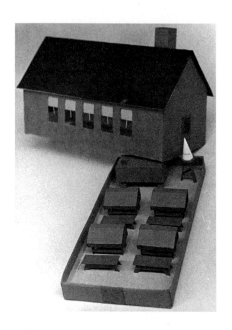

Pipe Cleaner Figures

procedure

1. Interesting stick figures can be created by bending and twisting the pipe cleaners.
2. Form and thickness can be added to the stick figures by wrapping additional pipe cleaners around the body, arms, legs, and so on.

supplies

1. White or colored pipe cleaners
2. Any cutting tool that can be used to cut the pipe cleaners to the desired length; use with care.

 Note: These figures may be used in shadow boxes, sand table displays, small stage sets, or for individual party favors or decorations.

supplies

1. Plaster
2. Small balloon
3. Yarn
4. Bowl for mixing plaster
5. Can of spray paint, if color
   is desired

Plaster Space Forms

procedure

1. Inflate the balloon, and tie the end closed.
2. Mix the plaster (see p. 119).
3. Holding one end of the yarn, immerse it in the plaster (if the yarn is too fine, use a double or triple strand). Pull the yarn from the bowl and through the fingers of one hand, wiping off the excess plaster.
4. Place the plaster-saturated yarn on the inflated balloon in a decorative manner, making sure the yarn crosses over itself frequently.
5. Allow the plaster to harden and dry thoroughly before puncturing the balloon.
6. Hold the plaster-decorated balloon in a wastebasket or large cardboard box to catch the numerous plaster chips that fall when the balloon is punctured.
7. Gently smooth any rough edges, and paint the plaster. Spray paint will work best. **Use spray paint with optimum ventilation.** Painting before the balloon is punctured will leave the inside pure white.
8. Additional decoration of various materials can be placed inside the space form.

 Note: Begin to clean up when the plaster begins to thicken—it will harden rapidly once the chemical reaction takes place. Any remaining plaster should be wiped from the pan immediately and rolled in newspaper so that it can be disposed of more easily. Do not wash plaster down any drain. When cleaning hands, tools, and mixing pan, be sure the water runs continuously. Teacher should handle the clean-up.

Salt and Flour Sculpture

procedure

1. Mix salt, flour, and alum to the consistency of putty. Add color if desired. Pinch pots, animals, and figures can be modeled from this mixture.
2. After the pieces have dried and hardened, they may be shellacked for permanence.

supplies

1. 1 cup salt
2. 1 cup flour
3. 1 tablespoon powdered alum
4. Mixing bowl
5. Food coloring or dry tempera (if color is desired)
6. Shellac and brush
7. Alcohol for cleaning brush

 Note: See other formulas on pages 125 and 343.

Sawdust Sculpture

procedure

1. Mix the sawdust and paste, stirring the mixture to the consistency of plastic clay.
2. Form the desired shape with the hands. An inner support of wire or wood is needed to brace large forms.
3. When dry, the sculpture can be painted with tempera paint.
4. A clear plastic spray or several coats of shellac will preserve the finish. **Spray in a well-ventilated area.**

supplies

1. Sawdust
2. Wheat paste
3. Brush
4. Tempera paint
5. Plastic spray or shellac

supplies

1. Molding plaster
2. Container for mixing plaster
3. Shallow box or container to be used as mold
4. Fine beach sand

Sand Casting

procedure

1. Fill the shallow container with moist beach sand, and pack it tightly.
2. Scoop out various shapes of different depths to form the necessary mold (if a beach is handy, the pattern can be made on the spot, rather than in a box).
3. Mix the plaster (see p. 119).
4. Allow the plaster to harden before removing from the sand mold.

 Note: Begin to clean up immediately after pouring the plaster in the mold—it will harden rapidly once the chemical reaction takes place. Any remaining plaster should be wiped from the pan immediately and rolled in newspaper so that it can be disposed of more easily. Do not wash plaster down any drain. When cleaning the hands, tools, and mixing pan, be sure the water runs continuously. Teacher should handle the clean-up.

supplies

1. 1 cup cornstarch
2. 2 cups baking soda (1 lb. box)
3. 1¼ cups water
4. Saucepan
5. Stove or hot plate
6. Aluminum foil
7. Food coloring
8. Plastic bag
9. Watercolor or tempera paint
10. Clear commercial spray

 Note: If it is desired to hang these decorative shapes, a hole may be punched in the top of the ornament while the clay is soft, or a Christmas ornament hook may be inserted in the back of the piece while the clay is soft. Teacher should do the cooking.

Soda and Cornstarch Sculpture

procedure

1. Combine the first three ingredients in a saucepan, and cook over medium heat, stirring constantly.
2. When the mixture is thickened to a doughlike consistency, turn out on a piece of aluminum foil or on a breadboard.
3. Food coloring may be worked into the clay when it has cooled slightly.
4. When not in use, keep the clay covered with aluminum or in a plastic bag, and store it in the refrigerator to keep it pliable.
5. Clay may be rolled and cut into shapes or may be modeled into small shapes.
6. Watercolor or tempera may be used to paint the clay objects when they are thoroughly dry.
7. The painted objects may be sprayed with clear plastic or clear shellac. **Spray in a well-ventilated area.**

Shadow Box

procedure

The procedure for this project will vary somewhat, depending upon the type of shadow box to be made. Scenes from children's stories, poems, or songs may be depicted in a shadow box. It is possible, too, to create make-believe aquariums (suspend the fish and other aquarium animals and objects from strings, and use colored cellophane over the face of the box to give the illusion of water). Shadow boxes can also be very effective as Christmas crèches and puppet theaters.

1. Design the background for the picture. Any one of the number of techniques may be used for this: potato printing, crayon engraving, chalk stenciling, finger painting, watercolor, and so on. A combination of several of these techniques will make an interesting background for the shadow box.

2. Many methods are available for making trees, houses, barns, figures, and so on. Cleansing tissue can be modeled into the foliage for trees. It may be tinted with colored inks or tempera paint. Twigs, match sticks, or paper cylinders can serve as the trunks of the tree. Bits of sponges also make suitable foliage when painted. One may choose to use paper sculpture as a method of making trees, shrubs, and so on.

   Houses, barns, and other buildings can be made from tiny boxes, corrugated cardboard, or paper sculpture. These, too, may be painted with colored inks or tempera paints.

   Figures and animals can be made from wire, pipe cleaners, clay, the salt and flour mixture, papier-mâché, clothespins, and so on.

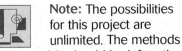

supplies

1. Drinking straws
2. Cardboard
3. Glue
4. Scissors
5. Box (to catch cut straws)

Soda Straw Relief

procedure

1. Make an outline drawing on cardboard with pencil.
2. Cut the straws into a box, and glue them perpendicularly to the cardboard, filling in areas or following pencil lines.

 Note: Straws of one length simplify the procedure, but straws of various lengths will create more interest. Straws may be combined with flat areas of construction paper to produce the image or add interest. *Paper* soda straws work best.

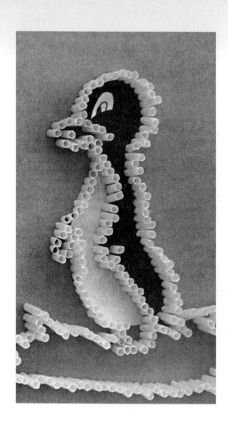

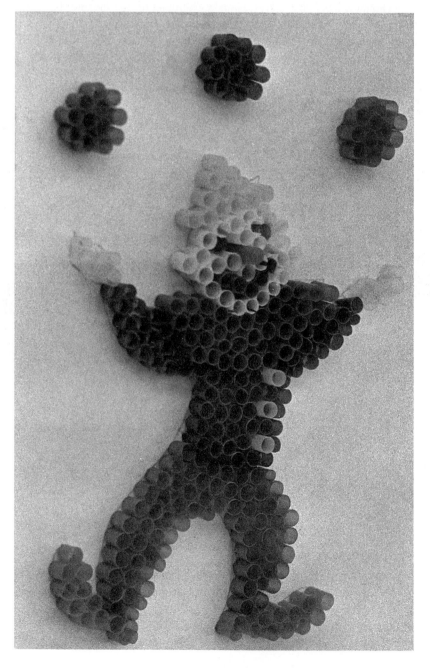

Spool Sculpture

procedure

There can be no prescribed procedure in this project, as each of the figures is made differently, according to the imagination of the artist. Basically, the procedure involves "dressing" the spool, which serves as a body. The materials are contrived to serve as clothing, and are adhered to, or sewn around, the spool. Many extras can be added, as shown by the illustrations. Facial features are usually added with drawing materials (pen, pencil, crayon, and so on). Doll hair may be used to crown the figure, or the hair may be fabricated from thread, string, or anything suitable.

supplies

1. Spools (a variety of sizes are useful) or pill bottles
2. Assorted fabrics
3. Needle and thread
4. Glue
5. Anything that will serve to simulate clothing accessories and other adornments

1. Newspaper or newsprint
2. Glue, rubber cement, or stapler
3. Paint (tempera, latex, watercolor, and so on)
4. Brush
5. Container for water
6. Clear spray, if necessary. Use with adequate ventilation.

Stuffed Newspaper Sculpture

procedure

1. Cut shape of intended design from at least four pages of newspaper.
2. Glue or staple two of the shapes together.
3. Glue or staple the remaining two pieces together.
4. Glue or staple the edges of these two sets together, leaving a space approximately 4 inches unglued somewhere along the edge. Allow the glue to dry thoroughly.
5. Stuff crumpled paper through the 4-inch opening until the design takes a three-dimensional form. Be careful not to tear the design by stuffing too tightly.
6. Glue or staple the opening together.
7. Paint the surface, and spray with clear spray to keep paint from smudging. **Spray in a well-ventilated area.**

Note: Punching and stitching may be used.

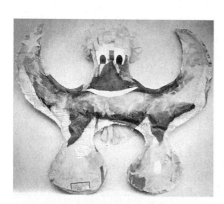

Toothpick Sculpture

procedure

Glue the toothpicks together to form various three-dimensional structures.

Note: Colored paper areas may be added as an experience in color and design.

supplies

1. Quick-drying glue, such as household cement. Some glues bond very quickly; be careful!
2. Toothpicks

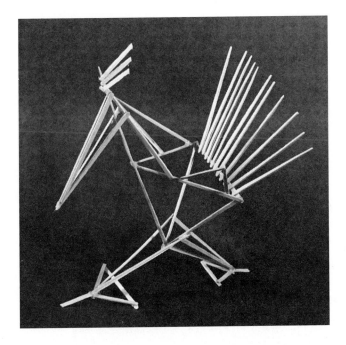

s u p p l i e s

1. Paraffin
2. Old double boiler or pan
3. Container to be used as a mold (jelly glass, small tin can, cardboard box, and so on)
4. Carving tools (penknife, nails, hairpins, sticks, and so on)
5. Turpentine and cloth

Wax Sculpture

procedure

1. Melt the paraffin in the pan over a low flame.
2. Pour the melted wax into the mold, and allow to cool and harden.
3. Dip the mold in hot water until the block of paraffin is released. If a cardboard mold is used, tear it from the wax.
4. Carve the paraffin block into the desired form. **Use carving tools with caution.**
5. Smooth the finished sculpture with a cloth dampened in turpentine.

 Note: Color can be added to the melted paraffin by mixing in waxed crayons. A relief wax carving can be made by pouring the melted wax into a shallow container. As this project involves the use of an open flame and hot wax, it should be executed by the teacher.

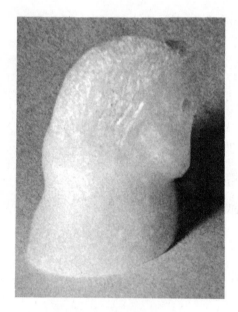

Wire Sculpture

procedure

1. Decide on a design or figure that can serve as a subject. It may prove helpful to use a pencil sketch, but it should be remembered that the drawing must be purely linear. Remember also that the drawing is to be transformed into a three-dimensional work and should not be followed too literally.

2. Bend and twist the wire into the desired shapes. Coils may serve as figure elements and these may be created by wrapping the wire around such objects as sticks, pencils, or bottles. Make sure the objects can be removed.

3. Wire sculptures are generally conceived as one continuous length of wire, but they may consist of several lengths joined together. If several pieces are used, they may be hooked, wound, or soldered together.

4. Paint may be added if it is felt that color will improve the appearance of the work. Other materials, such as wood, sponge, plastics, and so on, may also be combined with the wire. The American sculptor, Alexander Calder, did a great deal of work in this medium.

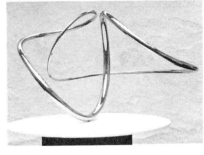

Graceful curves of the kind seen here can be produced with wire. José de Riviera, American, b. 1904, Brussels Construction, stainless steel, 1958, 118.1 × 200.6 cm, Gift of Mr. and Mrs. R. Howard Goldsmith, 1961.46. Photograph © 1996, The Art Institute of Chicago, All Rights Reserved.

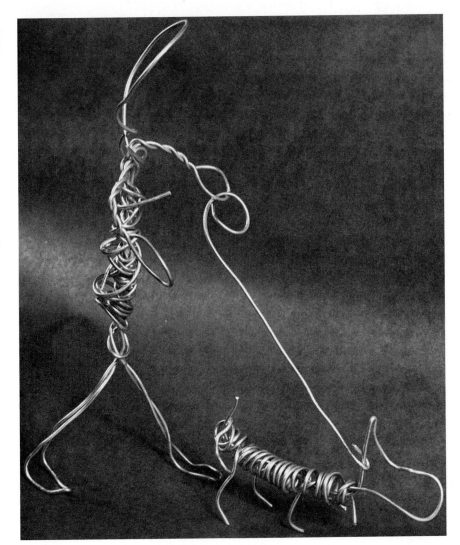

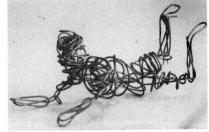

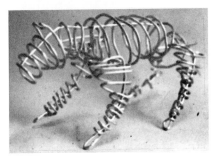

Wood Scrap Sculpture

procedure

1. From a generous supply of small pieces of scrap wood of various sizes and colors, choose those pieces that will work well together in creating a piece of sculpture.
2. When the arrangement is satisfactory, glue all the components together.
3. Paint or crayon decorations can be added to finish the sculpture.

 Note: A piece of sculpture should present interesting views from all sides.

This is an example of "assemblage" sculpture in which pieces of wood are modified, refined, and put together. Louise Nevelson, American, 1900–1988, America Dawn, painted wood, 1962, 548.6 × 426.7 × 304.8 cm. Grant J. Pick Purchase Fund, 1967.387, photograph © 1996, The Art Institute of chicago. All Rights Reserved.

Cylinder Forms

procedure

method a—head

1. Mark the center of a rectangle on the long side of the tag board or heavy paper with a light pencil mark.
2. Make light pencil dots where the features of the character will go on the paper when it becomes a cylinder, but do not glue it. Draw or cut out pieces of construction paper to make the features.
3. Overlap and glue the two ends to make a cylinder.
4. Add any other details that might be interesting such as eyebrows, hair, ears, moustaches, beards, glasses, and so on.

method b—full figure

1. Mark the center of a rectangle on the long side of the tag board or heavy paper.
2. Directly below the pencil mark, draw a figure with the top of the head at one edge of the paper and the feet at the other edge.
3. Draw all the details that would help make the basic figure into the desired character.
4. Add color.
5. Make into a cylinder by gluing and overlapping the two ends. Add other details.

method c—full figure with arms and legs

1. Put a pencil mark at the middle of a rectangle of tag board or heavy paper. Draw the head and body of the character directly under that point.
2. Pattern and color the head and body.
3. Overlap and glue the ends of the rectangle to make a cylinder.
4. Cut two smaller rectangles to make cylinder legs. Add color and pattern. Check their size with the body cylinder before gluing.
5. Cut, color and make two more small cylinders for the arms. Glue to the side of the body below the head. Add hands, feet, and any other details.

supplies

1. Tag board or heavy paper
2. Scissors
3. Glue, glue stick
4. Scrap paper
5. Crayons, oil pastels, markers

supplies

1. Tag board or heavy paper
2. Scissors
3. Glue, glue stick
4. Scrap paper
5. Crayons, oil pastels, markers

supplies

1. Tag board or heavy paper
2. Scissors
3. Glue, glue stick
4. Scrap paper
5. Crayons, oil pastels, markers

Method A

Method B

Method C

Sculpture   273

supplies

1. Strips of construction paper
2. Glue or glue stick

Note: This form is very flexible and strong. It is like a spring and can be used in paper sculpture forms. It makes great arms and legs for puppets. If the ends of the Jacob's Ladder are glued together it will form a rosette and can also be used in many ways.

Jacob's Ladder

procedure

1. Glue two strips of paper together to form a corner making sure they are square. For beginners, it is easier to use two different colors.
2. Fold one color straight across where the two colors are glued together. Fold the second color across at the same point. It is like weaving up, folding first one color and then another.
3. Fold the strips alternating the colors until the strips have been used. One may be used before the other and the longer one will need to be trimmed.
4. Glue at the top between the two color ends.

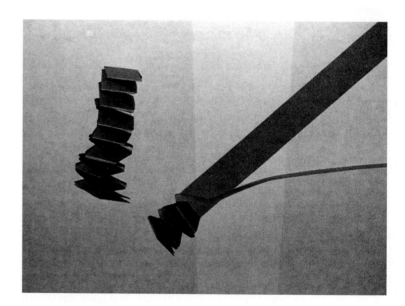

Totem Poles

Totem poles are carved by a particular group that associated themselves with specific plants or animals. The spirits of the chosen creatures are considered their ancestors and the group feels that they get strength and comfort from these creatures.

Kachina Dolls

Kachina dolls are found in Arizona and are not really dolls but are the representations of the masked dancer known as the kachina. This dancer becomes for a short time, through the use of costume and dance, the connection between the spirit world and the real world. The dolls are carved out of cottonwood root, coated with ground clay, and painted. Details such as fur, feathers, and so on, are fastened to the figures. These "dolls" are not playthings but are given to the women and children, who usually do not participate in the dances, as a sacred object. This doll is their connection to the spirit world.

Stencils

supplies

1. Wet media (stencil paper or a suitable substitute. The back of a typewriter stencil may be used or commercial stencil paper may be purchased. You may make your own stencil paper by drawing typing paper through paraffin melted in a flat pan.)

    Dry media (tag board works very well because of smooth surface)
2. Cutting tool (X-acto knife, scissors)
3. Cutting board (heavy cardboard or old drawing board)

Caution: Some activities in this chapter call for the use of X-acto knives. Extreme care and supervision must be utilized whenever X-acto knives are used. Safety instructions should be given before **EVERY** use of the knives. X-acto knives are now sold with safety caps, but separate caps may be purchased for older knives. Heavy corrugated cardboard should always be placed under the paper or material being cut. The X-acto knife is held like a pencil, with the fingers holding the knife on the textured ring. The slanted, sharpened edge should be directly over the line to be cut and the position of the knife or the paper should be changed if the line changes direction. Keep the fingers of the holding hand out of the way of the blade, usually above the cutting area. Remind students often to check themselves and the position of the knife and their hands.

Cutting a Stencil

procedure

1. Lay the stencil paper (Ill. 2) over a drawing (Ill. 1). Trace the parts you wish to cut out if the design cannot be seen through the stencil. (Holding the stencil against a window is the easiest method.) As a general rule, thin lines are not very visible in the final product.
2. Place the stencil paper on a sheet of heavy cardboard or cutting board, and cut around the outlines (Ill. 3). The paper from which the shapes have been cut is the negative stencil. The shapes that fall away from this stencil are the positive stencils. Illustration 4 demonstrates the completed stencil.
3. A separate stencil must be cut for each color to be used (Ills. 5 and 6).

Note: Safety precautions must be observed and there must be close supervision with the use of X-acto knives. Safety scissors should be used.

1   Original drawing

2   Stencil paper over drawing and cutting surface

3 Cutting stencil

Positive stencil. These are the sections removed from the negative stencil. Color is applied around them as they lie on another paper.

Original drawing

Cut stencil

Cutting surface

4

Negative stencil. The figurative areas are cut out of the sheet and color is applied through the openings onto the paper below.

Eyes, dress, legs

Hair, mouth, feet

Face and arms

5

6

1. Stencils
2. Wax crayons or oil pastels
3. Paper
4. Eraser or tissues

Crayon or Oil Pastel Stencil

procedure

1. Tag board stencils work well.
2. The stencil may be made by folding tag board and cutting one-half of a symmetrical shape from the fold. When the tag board is unfolded the shape will be complete. The shape piece is called the positive and the hole in the folded tag board is the negative. Putting crayon or oil pastel on the edge of any piece of scrap can work as a stencil if it is rubbed off on to another piece of paper.
3. Hold or fasten the stencil firmly in place over the drawing paper.
4. Color a heavy and thick line of crayon or oil pastel around the shape or around the edge of the negative shape. Rub the color off of the shape onto the paper and off the negative into the hole and on the paper. An eraser works as a transfer tool for crayon. Oil pastel is softer and a finger or a finger covered with tissue works well as a transfer tool.

 Note: Crayon may be stroked directly through the stencil onto the other paper as described under chalked stencils (p. 279).

Stencil with Chalk

procedure

1. Cut stencil.
2. Lay the stencil over the paper. Hold or fasten it firmly in place.
3. If you are using the positive stencil, make a series of strokes with chalk, working from the outside of the opening in so as not to curl the edges of the stencil.
4. If the negative, or the cutout stencil, is being used, stroke from the inside of this stencil out to avoid the curling of stencil edges. This system will also prevent the chalk from sifting under the stencil.
5. If a softening effect is desired, rub the chalk lightly with the piece of cotton or tissue, or with the fingers, being careful to rub from the stencil onto the surface of the paper.

 Notes: The chalk may be applied directly to the paper with the cotton or tissue. Simply make strokes with the chalk on paper, then pick up the chalk dust with the tissue or cotton, and proceed as directed in step four. A separate stencil must be cut for each color.

1. Stencil
2. Chalks
3. A piece of cotton or cleansing tissue (fingers may be used)
4. Paper
5. Fixative spray (Use spray with adequate ventilation.)

Negative stencil

Positive stencil

supplies

1. Tempera paint, colored inks, or pressurized spray paint
2. Stencil paper
3. Drawing paper
4. Small piece of window screen
5. Stiff bristle brush, such as an old toothbrush
6. Tape
7. Newspaper or wrapping paper

Spattered Stencil Design

procedure

1. Cut the stencil as directed on page 276.
2. Use the tape to fasten the paper in the center of the sheet of newspaper.
3. Pick up a small quantity of paint or ink with the brush (excess paint or ink will destroy the fine spatter effect).
4. Hold the screen above the paper, and rub back and forth across it with the brush, or spray with pressurized can or atomizer. In the absence of window screen, similar results may be obtained by drawing a stick across the brush bristles away from the paper.

Notes: Caution should be observed in using pressurized spray cans; spray in a well-ventilated area. A little experimentation on scrap paper is recommended before attempting the finished product.

It is possible to reproduce the image of various forms of plant life by simply pinning them to the drawing paper and spraying over them.

Chapter Fifteen

Sponged Stencil Design

procedure

1. Cut the stencil as directed on page 276.
2. Pick up the sponge with the clothespin or fingers, and dip it in the paint, making sure that the sponge is not fully saturated.
3. Put the stencil over the paper, hold or fasten it securely, and press the sponge lightly enough to utilize the sponge texture over the open portions of the stencil. Avoid scrubbing with the sponge, as this will work the paint under the stencil, creating ragged edges.

Note: A little experimentation on scrap paper is recommended before attempting the finished product.

supplies

1. Stencil paper
2. Tempera paint or colored ink
3. Small piece of sponge
4. Drawing paper
5. Clip-type clothespin

Original drawing

Stencil →

Paper →

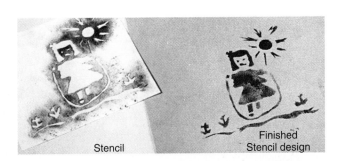

Stencil

Finished Stencil design

supplies

1. Thinned paint, ink, or a quick-drying commercial spray paint
2. Stencil paper
3. Insect sprayer, fixative sprayer, atomizer, or pressurized spray can
4. Drawing paper
5. Newspaper or wrapping paper
6. Tape or pins

Sprayed Stencil Design

procedure

1. Cut the stencil as directed on page 276.
2. The paper to be sprayed should be fastened to a newspaper or piece of wrapping paper. Secure the stencil over this so that it lies perfectly flat.
3. Place the newspaper on the floor, or tape it to the wall so that the stencil is at a convenient height.
4. Spray over the stencil, making sure that the open areas are fully covered with the paint. **Spray in a well-ventilated area.**

 Notes: Variety may be added by spraying some areas more heavily than others, by using different colors on the shapes, or overlapping the colors. In overlapping colors, it is generally advisable to permit complete drying of the first coat before attempting another.

It is possible to reproduce the image of various forms of plant life by simply pinning them to the drawing paper and spraying over them.

Thinned tempera paint is less messy than commercial sprays.

Positive stencil

Sprayed design

Negative stencil

Sprayed design

Stencil with Tempera

procedure

1. Cut the stencil as directed on page 276.
2. Hold or fasten the stencil securely in place.
3. Dip the stencil brush very lightly into the paint, and wipe the excess paint from the brush onto a paper towel or absorbent cloth. The brush should appear to be almost dry, for very little paint is needed.
4. Apply the paint with strokes, which start on the stencil and run off onto the paper, or dab, with the brush held vertically to prevent any paint from getting under the stencil.

Note: Try overlapping these or new shapes with new colors for a more interesting design. A separate stencil must be cut for each color.

supplies

1. Tempera paints
2. Stencil paper
3. Paper
4. Stencil brush (a brush with *short, stiff* bristles)
5. Jar of water and absorbent cloth for cleaning brushes
6. Tray for mixing paints

1. Stencils
2. Drawing board or flat, smooth surface to which fabric can be tacked for stenciling
3. Thumb tacks
4. Paper towels or absorbent cloths
5. Fabric that has been washed to remove sizing, such as linen, sailcloth, muslin, or gingham
6. Textile paints
7. Stencil brushes (preferably one for each color) with short, stiff bristles
8. Textile cleaner (usually included with commercial textile paint)

Textile Painting with Stencils

procedure

1. Cut the stencil as directed on page 276.
2. Press the cloth with a hot iron to remove any wrinkles. Tack the cloth to the drawing board or any other flat, smooth surface.
3. Place the stencil in position on the cloth, and tack it so that the stencil will not slip or slide on the material.
4. Touch the brush lightly in the paint; it is *especially* important in textile painting that a very, very small amount of paint be used. Too much paint will soak through the fabric and wash out when the material is laundered.
5. Wipe all of the excess paint from the brush with a paper towel or absorbent cloth. Running the brush back and forth across the towel or cloth will remove the excess paint and will also work the paint into the brush. The brush will appear to be nearly dry.
6. If an open stencil is being used, stroke or stipple with the brush, working from the outside of the opening in, so as not to curl the edges of the stencil. If you are using a positive stencil, stroke from inside of the shape out; this will prevent the paint from going under the edges of the stencil.
7. Experimentation will help to determine the proper quantity of paint to be used. Shading or painting one color over another in parts of the stencil will greatly enrich the design.
8. After stenciling all parts of the design (many colors may be used, but a separate stencil must be cut for each color), remove the stencil.
9. If the proper amount of paint has been used, the painted fabric will appear to be dry and the paint will not have soaked through the material. For all practical purposes, the fabric is now dry enough for handling; however, the paint should be allowed to dry thoroughly overnight before pressing with a hot iron for permanence. Be sure to read the directions on your textile paint to complete this last step.
10. Clean the brushes with a textile cleaner.

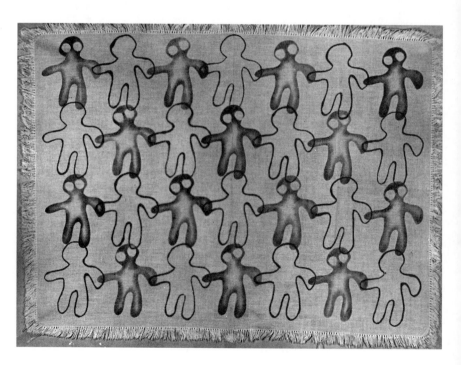

Fiber

Nature of the Medium

Weaving

Weaving has been used since ancient times because of the basic need for cloth. Weaving is the interlacing of fiber. The fiber running lengthwise is the warp and the fiber that crosses and is woven into the warp is called the weft. The first weavings were probably done with fingers and very primitive looms. Ancient people quickly learned to twine and twist fiber to produce different textures. They also used various natural dyes to produce many different colors. Now, very complicated and powerful looms produce all the fiber products needed for modern society. Computers are used to help plan the design and to render the weaving.

Still, people in many cultures cling to the old ways of producing fiber products. Hand looms are still used by many craftsmen, baskets are still woven by hand, and people still dye their own fiber. The use of color and texture, and the wide variety of available materials, have led many contemporary artists to reexamine and explore many aspects of the media. Plastics, paper, yarn, cloth strips, natural objects, reed, and cord have been used by artists. Many objects, such as bells, beads, branches, rods, and so on, are incorporated into the weavings. Almost anything that can be interwoven or wrapped is used to create both two-dimensional or three-dimensional forms.

Batik

Batik is a technique that uses molten wax to paint or draw on fabric, and then the fabric is dipped in or painted with wet dyes. The waxed areas repel or resist the dyes. Each time a new dye color is introduced on the fabric, parts of that color are waxed to preserve it until the desired color scheme is achieved.

It is difficult to pinpoint the exact origins of batik. Some fragments were found in first century Egyptian tombs, but that might have been obtained through trade. Evidence has been found that it originated in Asia and spread to the Malaysian area. Java and Bali are famous for batiks and batik garments are worn in Japan and China. Much of the paisley patterns of India and the symmetrical tribal patterns of Africa are batik.

Tie-Dye

Tie-dye probably began in ancient Asia and spread down the sub-Indian continent to Malaya and across Africa. On the American continent, the earliest tie-dyed fabrics date from pre-Columbian times. Tie-dyed fabrics come from Mexico, Guatemala, Peru, Bolivia, Paraguay, and Argentina. In North America, the Pueblo people and other Native Americans used the craft at a later time.

Tie-dye is a resist technique used with fabric. The fabric is gathered or folded in various patterns and held in place by tying knots, stitching, tying cords, or placing rubber bands. Objects can also be tied into the fabric. The unusual textures are caused by the dye as it seeps around the ties. Fabrics can be tied and dyed one color, untied and then retied a slightly different way and redyed another color. This can be repeated several times. The fabric is allowed to dry and all the knots are removed.

Coiling

Coiling is a method for making baskets employed for centuries by almost every culture. Although it is still usually used for making baskets, contemporary artists have made more sculptural forms using this technique. The weft or wrapping material is the thread that wraps around the core or warp and holds the core together in a form.

Stitchery

Stitchery is the technique of using a needle like a paint brush and the yarn like paint. Yarn comes in hundreds of colors, many different weights, and different textures. There are at least 300 different stitches but it is only necessary to learn a few of the simple basic stitches. These stitches can be varied by changing the size of the thread, changing the spacing between the stitches, distorting the stitches, and combining the stitches in patterns. Stitchery can teach color relationships, balance, good spacing, proportion, and texture.

Appliqué

An appliqué is a piece of fabric fastened on another larger piece of fabric. The edges may be turned under and hemmed down or left raw and held down with stitches near the edge or over it. Stitches may become important and be decorative or the stitches may be strictly to hold appliqués in place. Quilts are usually made in appliqué.

Appliqué may also be done in a reverse manner. Openings of any size or shape may be cut in the larger piece of fabric and another piece laid underneath to show through the opening. This may be done several times so that several colors show. The edges may or may not be turned in and stitched, and stitches may be added to the design. Molas are an example of reverse appliqué. They are unique to Panama, particularly the San Blas Islands. The oldest molas usually have three layers of black, red, and yellow, and the designs are simplified human, animal, or floral forms.

Cloth skirt (mola) made by the Chvenaque Indians of Panama. Courtesy of the National Museum of the American Indian Smithsonian Institution (Neg. #18670).

1. Paper
2. Scissors
3. Paste

Paper Weaving

procedure

1. Cut a series of slits in the paper, making sure a border is maintained (Ill. 1). **Use safety scissors if available.**
2. Cut strips of colored paper, magazines, wallpaper, and so on (Ill. 2).
3. Weave the strips through the slits in the paper (Ill. 3).
4. Hold strips in place with a spot of paste if necessary.

 Note: Numerous designs can be obtained through an inventive approach. The paper can be folded in half to cut a series of slits, as shown.

1

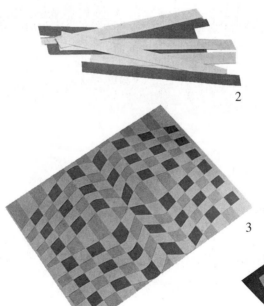

2

3

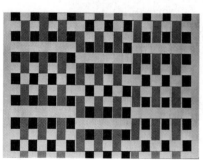

Appliqué

procedure

1. The edges of the background material may be fringed before starting the picture. This will give a more finished look to the piece.
2. When the design has been decided upon, the shapes to be used in the picture may be cut and laid on the background until the arrangement is satisfactory. **Use safety scissors if available.**
3. The pieces of cloth are appliquéd to the background by using a variety of stitches chosen by the designer. A long running stitch or an overcast stitch are perhaps the easiest for young children to use.
4. The picture may be pressed with a warm iron when finished.

 Note: The technique can be used to produce hats, pillows, decorative wall hangings, and so on.

1. A piece of loosely woven material cut to the size and shape of the finished picture (colored burlap is most satisfactory, as the open weave makes stitching easier)
2. Materials to be appliquéd to the background cloth (felt or any other type of material that will not ravel or fray too easily)
3. Large, blunt needles
4. Thread, colored yarn, raffia, or string for stitching
5. Scissors

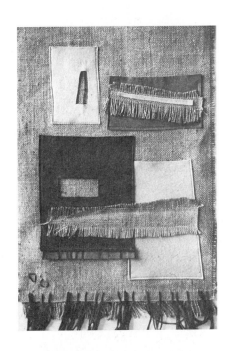

s u p p l i e s

1. Heavy cardboard, mat board, illustration board, or corrugated cardboard
2. Yarn
3. Scissors
4. Comb or fork
5. Ruler
6. Pencil

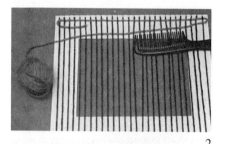

1

2

3

Cardboard Loom Weaving

procedure

1. Construct loom. The loom may be constructed by stapling four pieces of heavy cardboard at the corners to make a frame (Ill. 1), or use a solid piece of cardboard. Cut small notches ½ inch apart in two opposite sides of the square or rectangle. In the case of a circle loom (Ill. 1), cut notches ½ inch apart all around the edge. **Use safety scissors if available**.

2. String or warp the loom by placing a knot in one end of a small ball of yarn. Place the knot in the first notch, and bring it from the back to the front of the loom. Loop the yarn around the first tooth (formed by the notches) on the opposite end of the loom. Continue looping the yarn back and forth around the teeth until the loom is finished. Knot the end of the yarn at the back of the last notch. The yarn should lie flat on the front surface of the cardboard. Do not pull the string too tight or the loom will buckle when weaving.

3. String a circle loom in the same manner, looping the yarn around the teeth at opposite sides. Begin your weaving in the center of the circle loom.

4. Make a small ball of yarn to weave on the loom (weft). Begin weaving by using a simple over and under pattern (Tabby weave). It is not necessary to tie the yarn to the warp or to a new colored yarn. Just weave in the ends; they will stay in place. Push the rows of weaving together with a comb or fork (Ill. 2). (The comb or fork serves as a beater.)

5. Variety can be added to the weaving by adding loops or rya knots. (See number 7.)

6. To make loops, use a Tabby weave, moving from right to left and allowing extra yarn at the right side of the loom. Take the point of a pencil and lift the weft yarn where it passes *over* the warp yarns (every other strand). While the yarn is still looped over the pencil, weave another row of Tabby weave from left to right. Gently remove the pencil and comb and beat tight.

7. Rya knots are a good way to use short (3 inch to 4 inch) yarn scraps. Place three short pieces across two of the warp strands. Bring both ends of the short pieces down, around, and up between the two warp strands (Ill. 3). Make sure the short ends are pointing toward the existing weaving. Slide the knot up to the weaving by pulling the short ends. Continue to make knots until there are no more warp threads. To make a second row of knots, skip the first warp yarn and make the first knot, using the second and third warp yarns. This will lock the first row in place. If a third row is desired, make the first knot, again using the first and second warp yarns.

8. When the weaving is as large as you want, finish by removing the warp yarns from the teeth of the cardboard loom. Tie any loose ends.

9. Dowels or branches can be pushed through the warp loops on one end to use as a hanger.

10. Another possibility is to string the warp yarn around the loom so that the warp is on both sides of the loom. Weave on both sides to create a pouch.

Cloth Batik

procedure

1. Develop a full-scale drawing with pencil on paper.
2. Stretch the material tightly on a smooth board. Fasten it with thumbtacks or a staple gun.
3. Transfer the design from the paper to the cloth with pencil and carbon paper.
4. Remove the cloth from the board, and stretch it tightly over the wooden frame. Fasten with thumbtacks or staple gun.
5. Melt equal parts of paraffin and beeswax together in an old pan over an electric hot plate, or 150-watt light bulb. Wax need not be boiling—use only enough heat to render the wax liquid.
6. Add a quantity of toluene equal to the paraffin and beeswax—this will keep the wax from congealing too quickly.

 Note: Toluene is extremely volatile and should be handled with caution.

7. Place the frame on newspapers with the cloth side up.
8. Paint the melted wax on the cloth in areas that are to remain the natural color of the material. Make sure the wax penetrates through the cloth.
9. Remove the material from the frame. Crumple and submerge the material in the bowl of colored dye. Crumpling makes the crackle effective in the finished batik. Allow the cloth to dry.
10. Stretch the material on the frame again for each additional color that is needed.
11. Paint the melted wax over the areas just dyed to retain this color. Remove the cloth from the frame, and dye it in a second color. This operation can be repeated several times.
12. Remove the wax from the material in boiling water or by ironing it between newspapers or wrapping paper. If using the iron for wax removal, change the papers often.

supplies

1. Material to be decorated
2. Smooth board
3. Pencil and paper
4. Thumbtacks or staple gun
5. Carbon paper
6. Wooden frame or picture frame in the size of finished batik
7. Paraffin and beeswax
8. Old pan or can for melting wax
9. Toluene (Keeps wax from congealing too quickly. It should be available locally. It is extremely volatile.)
10. Electric hot plate or 150-watt electric light bulb
11. Brush
12. Dye
13. Bowl for mixing dye
14. Iron
15. Newspaper or wrapping paper
16. Rubber gloves for handling dyes

 Note: Clean the brush with mineral spirits and soap or detergent. The hot plate and warm wax should be handled by the teacher. Use rubber gloves when handling dyes.

s u p p l i e s

1. Fabrics with all kinds of pattern
2. Tag board or gray cardboard
3. White glue
4. Sharp scissors that will cut fabric
5. Permanent marker
6. Variety of lace scraps, trim scraps and buttons

Appliqué with Glue

procedure

1. Cut pieces of material into different shapes, such as squares, rectangles, triangles, egg shapes, free forms, and so on.
2. Lay the shapes on the cardboard and arrange the shapes. Try several arrangements before gluing.
3. Glue by putting glue on the cardboard and place the material pieces on top, one at a time.
4. Make sure all of the edges and corners are tight.
5. When the cardboard is completely covered with fabric, other materials such as trim can be glued in place.
6. A permanent marker can be used to simulate stitches on the edges of the material. The stitches should be different too.

Cotton Roving

procedure

1. Cover working area with newspaper.
2. Place construction paper on newspaper and cover large area of the construction paper with heavy layer of paste.
3. Lay the desired colored roving in the paste as if drawing an outline. Do not stretch the roving when applying.
4. Cut the roving when shape is completed. **Use safety scissors if available.**
5. Gently pat the roving into the paste.
6. Continue with a second line of roving inside the first outline.
7. Continue until desired result is obtained, changing colors if necessary.

 Note: Roving can also be wrapped around a paste-covered shape cut from cardboard or any other three-dimensional object.

supplies

1. Cotton roving (inexpensive, bulky cotton yarn)
2. Paste or media mixer (p. 343)
3. Newspaper
4. Paste applicator (brush, piece of cardboard, or folded paper)
5. Scissors
6. Cardboard or construction paper

Huichol Yarn Painting. 1978, Mexico. From the Girard Collection in the Museum of International Folk Art, a unit of the Museum of New Mexico. Photographer: Mark Schwartz.

supplies

1. Colored felt
2. Scissors
3. White or textile glue
4. Needle and thread (if design is to be sewn)

Felt Picture

procedure

1. When a design has been decided upon, the shape to be used in the picture may be cut directly from the felt, or patterns can be made of cardboard. **Use safety scissors if available.**
2. Arrange the cut pieces of felt on a felt background until satisfactory.
3. Glue or sew the pieces in place to complete picture.

Felt Mola

A mola is a reverse appliqué. The material is cut through to reveal the colors of the various layers underneath.

procedure

1. Using newsprint the same size as the first piece of felt, draw a design. Traditionally, the main shape is a bird, animal, reptile, insect, or human figure.
2. Cut the main shape from the newsprint to use it as a pattern to draw around on the first piece of felt.
3. Carefully cut the shape from the felt (save all of the cutout pieces).
4. Pin the cut top piece of felt to another piece of felt of a different color and mark both for additional cuts.
5. Cut and put a different color of felt under the two layers of cut felt and mark again for cuts through all layers.
6. A fourth layer of felt is put under all three layers of cut felt.
7. Pin in place and sew with small running stitches (see "Stitchery"). It is also possible to glue the layers of felt with Tacky Glue.

s u p p l i e s

1. Felt, 4 pieces of different colors
2. Needle and thread
3. Pins
4. Tacky Glue (to be used in place of stitching)
5. Newsprint and pencil
6. Sharp scissors

 Note: The extra pieces of felt can be used as an applied appliqué.

1. Wax crayons, with paper wrapping removed
2. Paper
3. Candle
4. Cloth (muslin or any material that will absorb dye easily; old bed sheets are ideal)
5. Masking tape
6. Commercial dye and sticks for stirring
7. Large glass jars (for storing dye)
8. Glass or enamel cooking utensils for mixing dye
9. Wooden board or heavy cardboard
10. Iron
11. Soft pencil
12. Brush
13. Rubber gloves
14. Newspaper
15. Baking soda should be kept nearby whenever hot wax is used in case of a fire.

Note: As this project involves the use of an open flame, it is suggested that every precaution be observed. Use rubber gloves when handling dyes.

Melted Crayon Batik and Print

procedure

1. Fasten cloth to board with masking tape, stretching the cloth as tightly as possible.
2. Draw a design on the cloth with a soft pencil.
3. Hold the crayon briefly over the flame of the candle until the crayon softens.
4. Press, drag, or drip softened crayon on the drawing.
5. A number of different colors can be used to complete the design.
6. Should the crayon become too short to hold over the candle flame, a long pin stuck into the crayon will solve the problem.
7. The cloth can then be dyed with dye mixed in bowls as indicated on the package of dye (see number 13 for painting a design).
8. Remove the cloth from the board, dip it in water (crumple if crackle effect is desired), and place it in the dye solution, stirring constantly with a stick or hand (use rubber gloves).
9. Remove the cloth from the dye, rinse it in cold water, and allow it to drip dry or wring out excess water.
10. Place the dyed cloth on pad of newspaper, and cover the design with a piece of paper. Cover with newspaper and iron until the crayon is transferred to the paper.
11. Remove the newspapers and printing paper, and a crayon print will be revealed (only one print can be made).
12. Store excess dye in an airtight glass container for further use.
13. Instead of dipping the cloth in the dye, various colored dyes can be painted over the crayon picture on the cloth. The crayon, being greasy, will resist the dye and make interesting effects.
14. Rinse the cloth in cold water, and allow it to drip dry or wring out excess water.
15. Press the cloth with a hot iron while it is still damp.

Paraffin Batik

procedure

1. Fasten the cloth to board with masking tape, stretching the cloth as tightly as possible.
2. Draw a design on the cloth with a soft pencil.
3. Put water into skillet and muffin tin into water of skillet to form a double boiler.
4. Place pieces of paraffin in muffin tin and melt.
5. Brush in desired portions of the drawing with liquid wax (portions painted with wax will remain the color of the cloth).
6. The cloth can then be dyed with dye mixed in bowls as indicated on the box.
7. Remove the paraffin-painted cloth from the board, dip it in water (crumple if crackle effect is desired), and place it in dye solution, stirring constantly with a stick or hand (use rubber gloves).
8. Remove the cloth from dye, rinse it in cold water, and allow it to drip dry. If a second color is to be used, repeat number 5 (but paint melted wax over desired areas just dyed), number 7, and number 8.
9. Place the dyed cloth on a pad of newspaper, and cover it with a pad of newspaper; then iron to remove wax.
10. Change newspaper pads often until all wax has been removed.
11. Rinse the cloth in cold water, and allow it to drip dry or wring out excess water.
12. Press the cloth with a hot iron while it is still damp.
13. Store excess dye in an airtight glass container for further use.

Note: As this project involves the use of an electric skillet and liquid wax, it is suggested that every precaution be observed. Use rubber gloves when handling dyes.

supplies

1. Paraffin
2. Electric skillet
3. Muffin tin
4. Brush
5. Cloth (muslin or any material that will absorb dye easily; old bed sheets are ideal)
6. Masking tape
7. Commercial dye and sticks for stirring
8. Large glass jars (for storing dye)
9. Glass or enamel cooking bowls for mixing dye
10. Wooden board or heavy cardboard
11. Newspapers
12. Iron
13. Soft pencil
14. Rubber gloves
15. Baking soda should be kept nearby whenever hot wax is used in case of a fire.

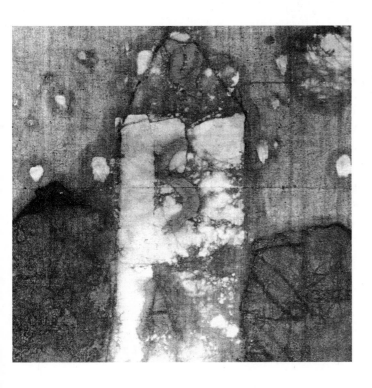

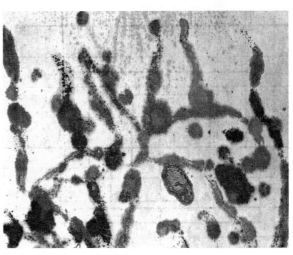

supplies

1. Popsicle or ice cream sticks (6 to 8 drilled sticks, 4 undrilled sticks)
2. Glue
3. Yarn
4. Pencil
5. Scissors
6. Comb

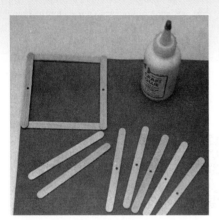

1

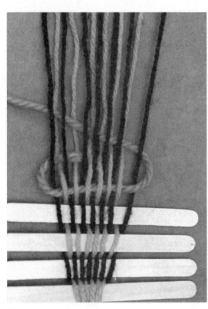

2

Popsicle Stick Loom Weaving

procedure

1. Construct the harness for the loom. Drill a hole in the center of 6 or 8 popsicle or ice cream sticks. Place 2 undrilled sticks in a horizontal position. Place and glue 1 drilled stick at each end of the 2 undrilled sticks in a vertical position to form a square. If the sticks are placed in the corner of a sheet of paper, it is very easy to have a straight square (Ill. 1). Arrange evenly, and glue the remaining drilled sticks in the space between the end sticks. Put a drop of glue at each end of the drilled sticks and place the 2 remaining undrilled sticks across each end. Place a book or weight on top until the harness dries completely.

2. String, or warp, the loom. Cut strands of yarn approximately 36 inches long. **Use safety scissors if available.** Cut one strand of yarn in one color for each hole in the harness. Cut another set of strands in another color for each space between the drilled sticks in the harness. Gather all the yarns together, and tie an overhand knot at one end. Comb the loose ends to straighten, and thread through the harness using the same color yarn for all the holes in the sticks and the other color for all the spaces between the sticks. Comb the yarn again to straighten, and tie the ends together with another overhand knot.

3. To begin weaving, fasten each end by overhand knots to something solid (chair leg, desk leg, door knob, hook). This will keep the warp yarns tightly stretched, which will allow the harness to work properly.

4. Check the loom by raising the harness. All of the yarn going through the holes will be lifted. This forms a space, or shed, where the yarn being woven will go. Lower the harness, and all the strands going through the spaces will be in a raised position, also forming a shed.

5. To space the warp threads and establish the width of your weaving, it is advisable to insert 4 popsicle sticks in the warp threads between one of the overhand knots and the harness. Simply weave the sticks into the warp by raising the harness, and insert a stick. Lower the harness and insert a stick, etc. (Ill. 2).

6. Begin weaving. Make a shed again, and insert the end of a ball of yarn, allowing 2 inches to hang out the left side, with the ball on the right. Change the position of the harness and push the 2-inch end into the shed. Pass the ball of yarn from right to left (this weaves the end in). Continue passing the ball of yarn back and forth as the harness is changed. The yarn should be loose on the edges so that the warp is not distorted. Push the yarn together by using a comb or fork. This simple weaving is a Tabby weave. Variety can be obtained by using different colors, different weight, and texture yarns. Other materials can also be woven into the warp strands.

7. Loops and rya knots may also be added. (See "Cardboard Loom Weaving.")

8. To finish the weaving, cut or untie the overhand knot furthest away from the weaving. Gently remove harness. A simple overhand knot may be tied close to the weaving with the loose ends, or two warp yarns at a time may be tied together in an overhand knot close to the weaving.

Straw Weaving

procedure

1. Use 4 or 5 straws. Any number may be used; from 2 to as many as 10 can be held in the hand.
2. Cut as many pieces of yarn as you have straws. **Use safety scissors if available.** They should be equal and as long as you want the finished weaving to be.
3. Thread or suck each yarn through its own straw. Turn over the yarn at the end of the straw, and fasten it at the top by using a piece of tape wrapped around the yarn end and the straw (Ill. 1).
4. Keep the tape as smooth as possible.
5. Tie all the loose ends together with an overhand knot.
6. Begin weaving by tying the end of a small ball of yarn to the first straw. (Any yarn may be used, but variegated yarn will make an automatic pattern.)
7. Work the yarn over and under the straws, moving back and forth with the yarn moving up on the straws (Ill. 2).
8. To add a new color, simply tie it on and continue weaving.
9. As the weaving progresses, gently push the weaving down on the straws. If the weaving is tight, gently pull the straws up—this allows more room for weaving on the straws. Do *not* push the weaving completely off the straws; although as the weaving builds up, it will gradually go onto the yarn by itself.
10. Continue weaving until the weaving reaches the overhand knot and is tight.
11. Finish by pushing all the weaving off the straws. Cut the end of the straws where the tape holds the yarn. This allows enough yarn for another overhand knot to be tied to hold the weaving in place.

supplies

1. Common soda straws, cut in half
2. Yarn
3. Transparent tape
4. Scissors

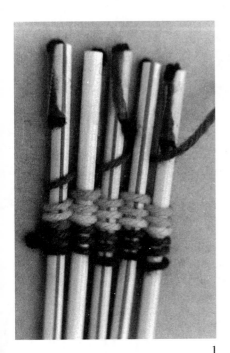

1

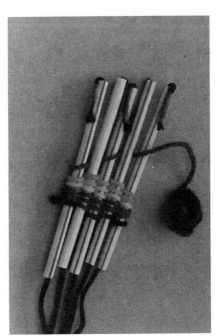

2

supplies

1. Colored burlap
2. Assorted colors and sizes of yarn
3. Tapestry needle

Note: Additional fringing can be added at the bottom for wall hangings. Small curtain rods, doweling, or sticks can be attached to the top so the material will be held straight and can be attached to the wall.

Stitchery

method a

1. Remove the selvage (the edge on either side of a woven fabric finished to prevent raveling) and pull the threads on the burlap so the sides are straight.
2. Put a dab of white glue on each corner to prevent raveling.
3. Pull interior threads and fill vacated space with colored yarn.
4. Patterns and variations can be achieved by going over two warp threads, under one, or any other combination.
5. Felt or fabrics can be appliquéd.
6. Various stitches, such as chain stitching, can be used.

STITCHES

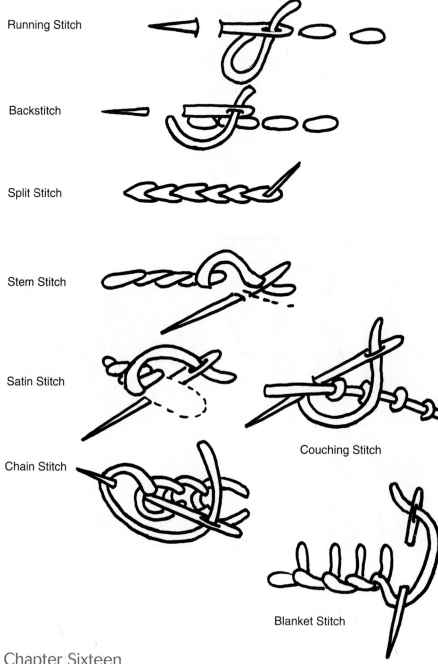

Running Stitch

Backstitch

Split Stitch

Stem Stitch

Satin Stitch

Couching Stitch

Chain Stitch

Blanket Stitch

method b

1. Remove the selvage (the edge of the fabric finished to prevent raveling) and pull threads so that the sides are straight.
2. Put a dab of glue on each corner to prevent raveling.
3. Draw a design on newsprint the same size as the burlap.
4. If the main object is large enough, cut it out and use it as a pattern by drawing around it with chalk or an erasable fabric pencil or marker.
5. Complete the drawing of the design on the burlap.
6. Thread the needle with one end of the yarn long and one end short. The knot goes in the long end.
7. Bring the needle from the back of the burlap when beginning so that knot will be on back of fabric.
8. Use any of the stitches.

supplies

1. Colored burlap
2. Assorted colors and sizes of yarn
3. Tapestry needle
4. Newsprint and pencil
5. Chalk or erasable fabric marker or pencil

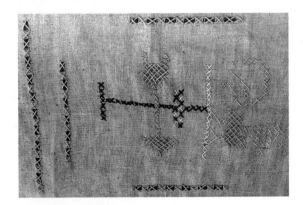

© James L. Shaffer

1. Enamel, glass, copper, or brass cooking utensil
2. Jars for storing dye
3. Sticks for stirring dye
4. Hot plate
5. Iron to press finished material
6. Commercial dyes
7. Cloth, such as muslin, silk, or any material that will absorb dye easily
8. String or cord
9. Marbles, small stones, or pieces of wood
10. Rubber gloves

Note: Use rubber gloves when handling dyes.

Tie and Dye

Tied and dyed material is made by dipping cloth in a dye bath after having wound parts of the cloth tightly with string or cord. The tightly wound string prevents the color dye from reaching parts of the fabric, creating a resist retaining the original color of the cloth. The tied and dyed method is suitable for numerous possibilities, including scarfs, blouses, T-shirts, aprons, and so on.

procedure for tying

1. *Concentric squares*
   Fold materials on the two diagonals of the cloth shape, and wind string tightly at intervals from the middle.
2. *Concentric circles*
   Pick up the cloth from the middle, and fold as evenly as possible away from the middle point, tying string tightly around the cloth at several intervals. When dipped in dye, the areas where the string was tied will create concentric circles and remain the color of the cloth.
3. *Varied shapes*
   Marbles or pebbles tied in the cloth will create interesting effects. Blocks of hard wood cut in various shapes and tied in the cloth (so not so much dye is absorbed) also create different designs.
4. *Stripes*
   Roll the cloth into a small tube and tie it with strong knots. Cloth folded accordion-style and tied tightly with string at intervals will also create stripes.

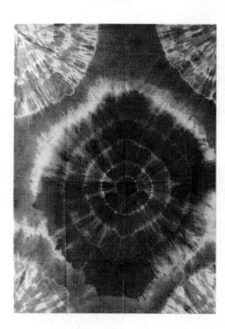
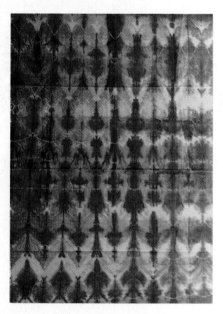

procedure for dyeing

1. The fabric to be dyed must be clean. Make sure all sizing is removed by washing vigorously with soap and hot water.
2. Plan your design by tying cloth in any combinations (Ill. 1). It may be wise to first experiment with a scrap piece of cloth.
3. Mix the dye as indicated on box.

4. Dip the material in warm water before dyeing. This will tighten the tied string and also conforms to the dyeing instructions on the dye box. Wring out excess water.
5. Place the cloth in dye solution, and stir constantly with a stick or hand (use rubber gloves) so materials will be dyed evenly (Ill. 2).
6. Leave the material in dye for only a few minutes or dye will penetrate the tied places.
7. Remove from the dye, and rinse in cold water (Ill. 3). Put the dye in a glass container to keep for future use.
8. If another color is to be used, untie the strings desired, retie at other spots, and put in the next color dye solution.
9. Allow the cloth to drip dry or wring out excess water.
10. Press the cloth with a hot iron while it is still damp. This will also help set the color.

Variation: Tie-Dye Color Cords are another way of doing tie-dye. The cords are impregnated with color dyes and the color transfers from the cords to the fabric, thus making designs. The designs are dependent upon the way the cloth is folded or tied and if cords are laid inside the folds along with being used for the tying. The color cords can be used on all cotton and rayon fabrics or cotton or rayon fabric blends. There are selected colors available in packages of 30 cords that are about 3 feet long. It takes at least 4 cords per yard of material (1 T-shirt) for a simple design and more for anything complex.

1

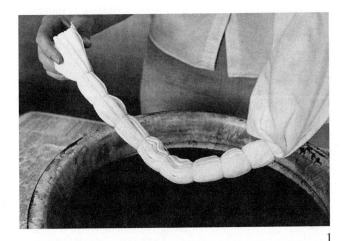

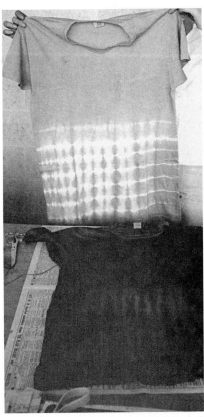

2

3

s u p p l i e s

1. Yarn. Variegated yarn will make an automatic pattern. Even short scraps of yarn can be used.
2. Popsicle sticks, tongue depressors, or dowel sticks
3. White glue

God's Eye—Ojo de Dios

This Mexican craft involves the organized wrapping of yarn around a crosspiece of some material, usually wooden sticks. They can be wrapped in different ways to create different patterns and they can be as small as toothpicks or as large as you care to make them.

procedure

1. Glue sticks together in a crossed position.
2. Cut a piece of yarn about 6 feet long.
3. Hold one end of the yarn next to the center on one of the spokes. Bring the long end of yarn around the same spoke on top of the yarn end to hold it in place.
4. Turning the crosspiece in a counterclockwise direction, wrap the long end of yarn around the next spoke, going under and around.
5. Turn and wrap under and around the next spoke.
6. Turn and wrap under and around the next spoke.
7. At the place of beginning, lay the next wrap beside the first wrap so that the yarn will build up toward the end of the spoke.
8. Continue wrapping, always in the same direction.
9. When the spokes are filled almost to the end, put the end of the yarn through the last string and make a knot near one of the spokes.

 Note: The front side should have a diamond pattern.

Variation: A tree branch in the shape of the letter Y (like a slingshot) works very nicely as a base for the wrapping of a God's Eye.

Variation: With a larger God's Eye, at the midpoint of wrapping, turn the sticks over and continue to wrap the yarn from under or behind and around the sticks in a counterclockwise direction. The diamond design will appear on both the front and the back of the God's Eye.

Batik

procedure

1. Develop a design on a piece of newsprint the same size as the fabric.
2. Transfer the design to the fabric with a light pencil line.
3. Smooth the material as much as possible. The fabric can be stretched on a frame or board with tacks, staples, or tape or keep it straight.
4. Melt equal parts of paraffin and beeswax in a double boiler or an old pan floating in water in an electric skillet. Use only enough heat to render the wax liquid. Pour wax carefully into a Crock-Pot if one is available. **Only the teacher should pour hot wax.**
5. With newspaper under the fabric, paint the wax on the areas that are to remain the natural color of the material.
6. Check the underside of the material to make sure the wax is penetrating the cloth.
7. Mix the dye as directed on the package. Cold water dye is a necessity.
8. Remove the cloth from the board and dip in cool clean water. Crumple the cloth if a crackle effect is desired, and then place it in a dye bath, stirring constantly with a stick.
9. Remove the cloth from the dye, rinse it in cold water, and allow it to drip dry.
10. Smooth the fabric when it is dry or place it on the frame and fasten in place.
11. Paint the melted wax over the areas just dyed to retain this color. Remove the cloth from frame, and dye it in a second color. This operation can be repeated several times. As you can see, lighter colors of dye should be used first with darker colors coming later in the sequence. Remember the colors will mix in the second bath with the color of the first bath creating a different color on the material.
12. Remove the wax from the material by ironing it between newspapers or paper towels. Change the paper often because the paper absorbs the wax.

Variation: Stamps can be dipped in the molten wax and printed on the fabric. There are metal stamps available commercially, but simple stamps can be made from pipe cleaners bent into shapes. Make sure there is an end left for a handle. Clothespins can be used as handles for objects dipped in wax and printed. Tjanting tools, made of metal, are small cups with a spout that trails the hot wax in lines on the fabric. Wax paper is very helpful in masking areas so that wax doesn't accidentally drip in an unwanted place on the fabric.

supplies

1. Fabric. Unbleached muslin works very well. Natural fibers absorb dyes easily.
2. Electric skillet and an old pan or a double boiler for melting the wax.
3. Small Crock-Pot keeps wax molten.
4. Brushes. Use old brushes because they can only be used for wax.
5. Paraffin and beeswax
6. Newspapers
7. Newsprint paper and pencil
8. Frame or board with tape, tacks, or staples that can be used to stretch material
9. Large jars or buckets to hold dye
10. Stir sticks for dye baths
11. Iron
12. Cold water dye
13. Rubber gloves, always used in handling dye
14. Baking soda should be kept nearby whenever hot wax is used in case of a fire.

1. Core material, Fiber Flex, or cotton clothesline
2. Yarn of all textures and colors or material cut into strips
3. Tapestry needle

Coiling

procedure

1. Taper the core end. Cut the core at an angle for 1½ inches.
2. Cut 3 or 4 feet of colored yarn or cloth and thread on a tapestry needle.
3. Lay the other end of the wrapping yarn along the core for about 1 inch and ½ inch from the tapered end. Wrap around the core and yarn end until it is long enough to bend back on itself.
4. Wrap the core and the tail end of the core together. This forms the center of the spiral. Wraps need to be tight.
5. There should be a very small opening in the center of the loop. Wrap the yarn around the cord away from the loop 5 times to hold it in place. Place two stitches through the hole in the loop.
6. The Lazy Squaw stitch goes directly across from one coil, around the previous coil and back to the outer coil to begin wrapping again. The Figure Eight stitch follows the contour of the coil being wrapped, goes between the two coils and around the previous coil, between the two coils again and begin wrapping the outer coil. From the edge, the stitch looks like a number 8 and blends with the coils.
7. Plan the number of wraps before going on, usually 5 to 7 wraps for double yarn and 8 to 10 wraps for single yarn.
8. The core should be placed in a spiral form as it is wrapped, taking stitches at regular intervals.
9. A hot pad may be made of a coiled spiral.
10. If a basket is desired, the bottom of the basket is at least 3 inches wide before coiling the walls. To make the walls, as the stitch is taken, the coil is placed on top of the previous row rather than beside it. If the coil is placed directly above previous row, a straight-sided form will result. A sloping side results when the new coil is placed slightly to the outside of the previous coil.
11. To add yarn or change color, make sure there are 6 to 8 wraps left on the old yarn. Place the end of the new yarn along the core so that both yarns are together. Wrap the new yarn around both ends and the core several times and take a stitch.
12. To finish, cut a tapered end on the core material. After wrapping to the end, take several stitches and with the needle pull the end of the yarn between the core and the wrap to hide and hold the end of the yarn.

Masks and Puppets

Masks

The paintings in the caves of France, dating between 30,000–13,000 B.C., show humans wearing animal masks. Masks have been used by humans for one reason or another in almost all parts of the world. There seem to be three main ideas that masks represent: Ancestors and Tradition, Spirit Helpers, and Theater.

African masks are used as a bond between a group of people and their ancestors, and become a guarantee of continuity. The death masks found on the mummies in central America, northern China, Egyptian, and Mycenaean civilizations, and ancient Africa were all crafted to help the spirit continue in the afterlife.

The masks of Native Americans often took the form of animals or a totemic symbol. The totem pole of the tribes of North America is an example of the use of the bird, fish, and animal symbols as special spirits to protect and provide for their people. The mask in the hands of a shaman or medicine man acted as a "spirit helper" and had the magic quality not only to represent an animal or character but to change the wearer into that character.

Theater masks were used in Classical Europe and are still used extensively in Indonesia and Japan. Some of the most beautiful masks come from Japan where theater masks were developed to a very high level.

Many of the masks seen today (Carnival or Halloween) are used as a disguise and can be classed as funny or scary folk art.

Masks may be held in front of the face, worn over the face, or on the head like a helmet or hat. They may include coverings for some or all of the body, or additions may be well above the head. They may have a lot of color or very little color and they can be made from almost any material that can be manipulated and decorated.

Kwakiutl Indian Mask. One example of masks made by cultures throughout the world. Courtesy Department of Library Services, American Museum of Natural History (#2A 21548).

Masks have been used by many cultures for many reasons. This one is quite complex. Areogun, African, Nigeria, Yoruba Ekiti People, Epa Society Mask, 1930s, wood with polychrome painted decoration, Ht. 49½ in. (125.7 cm) (1977.22) The Toledo Museum of Art, Purchased with funds from the Libbey Endowment, Gift of Edward Drummond Libbey.

Materials and Tools
for Masks and Puppets

1. Material, such as felt (does not fray and can be glued)
2. Yarn
3. Feathers, for example, marabou or feather boas
4. Cardboard or tag board
5. Pipe cleaners
6. Buttons
7. Sequins
8. Beads
9. Costume jewelry
10. Trim of any sort
11. Plastic that can be cut
12. Styrofoam
13. Polyurethane carpet padding or thick foam for cushions
14. Pins and pin cushion
15. Needle and thread
16. Tacky Glue (a thick white glue which holds things in place while they dry)
17. Chalk
18. Acrylic or tempera paint
19. Brush
20. Fun fur
21. Eyes
22. Polyester
23. Pom-poms
24. Any material is fair game to use for puppets or masks

One of the most helpful tools to have when doing masks and puppets is a low-heat glue gun. This glue gun does not get as hot as the hot glue gun but the nozzle and the glue itself do get hot. If safety rules are followed and if there is supervision it is possible to have things stick instantly. The teacher could keep one glue gun on hand to help with parts that will not hold with regular glue. This type of glue gun should use the oval glue stick. (Do not get the dual heat glue gun.)

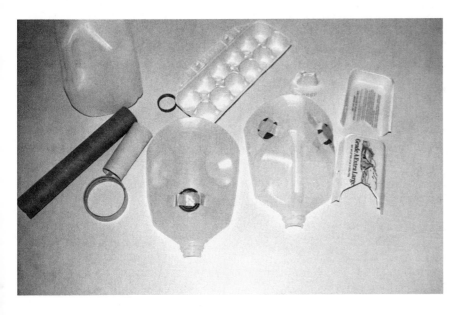

Puppet Stages

- A table can be turned on its side.
- A card table or a piece of cloth can be put across a doorway.
- A pressure curtain rod with a curtain can be a theater for hand or rod puppets, or the curtain can be raised to become a marionette theater.
- A broomstick or dowel can be placed between the backs of two chairs with a blanket or a cloth placed over it.
- Tabletop
- Cardboard box with a hole cut in it.
- Folding screen

Shadow Puppet Stages

- Frame made from a big box with enough space below for the puppeteer to work and not obstruct the light.
- Picture frame with muslin. Use tape or staples to pull and secure material with no sags or wrinkles.

Light Sources

- Daylight. Put the screen with its back to a window.
- Fluorescent tube placed behind the screen.
- Gooseneck lamp to the side of the screen.
- Overhead projector or a slide projector allows scenery to be added easily.

Keep the puppets close to the screen if you want the shadow to be the same size as the puppet and in sharp focus. If you want the puppet to appear bigger, move the puppet away from the screen and closer to the light source. The shadow form will also be more diffused.

Paper Bag Mask

procedure

1. Slip the bag over the child's head. The *bottom* of the bag will be the *top* of the mask. You may need to cut out sections at the sides of the bag so that it will fit more comfortably over the shoulders. **Use safety scissors if available.**

2. Locate the eyes and mark them with a blunt crayon. Remove the bag and cut the openings for the eyes. Add the nose, mouth, and, if you wish, ears.

3. Decorate the bag with any of the media and materials listed.

supplies

1. Paper bag large enough to slip over child's head
2. Scissors
3. Rubber cement, paste, or glue, and a stapler, if one is available.
4. Watercolors, tempera paint, or colored inks
5. Materials to be used for decorating mask, such as bits of colored paper, felt or cloth, bottle caps, buttons, yarn, ribbons, and so on.
6. Paint brush and container for water, if paint is used

1. Heavy-duty paper plate
2. Safety scissors or X-acto knife
3. Cardboard
4. Markers, watercolors, tempera, or acrylic
5. Scrap construction paper, string, yarn, feathers, and material of all sorts
6. String or yarn, or a short stick

Paper Plate Mask

procedure

1. Put the paper plate over the face and gently mark the position of the eyes with a pencil.
2. Cut the holes for the eyes carefully using safety scissors or an X-acto knife. **X-acto knives must be used with caution and supervision.** Make sure there is a sheet of cardboard or a board under the plate.
3. Draw any other features needed for the mask. Scrap construction paper may be used and any kind of material can be used to make the features or decorate the mask.
4. Other materials may be added to the edge of the mask to build it out and away from the face.
5. Punch a hole on each side of the mask and insert a string or yarn if the mask is to be worn. If it is a handheld mask, glue a stick on the bottom.

Papier-Mâché or Paris Craft Mask

procedure

1. Cut the one-gallon jug in half and choose the side to use and which way it should be oriented.
2. Experiment with tubes, cutting and taping to decide where to place them. Use any shape to attach to the plastic surface. Holes can be cut in the plastic surface but it must be done carefully. **Teacher should do the cutting if done with a knife of any sort.**
3. Tape the shapes securely in place by putting tape on all four sides. Larger things, such as horns or ears, should be added later so that the mask will not be too heavy.
4. Papier-mâché—Mix the paste and cut newspaper strips. Dip strips of paper in paste and lay over the entire form, with the strips going in different directions. It is helpful to use different colors of paper to be able to see the number of layers. It requires about six layers for papier-mâché.
5. Paris Craft—Dip the strips into warm water, laying the strips in different directions and smoothing each strip before putting on the next strip. Check for holes. It requires three layers of Paris Craft.
6. Allow the mask to dry.
7. Decorate with paint. Attach other materials, such as feathers, beads, pipe cleaners, pom-poms, foam, fun fur, scrap paper, seeds, and so on. **If a fixative spray is used, ensure optimal ventilation.**

supplies

1. Papier-mâché materials (p. 343)
2. Paris Craft, cut into appropriate strips
3. Water container with warm water, if using Paris Craft
4. Newspaper
5. One-gallon plastic jug (cider, water, or milk) cut in half
6. Anything to build up the surface where protrusions are desired (cut up egg cartons, paper tubes, small plastic containers, lids, or tag board to make into shapes)
7. Masking tape
8. Paint, latex, acrylic, or tempera
9. Brush
10. White glue, Tacky Glue, or low-heat glue gun

supplies

1. Tag board or heavy paper
2. Scissors or X-acto knife with cardboard
3. Pencil
4. Markers, crayons, oil pastels, scrap construction paper, and all kinds of scrap materials
5. Glue or glue stick

Cardboard and Paper Mask

procedure

method a

1. Fold paper or tag board in half.
2. Draw lightly with a pencil a shape that will cover the eyes and part of the face with a place for the nose. The fold of the paper will go between the eyes.
3. Open the folded shape and check for eye position and mark it gently with a pencil.
4. Put the shape back in a folded position and cut the eye holes. X-acto knife works the best. **Use X-acto knives with extreme care and supervision.** Make sure there is cardboard under the knife while cutting.
5. Punch holes in the sides so that the mask can be worn over the face.
6. Decorate the mask.

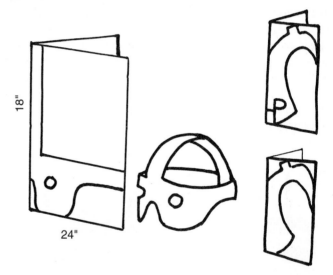

supplies

1. Tag board or heavy paper 12″ × 18″
2. Scissors or X-acto knife
3. Glue or glue stick
4. Pencil
5. Markers, crayons, oil pastels, construction paper scraps, and scraps of any materials

method b

1. Fold the 12″ × 18″ paper in half vertically.
2. Draw the desired shape on the side of the open edges (the fold will be the center of the mask).
3. Find and gently mark the eye after opening the shape.
4. Fold down nose or beak shape.
5. Add pattern, color, and other things to finish the mask.

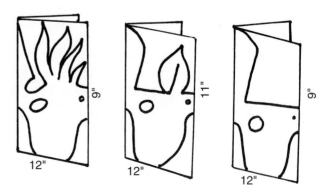

Simple Foam Mask

This mask allows the face to be open for talking or singing.

procedure

1. Measure around the head of the wearer at the forehead or around the face, depending upon the type of mask desired; then add another inch.
2. Cut a piece of foam 1½ inches wide and as long as the measurement.
3. Cut each end at a slant and glue the two ends together with a glue gun.
4. Round the edges of the foam ring with scissors.
5. Cut other parts to be added, such as ears, horns, and so on, from the foam scrap or chunks of foam.
6. Color all the parts with acrylic paint or chalk. If acrylic paint is used, mist the foam first with water so that the paint will spread. A scrap piece of foam can be used as a brush. If chalk is used, use the side of chalk and spray with hair spray when completed. **Use hair spray with optimal ventilation.** Allow all pieces to dry.
7. Put the pieces together using a low-heat glue gun. **Observe safety rules for the glue gun.**

 Note: Acrylic paint makes the surface of the foam hard. Chalk color is much easier and the foam stays spongy.

Variation: A muzzle mask can be made by measuring around the head at the nose and cutting a strip of foam 2 inches wide to cover the nose, cheeks, and ears of the wearer of the mask. It may be necessary to cut some of the foam out of the back side to make room for the nose. Other pieces are attached after they are colored.

1. Polyurethane foam or polyfoam carpet padding. Use the smooth type, not the type with compressed pieces.
2. Chunks of foam, such as that used in upholstery or mattresses
3. Sharp scissors, such as Fiskas
4. Permanent markers
5. Low-heat glue gun
6. Chalk or acrylic paint
7. Hair spray
8. Electric meat knife to cut chunk foam into basic shapes (teacher use only)

Puppets

Puppetry seems to have had its beginning in religious ceremonies. The shaman or medicine man used the puppet as a means of communication to influence the people. Puppets may have begun as a mask with the jaw hinged so that it would move and seem to bring the ancestor spirits to life. Unfortunately, most of the ancient puppets were made out of perishable material and thus have disappeared. A few figures made of clay by the Egyptians and the people of India have survived. Aristotle writes in 400 B.C. about the use of puppets in Greece.

Puppets are very diverse, ranging from found inanimate objects used as a character, to very complex and detailed characters. They may be as small as a finger or larger than life. Any material may be used to build the puppet. They have been moved by using the hand, rods, or strings attached to the body, head, and other parts. Puppets are controlled by a computer, in the modern age of movie special effects.

Designing, sculpture, painting, sewing, directing, acting, writing, music, and choreography are all combined in puppetry. Perhaps this is why artists such as Paul Klee and Wassily Kandinsky were involved in puppetry. Many fine puppeteers, such as Jim Henson, have passed on the traditions of puppetry and added contributions of their own.

Crafting the puppet is only one stage in the art of puppetry. Before the puppet can be made, thought must be given to the character of the puppet. Is the puppet human or animal? Is the puppet male or female? Is the puppet a particular character in a play or a story? Is the puppet a hero or a villain? Is the puppet going to sing or dance? All of these kinds of questions need to be answered before a puppet can be crafted because it will make a vast difference in the form of the puppet. At this stage, the puppet is only a doll until the puppeteer gives it life through movement, and that movement is determined by the kind of character needed for the show. After direction and a great deal of practice, the puppet and puppeteer will be ready to perform for an audience.

Paper Finger Puppet

procedure

method a

1. Cut a strip of paper to form a tube that will fit the finger snugly. **(Use safety scissors if available.)** A small paper tube will also work.
2. Tape or paste the tube together.
3. Add features with paper, paint, crayons, felt tip pens, or by cutting or folding the paper tube itself.

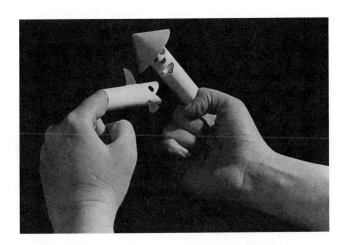

method b

1. Cut a rectangle of tag board wide enough so that the first two fingers will fit with space to spare.
2. Fold under one end of the rectangle. Draw two half circles on the fold and cut. Fit the first two fingers through the holes in the fold. If the holes aren't big enough, refold and cut to fit. Make sure that there is space between the holes and on each side. The two fingers will be the puppet's legs.
3. Make the character's torso, arms, and head in the space above the holes.

supplies

1. Paper
2. Paste or white glue
3. Tape
4. Scissors
5. Paint, crayons, or felt markers

Note: Finger puppets can also be created from the fingers cut from an old glove and decorated. Try a paper cup with an opening cut for the nose through which a finger is protruded. A paper plate folded in half to form a large mouth and decorated has possibilities.

supplies

1. Tag board
2. Paste, glue, or glue stick
3. Scissors
4. Crayons, markers, scrap paper, and any other scrap materials

supplies

1. Paper bag with a flat bottom, the size to be determined by the size of the hand (paper lunch bag works well)
2. Colored construction paper
3. Glue or glue stick
4. Markers
5. Scissors

Paper Bag Puppet

procedure

1. Put a hand in the bag, find the fold, and use the hand to open and close the fold. This is the moving part of the puppet and the flat bottom of the bag will be an area of the face or the top of the head.
2. The face can be drawn or glued directly on this flat bottom or another piece of paper can be shaped and glued onto the bottom. Don't forget to put color and details inside the fold. This could be either the mouth or the eyebrows.
3. Three-dimensional additions are excellent. Noses or beaks to stick out and Jacob's Ladders for the arms and legs may be used. Cut paper can be fringed or curled to make hair or feathers. Other materials can be added to enrich the puppet form.

Paper Bag Puppet on a Stick

procedure

1. Fill the bag with small pieces of torn or shredded newspaper.
2. The dowel or stick should be inserted in the open end of the bag until it touches the bottom of the bag. Gather the open end of the bag around the stick and tie the string tightly to form a neck. Make sure the stick extends far enough out of the bag to make a handle.
3. The features of the face can be added with paint, crayons, or with pieces of colored paper cut to shape.

 Note: Faces or animals can be cut from paper and mounted to a stick; they also make simple puppet heads.

s u p p l i e s

1. Paper bag
2. Newspapers
3. Wooden stick or dowel
4. String
5. Colored paper and scissors
6. Paints or crayons
7. Paste

supplies

1. Newsprint and pencils
2. Scissors
3. Variety of felt colors. Each puppet will need a 9″ × 36″ piece.
4. White glue, Tacky Glue, or a low-heat glue gun with compatible glue sticks

Felt Hand Puppet

procedure

1. Place the hand on newsprint in the desired puppet position and draw around with at least one inch extra around the hand.
2. Cut out newsprint pattern and pin it on a folded over piece of felt with the head touching the fold. Draw around the pattern with chalk.
3. Turn the felt with the chalk line to the inside and sew or glue the edges of the felt pieces making sure the bottom is open. An over and under or running stitch can be used. Low-heat glue guns are instant. **If glue guns are used, supervise to ensure that safety rules are followed.** Machine stitching is fine.
4. Using the scraps from the main bodies, cut a face or head from a contrasting color and glue it in place. Place all other features and details to make the puppet into the selected character.

Papier-Mâché or Paris Craft Puppet Head

procedure

method a—papier-mâché

1. Create a puppet head and neck with the plastic clay. The neck will eventually serve two purposes: first, a place to fasten clothing and secondly, a place for the middle finger to control the puppet. When forming the head, exaggerate the features, as the thickness of the applied paper strips tends to reduce feature recognition.
2. Cut newspaper or paper toweling into strips, approximately ½ inch wide. **Use safety scissors if available. Paper cutter should be employed by the teacher.**
3. Mix the paste in a bowl or pan to the consistency of cream.
4. Place a strip of paper into the paste until it is saturated. Remove the strip from the bowl, and wipe off the excess paste by pulling the strip between the fingers.
5. Apply the paste-saturated strip directly to the puppet head.
6. Continue to apply strips until the entire head is covered. Repeat until at least six layers of paper strips are applied. The number of layers can be readily counted if a different kind or color of paper is used for each layer. The strength of the finished puppet will be much greater if each strip is applied in a different direction. Also, make sure that all wrinkles and bubbles are removed after each strip is added.
7. Place the puppet head on a crumpled piece of paper, and allow it to dry thoroughly. The crumpled paper allows the air to circulate around the puppet head.
8. When the puppet head is dry, cut it in half with a sharp knife or saw to remove the clay (Ill. 1). **Use knives and saws with extreme care and supervision.**
9. Place the two halves together and fasten with additional strips. It may also be necessary to apply several strips over the bottom edge of the neck for strength.
10. When thoroughly dry, sandpaper until smooth, and then decorate (Ill. 2).
11. If tempera paint is used for decoration, the surface should be sprayed with clear plastic, or painted with shellac or varnish for permanence. **Use sprays with optimum ventilation.**
12. Additional material such as yarn for hair, buttons for eyes, and so on, can be added to further enhance the finished product (Ill. 3).

supplies

1. Newspapers, paper toweling, or any absorbent paper
2. Scissors or paper cutter
3. Paste thinned to the consistency of cream, such as wheat paste, library paste, or modeling paste. Methylan paste is widely used.
4. Container for mixing paste
5. Plastic clay
6. Sandpaper
7. Knife, saw, or single-edged razor blade
8. Paint (tempera, enamel, oil paint, acrylic, and so on)
9. Brush
10. Clear plastic spray, shellac, or varnish for protective finish if tempera paint is used

1   2   3

Paris Craft and warm water in a plastic container replaces the paste and newspaper strips. All other supplies are the same.

Variation of method a: Paris Craft

1. Cut the Paris Craft into appropriately sized strips and pieces.
2. Dip the strips into warm water and lay them in different directions over the base form. Smooth each strip before putting on the next strip. Three or four layers would be sufficient but always check for holes. Check edges to make sure they are smooth.
3. It is possible to crush a piece of wet Paris Craft and shape it to form some features but not large parts. Lay strips over the crushed piece to make sure it will not come off.
4. Finish the form as you would for papier-mâché.

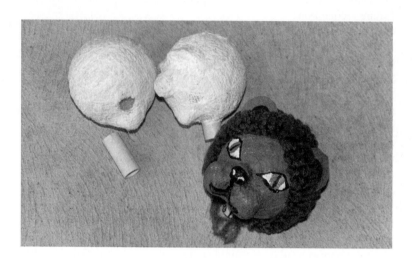

method b

Method B is the same as Method A except the base form of the puppet head is a small 5-inch balloon almost inflated with a tag board or cardboard cylinder securely taped over the air intake to make a neck. Crushed tissue paper is taped in place on the balloon for noses, muzzles, and so on. Three layers of Paris Craft or six layers of papier-mâché are necessary to cover the entire form, including the neck. (The hole in the bottom stays open.)

method c

A Styrofoam shape (oval, circle, and so on) is the base form for the puppet head with Styrofoam pieces attached by using Tacky Glue and broken pieces of tooth-pick to hold them in place. (Place toothpick pieces at an angle on each side of the piece to be attached going through the piece and into the base.) If Paris Craft is used, wet pieces of Paris Craft can be wadded up and held in place with strips of wet Paris Craft put over the entire base form. The neck can be a cylinder of card-board or a 2-inch piece of PVC pipe pushed into the Styrofoam base form. (Remove center piece of Styrofoam so that there will be room for the finger.) Use two layers of papier-mâché or one layer of Paris Craft.

A quick and easy material that can be used with Method C is torn tissue paper strips and diluted white glue. Brush the glue over the Styrofoam and lay strips of tissue on top, pushing the strips down with a brush full of the diluted glue. Cover everything including the neck. (Leave space to insert a finger in the neck.)

Hand Positions for Puppets

Try out the finger positions to find the one that is the most comfortable and allows the most movement. Sometimes this needs to be decided before the puppet is crafted.

These puppet heads need to have a mitt or hand covering to help make them the chosen character. Make a pattern for the mitt by drawing around the hand in the chosen position to be used with the puppet. Allow at least 1 inch additional all around. Lay the pattern on the material (felt works well) and draw around it with chalk. Cut out two pieces of the mitt and sew or glue the edges together but leave the bottom open for the hand and the small top open to attach to the puppet neck. Glue the small top to the neck of the puppet. Many things can be added to this mitt, such as aprons, ties, pockets, belts, buckles, bows, collars, spots, and so on. If a tail is added, put it in the middle of the back halfway from the bottom so the audience will be able to see it.

supplies

1. Tagboard
2. Markers, crayons, oil pastels, or colored pencils
3. Scissors
4. Paper punch, ¼ inch is good
5. Brass fasteners
6. String or yarn

Jumping Jacks

procedure

1. Draw the character's head and body on a rectangle of tag board. It must be large enough to attach legs and arms.
2. Draw the upper arms and lower arms, including the hands, separately on another piece of tag board.
3. Draw the upper and lower legs, including the feet, separately on a piece of tag board.
4. The arms and the legs need to be wide enough to punch in the holes, especially the tops of the upper arms and legs.
5. Add color. Remember the features of the face and the details needed for the character.
6. Overlap the upper and lower legs, punch holes, and put in brass fasteners with the smooth side to the front. Connect the arms in the same way.
7. Turn the body piece face down and lay the legs and arms in position. Make sure to overlap them. Punch the holes close to the outside of the body leaving room on the upper legs and upper arms for an additional hole that will be punched for the control string.
8. Put brass fasteners in place to connect the arms and legs with the body piece. Do not press the fasteners too tight, since they need to move.
9. Punch holes in the upper legs and arms slightly above and toward the center of the body.
10. Cut a string or piece of yarn about 18 inches long. Tie one end in the control hole in the upper arm and the other end in the other upper arm.
11. Cut another string about 14 inches long and tie each end in the control holes of the upper legs.
12. The puppet's arms and legs can move separately or the strings can be tied together and they can move at the same time.

 Note: A simple variation is to create any kind of bird and make only the wings move.

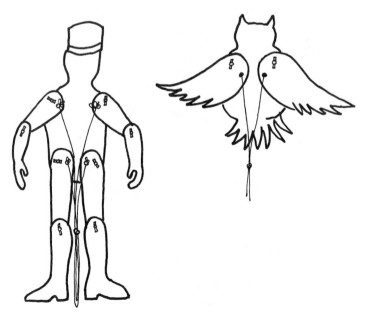

Shadow Puppet

procedure

1. Make a pattern using a piece of newsprint. Make a silhouette that is recognizable, usually a side view of any character.
2. Make any moving parts larger so that there will be enough space to overlap and fasten. One or two parts may be made to move.
3. Using the pattern, draw the pattern on tag board or cardboard and cut carefully. **If X-acto knives are used, all safety rules must be observed.**
4. Overlap the moving parts, punch holes and put in brass fasteners so they can move.
5. If the shape is small, a large soda straw can be taped to the back of the main body and taped in place. If the shape is large, use a clothes hanger wire and bend it so that it can be taped in place. **A wire cutter is helpful but use only with supervision.**
6. Soda straws can be taped in place coming down from the moving parts. Some parts may not need control if the brass fasteners and the puppet is moved so that there is a pendulum movement. For example, a human puppet is made with a stable body, head, and one leg. The other leg is attached with a fastener and will swing when the rest of the body is moved. Controls could be used on one arm or both arms.

supplies

1. Tag board or cardboard
2. Wire (clothes hangers work well)
3. Soda straws, straight or bendable
4. Tape
5. Markers
6. Colored tissue or cellophane
7. Brass fasteners
8. Paper punch
9. Scissors (X-acto knives could be used to cut small designs within the silhouette)

s u p p l i e s

1. Styrofoam ball, individual cereal box, or chunk of polyurethane foam (used in upholstery or mattresses). Smaller Styrofoam ball or oval for head.
2. Flexible material for legs and neck (string of pom-poms, tubes of material, heavy cord, or strips of polyurethane)
3. Felt scraps, construction paper scraps, feathers, and any other scraps available
4. Markers or acrylic paint
5. Weights, for feet, such as washers, pennies, or fishing weights, for example
6. Buttonhole thread for stringing the marionette
7. Tongue depressors, popsicle sticks, or screen molding for the controls
8. Tacky Glue or low-heat glue gun
9. Cut bobby pins (four will be needed)

Simple Marionette

A marionette can be anything that moves and is controlled by strings. The puppet may be as simple as a scarf or a gathered piece of cloth controlled by one string. It can be a very complex form controlled by as many strings as can be handled by the puppeteer.

procedure

method a

1. If Styrofoam shapes are used, they should be sealed by brushing watered-down white glue and putting tissue paper scraps on top. Brush additional glue mixture on top of tissue to smooth the tissue. Two layers should do. Allow to dry.
2. If polyurethane foam is used, smooth it with sharp scissors.
3. If cereal box is used, cover it with tissue papier-mâché or by covering it with construction paper or fabric. Allow to dry.
4. Color the body and head if they are not covered by material.
5. Color two triangles for the beak with markers, felt, or paper scraps. Reinforce with tag board if necessary.
6. Cut out four feet for the creature (actually two layers for each foot). Put the weight between them and glue in place.
7. Wings can be added by use of construction paper, feathers, and so on.
8. Connect all parts.
9. Make main control by gluing two popsicle sticks or pieces of screen molding together in a crossed position. Holes can be drilled in the ends and in middle of cross. Saw slots near holes.
10. Glue the short pieces of bobby pins in the sides of the head and the sides of the body. If Styrofoam, push into shape and glue.
11. String puppet by starting with the body. (See diagram.) String head and finally string feet.
12. Put the strings through the holes from the bottom and through the slot. Adjust and make a knot in the string. If the puppet tangles it can be untangled simply by dropping the strings and restringing.

method b

1. Cut the body into a shape that is a rounded triangle. The wide part is the shoulders and the more pointed end will be where the legs are attached.
2. Cut four pieces of foam that are long and thin, and that can be rounded on the edges and narrowed on the ends. These pieces are the upper arms and upper legs.
3. Cut the lower legs to include the feet.
4. Cut two more long, narrow pieces for the lower arms.
5. Hands can be made from felt scraps, cutting them like mittens. Small pieces of rug foam can be used also and fingers may be cut if desired.
6. Color with chalk or acrylic paint all parts that will show. If acrylic is used, mist the foam before applying the paint. Use hair spray to protect chalk colors. **Provide for optimal ventilation.**
7. Position all the parts in relation to body and make cuts in the body and the appendages where they will join. Use cut strips of material to join the pieces together. Glue them in place with a low-heat glue gun. **Observe safety rules for the glue gun.** Make sure the joints have free movement.
8. Cut a piece of the 2-inch foam into a head by rounding with scissors. Pieces can be glued on for noses, chins, and so on.
9. Color the head and add anything necessary to make it into the selected character.
10. Cloth can be draped or glued in place to make a costume.
11. Cut small slits in the side of the head to insert either small loops of material or shortened bobby pins for the stringing.
12. Make small slits in the shoulders and put loops in place or if material has been used, string through the fabric.
13. String the puppet beginning with the shoulders. The string goes from one shoulder, up through the control from the bottom, down through the other hole and fastened to the other shoulder.
14. The strings from each side of the head go to the holes at the end of the cross piece. The string goes through the hole from the bottom and through the slot. Adjust and tie a knot in the string and slide the string in the slot.
15. Tie the end of a string around one wrist. Pull the other end of the string up through the hole in the front of the control and down to the other wrist, where it is tied.
16. Fasten a string to each knee and up to the holes on the end of the added stick on the front of the control.
17. The final string goes from the lower back of the character to the hole in back of the control.

supplies

1. Polyurethane foam, 1 inch thick for appendages and 2 inches thick for body and head.
2. Material for joints and costume
3. Low-heat glue gun and glue sticks
4. Chalk and hair spray. Acrylic paint can be used.
5. Permanent markers
6. Scrap materials, buttons, pipe cleaners, eyes, yarn, and so on.
7. Buttonhole thread
8. Control made with popsicle sticks, tongue depressors, or screen molding

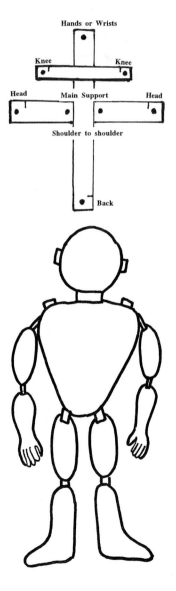

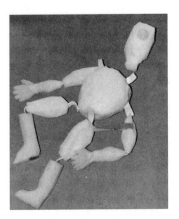

1. Cardboard cylinder such as a toilet paper roll or a cylinder made from cardboard or tag board
2. Colored construction paper, markers, material, or felt to cover tube
3. All kinds of scraps
4. White glue, Tacky Glue, or a low-heat glue gun
5. Tongue depressors, chop sticks, or pieces of screen molding
6. Scissors

Cardboard Cylinder Rod Puppet

procedure

1. Cover cylinder with color or material, remember the face is on one end of the cylinder.
2. Add features for the character selected.
3. Add arms and costumes. Legs could be attached at the bottom of the cylinder.
4. Glue the main support stick inside the cylinder with the handle sticking out of the bottom of the cylinder. **If a glue gun is used, observe all safety rules.**
5. If desired, the arms can be made longer and skewers can be used as controls. **Care should be taken because the skewers are sharp on one end.**

Matting and Framing

Mat Proportions

The matting of display material is an additional cost, but it makes displays more effective and is a practical method of retaining and storing outstanding material. It should be pointed out that display material of similar size is interchangeable, enabling the mat to be used more than once.

For effective and proper matting of creative artwork and other display material, the following rules generally apply:

1. In matting a square illustration, the top and sides of the mat should be equal, with the bottom margin wider (Ill. 1).
2. In matting a vertical rectangular illustration, the bottom margin is the widest, and the top margin wider than the sides (Ill. 2).
3. In matting a horizontal rectangular illustration, the bottom margin is the widest and the top margin should be smaller than the sides (Ill. 3).

The optical center of a picture area is always a certain distance above the measured center. Measured centering of a work in a mat therefore creates a topheavy appearance, whereas optical centering creates greater frontality and balance, and more comfortable viewing. Precut mats are often available.

1

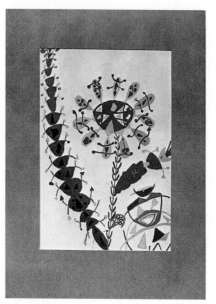

2

3

Cutting a Mat

procedure

1. Cut the mat board large enough to accommodate the picture to be matted, including a generous margin (Ill. 1).
2. Cut a piece of cardboard of equal dimensions. This piece will be the backing for the finished mat (Ill. 2).
3. Using the suggestions for square, horizontal, or vertical pictures mentioned earlier, measure and draw a light line the size of the opening to be cut on the face of the mat board (Ill. 3). Be sure that these lines are drawn at least ½ inch smaller than both the length and width of the actual picture to be mounted. This will allow the mat to overlap the picture on all sides.
4. Place a piece of heavy scrap cardboard under the line to be cut. Cut carefully along the pencil lines with a sharp mat knife or single-edged razor blade. Apply enough pressure on the tool to cut through the mat with one cut if possible. A ruler held firmly will serve as a guide while cutting. If the cutting tool is held at a 45° angle, a beveled edge can be cut—but only after considerable practice (Ill. 4).
5. Turn the mat over and butt the top edges of the mat and the cardboard backing. Hinge the two pieces together with gummed tape (Ill. 5).
6. Close the mat on the cardboard with the window opening facing up. Mark the four corners of the opening on the cardboard backing with a sharp pencil. This will help in locating the picture directly behind the window (Ill. 6).
7. Open the mat again and center the picture behind the window, making sure that the closed mat overlaps the picture on all four sides (Ill. 7).
8. Fasten the picture to the cardboard along the top edge with gummed tape (Ill. 8), making sure that the tape does not overlap the work far enough to be seen when the mat is closed. A picture fastened this way is easily removed and replaced with another without harm to the mat.
9. Finished matted picture (Ill. 9).

Caution: Young children using sharp tools should be under constant supervision; teacher should probably do the cutting.

1. Mat board (pebbled or smooth, colored or white)
2. Cardboard (which should be of the same rigidity as the mat board)
3. Pencil
4. Ruler
5. Mat knife or single-edged razor blade
6. Gummed tape

1

2

3

4

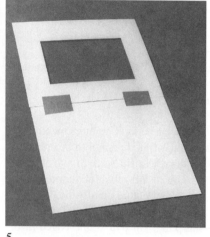

5

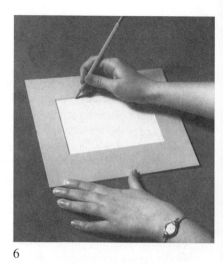

6

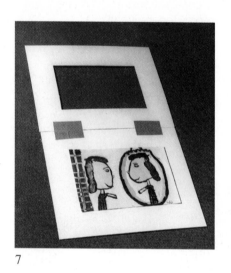

7

8

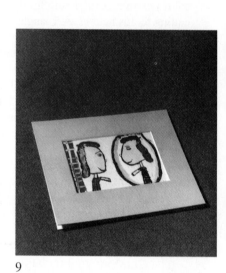

9

Covered Mat

procedure

1. Cut the mat as instructed on pages 331 and 332 (Ill. 1).
2. Select a piece of material that is larger than the mat (Ill. 2).
3. Cut the material so it exceeds the measurements of the mat by about 1 inch or less (Ill. 3).
4. Cut the corners of the material diagonally up to the corners of the mat (Ill. 3).
5. With the mat face down on the material, cut the inside corners of the material diagonally from the corners of the mat (Ill. 3). Leave about ½ inch of material around the window.
6. With the finger, smooth white glue over the entire one side of the mat. Allow the glue to dry.
7. Place the material on top of the mat with the backside toward the glue side of the mat.
8. With a steam iron, carefully iron the material to the mat. The glue reactivates and bonds the material to the mat.
9. Turn the mat face down. Smooth glue in a 1 inch band around the window and allow it to dry. Fold the edges of the material tight over the window edge and iron in place. Do all edges (Ill. 4).

supplies

1. Mat board or corrugated cardboard (see p. 331)
2. Pencil
3. Ruler
4. Mat knife or heavy scissors
5. White glue
6. Cloth, wrapping paper, wallpaper, or contact paper
7. Steam iron

 Note: Decorative trim, cord, or strips of paper may be added to the front of the mat around the window as desired to make it more decorative (Ill. 5).

 Caution: Young children using sharp tools should be under constant supervision.

1

2

3

4

5

supplies

1. Picture to be matted
2. Mat board or colored cardboard
3. Rubber cement
4. Scissors, sharp knife, or single-edged razor blade
5. Pencil
6. Ruler

Mounted Picture Mat

procedure

1. Choose a picture to be mounted, and cut it to the desired size.
2. Cut the material to be used as a mat large enough to accommodate the picture to be mounted, including a generous margin. Use matting proportions for square, horizontal, or vertical pictures on page 330 as a guide.
3. Place the cut picture on the mounting material, and use a ruler to make sure the border proportions are correct.
4. Draw around the picture with a light pencil line.
5. Remove the picture, and apply rubber cement to the pencil enclosed area. Allow to dry.
6. Apply rubber cement to the back of the picture. Allow it to dry.
7. Carefully replace the picture in the penciled shape. Lay a clean piece of paper over the illustration, and smooth it with the hand.

Caution: Children using sharp tools should be under constant supervision.

Shadow Box Frame

procedure

1. Select a box larger than the picture to be framed (Ill. 1).
2. Mount the picture of print (Ill. 2) to be framed on a piece of cardboard the size of the interior of the box. The cardboard left exposed will form a mat around the picture (Ill. 3).
3. Cut four cardboard strips with a 45° angle at each end (Ill. 4). The shortest dimension of each strip should be slightly shorter than the box.
4. Glue these four strips at the corners to form a flat frame (Ill. 5).
5. Glue the decorative trim (Ill. 6) to the flat frame (Ill. 7).
6. Glue the mounted picture in the bottom of the box (Ill. 8).
7. Glue the decorative flat frame (Ill. 7) to the top edge of the box (Ill. 9).
8. Glue a picture hanger or cardboard support (Ill. 10) to the back of the box.

Caution: Children using sharp tools must be under constant supervision.

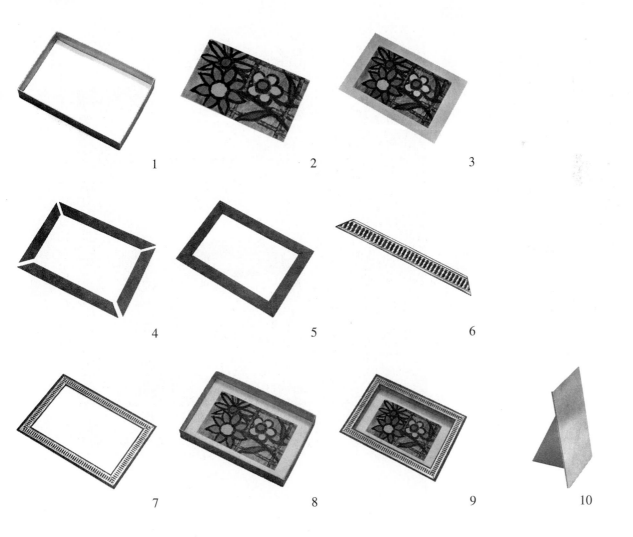

1

2

3

4

5

6

7

8

9

10

s u p p l i e s

1. Cardboard
2. Ruler
3. Scissors, single-edged razor
4. Pencil
5. Rubber cement

Caution: Children using sharp tools should be under constant supervision.

Three-Dimensional Picture Frame

procedure

1. Choose the picture to be framed, and mount it with rubber cement on a piece of cardboard, allowing at least 1½ inches of cardboard on all sides (Ill. 1).
2. Score around the edge of the mounted picture deep enough so it can be bent forward (Ill. 1).
3. Cut out four V-shaped corners. The larger the V, the deeper the frame (Ill. 2).
4. Turn up all sides until corners meet.
5. Hold corners together and tape on back (Ill. 3).
6. To hang, place a piece of tape across two ends of a loop of string, fastening them toward the top of the back.

Formulas
and Hints

Antique Plaster Finish

Soak the plaster in linseed oil. Remove and dust with dry umber or yellow ochre while still wet. Wipe off excess with a cloth until antique finish is obtained.

Art Tool Holder

Paper, folded several times, will make a holder that keeps tools from rolling.

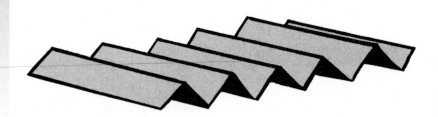

Blown Eggs

Raw, whole eggs can be emptied, and the shells, when kept intact, can be decorated and used in many attractive ways. If eggs are blown, exercise caution; salmonella is a possibility.

With a needle, gently pierce a hole about the size of a grain of rice into both ends of a fresh raw egg at room temperature. Make sure the yolk is broken.

Blow hard into one end of the egg, which is held over a bowl, and the contents will leave the other end.

Let water run inside the eggshell, and rinse well until all of the contents of the egg are removed. Allow it to dry before decorating.

The holes at each end can be covered with melted paraffin or candle wax applied with an old brush.

Proceed to decorate the eggshell with dye, ribbon, decorative braid, crepe paper, colored tissue paper, paint, beads, and so on.

 Note: Wax crayon drawn or melted wax painted on the surface of the egg will resist colored dye for interesting effects.

Dye the light colors first, then add more wax and dye darker colors.

A larger opening may be made in the front of the egg by first coating the area to be cut away with colorless nail polish. The opening then may be cut with sharp nail scissors. If the egg cracks around the opening, the cracks can be covered with beads, braid, and so on.

A scene or decoration may then be glued in place inside the egg. Such decorative eggs are especially nice on the Christmas tree or Easter tree.

Bread Dough Clay

Remove crusts from four slices of bread.
Tear bread into small pieces.
Mix pieces of bread with 3 tablespoons of white glue and 2 drops of lemon juice.
Allow one or two days for drying before decorating.
Preserve the clay in plastic bag, and place in refrigerator.

Candle Wax

Wax from an old candle is best.
Paraffin alone is good but melts rapidly.
Beeswax alone is excellent but expensive.
Mutton tallow makes excellent hard candles but becomes rancid.
Two formulas that work well are:

1. 60% by weight of paraffin
   35% stearic acid
   5% beeswax
2. 10 oz. mutton tallow
   4 oz. beeswax
   2 oz. alum
   ½ oz. gum camphor

Carving Gesso

Mix whiting and shellac to the consistency of thick cream. Add powdered tempera as needed to color.

Carving Material

1 part modeling plaster
1 part sawdust

Mix ingredients. Pour into a cardboard box, and allow to harden. Soak the block in water if it becomes too hard to carve.

Carving Paste

5 parts whiting
1 part liquid glue

Mix with water, thinning to the consistency of cream, and add powdered tempera for color.

Casting Cement

3 parts sand
1 part portland cement

Mix with water to a smooth consistency.

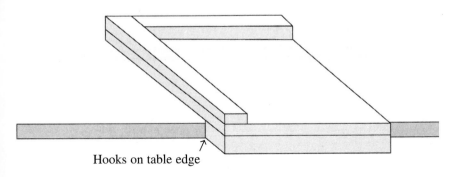

Hooks on table edge

Stop-block. This easily constructed (or bought) item secures linoleum or wood blocks for cutting. When built, three-quarter-inch wood is generally used.

Clothesline

Hang finished work on a clothesline with clothespins for drying work.

Drying Rack

Drying racks for wet artwork are ideal if space is at a premium. A number of uniform wooden sticks tacked or stapled to uniform pieces of corrugated cardboard will make a drying rack. If pieces of wood are not available, substitute two, three, or four pieces of corrugated cardboard and tape together, then tape to the base cardboard.

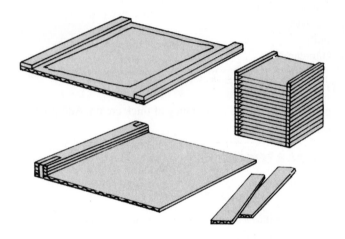

Encaustic Paint

1 oz. beeswax
2 teaspoons dry pigment or dry tempera for each color

Heat the beeswax and stir in the color with a stick.
Transfer hot encaustic color to picture with brush or palette knife. Wipe wax from brushes while still warm. Turpentine or mineral spirits will act as a solvent.

Felt Applicator

A piece of felt held to a stick by a rubber band will ease application of chalk dust to a picture, and keep it a bit more permanent.

Finger Paint

1. 1 cup liquid starch
   6 cups water
   ½ cup soap chips (nondetergent)

   Dissolve the soap chips in the water until no lumps remain; then mix well with the starch and remaining water. Color with dry or wet tempera or food coloring.

2. Mix wheat paste (wallpaper paste) into cold or lukewarm water. Stir until smooth. Pour into containers, one for each color, and stir in color pigment.
3. Small pieces of colored chalk finely ground and added to paste of a smooth consistency makes an inexpensive finger paint.
4. Two quarts boiling water and 12 tablespoons starch first dissolved in cold water. Stir until thick. Pour into containers, one for each color, and add pigments and a few drops of oil of clove to prevent distressing odors. Keep in cool place.

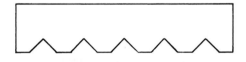

A piece of notched cardboard, when pulled and/or twisted through the finger paint, will produce interesting patterns.

5. Finger paint can be made from toothpaste or thick hand lotion and food coloring.
6. Mix nondetergent soap flakes, food coloring or dry tempera paint, and water to a creamy consistency for an ideal finger paint.
7. Liquid starch mixed with tempera paint to a creamy consistency is also a suitable finger paint.

Fixative (to Keep Work from Smearing)

Dissolve gum arabic in water to the consistency of thin cream. Spray through an insect sprayer or atomizer. Commercial hair spray may also be used. **Spray in well-ventilated areas.**

Glossy Plaster Finish

Dissolve white soap flakes in a pan or bowl to the consistency of thin cream. Soak the plaster cast or carving thoroughly in the solution for at least thirty minutes. Remove and polish with a dry cloth.

Hyplar Modeling Paste

(M. Grumbacher, Inc., New York). This is a water-based paste that dries and hardens quickly. It can be used for papier-mâché or can be modeled, shaped, carved, chiseled, or sawed when dry. The paste can be colored with acrylic watercolors that will dry to be waterproof.

Liquitex

(Permanent Pigments, Inc., Cincinnati, Ohio). A modeling paste with a water base, this is quick drying and can be modeled, carved, tooled, textured, and tinted with acrylic watercolor paint that dries to be waterproof. Thinned with water, it can be used for papier-mâché.

Methylan Paste

(The Standard Chemical Products, Inc., Hoboken, NJ). This water-based paste is colorless, odorless, nonstaining, nontoxic, and stays fresh indefinitely in a container that will not rust. It is suitable for use on papier-mâché, collage, découpage, and so on. One-fourth pound makes approximately the same amount of paste as 2 pounds of wallpaper paste.

Modeling Cement

1 part portland cement
1 part asbestos cement
1 part powdered clay that has been sieved

Mix with water to consistency of putty.

Nonsmearing Chalk

Add 6 to 8 tablespoons of sugar to an inch of water in a pan. Mix well until all of the sugar is dissolved. Soak chalk in the solution for ten to fifteen minutes. Draw with the chalk.

Paint Container

Paper milk containers stapled together with tops removed and with a cardboard handle make an ideal container for colored paint and water.

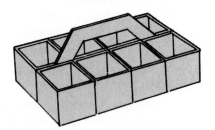

Paint Dispensing

Plastic mustard or ketchup containers make good paint dispensers. An aluminum nail in the top of each will keep the paint fresh. In some cases the plastic containers can be used for painting. Syrup pitchers make good paint dispensers and are ideal for storing paint.

Papier-Mâché

1 box Knox Gelatin
3 oz. white glue
2 oz. water

Mix ingredients and stir until mixture is smooth and creamy. Tissue paper or paper toweling strips, saturated with water, are placed over the object to the desired thickness. Papier-mâché will dry translucent and with a shiny surface.

Parchment Paper

Brush the surface of a piece of cream-colored manila paper with burnt linseed oil; brush the back of the paper with turpentine, and allow to dry.

Plastic Foam

6 tablespoons of plastic starch
1 cup dry detergent—for tinting, add powdered color

Mix with water, and whip to the consistency of marshmallow cream. This can be used in decorating Christmas ornaments, puppet heads, and so on.

Plastic Spoon

Keep plastic spoons in cans of powdered tempera for easy paint dispensing.

Prang Media Mixer

(American Crayon Company, Sandusky, Ohio). This water-based mixer is a colorless, odorless, gelatinlike formula for converting liquid or dry tempera into colored finger paint. Used in a clear form, it will act as a binder for papier-mâché and as an adhesive for paper collage.

Printing Gimmicks

Glue heavy string or scraps of felt to a cardboard tube. Slip this tube over a painting roller so that it fits snugly. Roll it in paint and then over a piece of paper, possibly in various directions, to produce a design.

Salt and Cornstarch Modeling Mixture

1 cup salt
½ cup cornstarch
¾ cup water

Cook in an old double boiler for two minutes; mixture will form a glob or mass. Place the mass on wax paper until it is cool enough to handle, then knead (as bread dough) for three minutes. The material can be wrapped in foil until time for use. It will keep several days but must be kneaded again before using. It works well around wire or armatures.

Salt and Flour Beads

2 parts table salt
1 part flour

Mix the salt and flour and water to a doughlike consistency. If color is desired, add dry pigment or food coloring. Break off small pieces and form into beads. Pierce each with a toothpick, and allow to dry, then string.

Salt and Flour Gesso

2 cups flour
1 cup salt
1½ to 2 cups water

Mix until it is smooth and does not stick to the fingers.

Salt and Flour Modeling Mixture

1 cup salt
1 cup flour
1 tablespoon powdered alum

Mix with water to the consistency of putty.

Salt and Flour Relief Mixture

3 parts salt
1 part flour

Mix with water for the desired consistency.

Sawdust and Wheat Paste for Modeling

2 parts sawdust
1 part wheat paste

Add paste to cold water to form a smooth and creamy mixture. Add sawdust and more water, if necessary, until paste becomes like putty.

Silk Screen Paint

Combine liquid or powdered tempera mixed with a stiff mixture of nondetergent soap flakes and warm water, or with Prang Media Mixer (mentioned earlier in this section).

Simulated Marble

1 part Vermiculite
1 part modeling plaster

Mix ingredients and add water, stirring constantly until the mixture becomes creamy. Pour into a cardboard box, and allow to harden. Model with knife, rasp, sandpaper, or any similar tool.

Simulated Stone

formula a

1 part sand
1 part cement
4 parts Zonalite
1 part modeling plaster

Mix ingredients, then add water to form a thick paste. Pour into a cardboard box and allow to harden.

formula b

2 parts sand
2 parts cement
4 parts Zonalite

Mix ingredients, then add water to form a thick paste. Pour into a cardboard box, and allow to harden.

Soda and Cornstarch Modeling Mixture

1 cup cornstarch
2 cups baking soda
1¼ cups water
Food coloring
Aluminum foil or plastic bag

Combine the first three ingredients in a saucepan and cook over medium heat, stirring constantly. When the mixture is thickened to doughlike consistency, turn out on a piece of aluminum foil or on a breadboard. Food coloring may be worked into the clay when it has cooled slightly.

Keep the clay in a refrigerator covered with aluminum foil or in a plastic bag to keep it pliable when not in use.

Clay may be rolled and cut into shapes or may be modeled into small shapes.

Stencil Paper

Typing paper pulled through melted paraffin in a flat pan makes an ideal stencil paper. Melt paraffin in a large, shallow pan over a *very low* fire. Holding the end of the typing paper with tweezers, run the paper through the melted paraffin. Allow the paraffin to set by holding the paper over the pan for just a short time. Recoat the paper in the same manner and allow to dry. The stencil paper is now ready to be used.

Synthetic Oil Paint

Add dry color to regular wheat paste that has been mixed to thin, smooth consistency. Apply with a stiff brush.

Tempera Paint for Glossy Surfaces

Liquid detergent, or a few drops of glycerine mixed with tempera paint, enables the paint to adhere to shiny or oily surfaces, such as aluminum foil, glass, and so on.

Translucent Paper

2 parts turpentine
1 part linseed oil

Brush or wipe the mixture on the paper, and allow it to dry.

Transparent Paper

Two parts linseed oil and one part turpentine applied to the back of a drawing with a brush or rag will cause the illustration to become transparent.

Zonalite Sculpture Cement

1 part cement
5 parts Zonalite

Mix cement and Zonalite with water until smooth. Pour into a cardboard box or mold to harden. Zonalite cement is lightweight and can be cut with a saw or carved with any metal tool.

Appendix: Art Resources

The material listed in this section should be helpful in achieving an improved level of art understanding. The listing is, of course, by no means exhaustive. Those books indicated by an asterisk (*) are out of print: it is recommended that libraries be searched for them.

Books and Journal Articles

Introduction to Art

Canaday, J. *What Is Art?* New York: Alfred A. Knopf, 1980.

*Clark, K. *Civilization: A Personal View.* New York: Harper & Row, 1970. This is an introduction to the visual arts as part of historical cultures.

———. *What Is a Masterpiece?* Magnolia, Mass.: Peter Smith, 1983.

Cleaver, D. G. *Art—An Introduction,* 4th ed. New York: Harcourt, Brace & World, 1985.

Gombrich, E. H. *The Story of Art,* 14th ed. Ithaca, N.Y.: Cornell University Press, 1985.

*Knobler, N. *The Visual Dialogue,* 3d ed. New York: Holt, Rinehart & Winston, 1980.

*Myers, B. S. *Art and Civilization,* 2d ed. New York: McGraw-Hill, 1967.

Ocvirk, O. G.; Bone, R. O.; Stinson, R. E.; and Wigg, P. R. *Art Fundamentals,* 6th ed. Dubuque, Iowa: Wm. C. Brown Publishers, 1990.

*Seiberling, F. *Looking into Art.* New York: Henry Holt & Co., 1959.

Art Education

Anderson, Frances. *Art for All the Children.* Springfield, Ill.: Charles C Thomas, 1978.

*Battock, G. *New Ideas in Art Education.* New York: E. P. Dutton, 1973.

Blandy, D., and Congdon, K. *Art in a Democracy.* New York: Teachers College Press, 1987.

*Brittain, W. Lambert. *Creativity, Art and the Young Child.* New York: Macmillan, 1979.

Brookes, Mona. *Drawing with Children.* Los Angeles: Jeremy P. Tarcher, 1986.

* Brouch, V. M. *Art Education: A Matrix System for Writing Behavioral Objectives.* Phoenix: Arbo Publishing, 1973.

Cane, F. *The Artist in Each of Us.* New York: Art Therapy Publications, Basic Books, 1983.

*Chapman, L. *Approaches to Art in Education.* New York: Harcourt Brace Jovanovich, 1978.

*Churchill, A. R. *Art for Pre-adolescents.* New York: McGraw-Hill, 1971.

*Colter, L. R. *Junior Art Museum.* J.A.M. Printing, 1977.

*DeFrancesco, Italo. *Art Education.* New York: Harper & Row, 1958.

*Dimondstein, G. *Exploring the Arts with Children.* New York: Macmillan, 1971.

Edwards, Betty. *Drawing on the Right Side of the Brain.* Los Angeles: Jeremy P. Tarcher, 1979.

Eisner, E. *Educating Artistic Vision.* New York: Macmillan, 1972.

*Erdt, M. H. *Teaching Art in the Secondary School.* New York: Holt, Rinehart & Winston, 1962.

*Fukurai, S. *How Can I Make What I Cannot See?* New York: Van Nostrand Reinhold, 1974.

*Gaitskell, C. D., and Hurwitz, A. *Children and Their Art,* 4th ed. New York: Harcourt Brace Jovanovich, 1982.

Gardner, H. *Artful Scribbles.* New York: Basic Books, 1980.

Gentle, K. *Children and Art Teaching.* London: Croom Helm, Ltd., 1985.

*Greer, D. W. "Discipline-Based Art Education: Approaching Art as a Subject of Study." *Studies in Art Education* 25 (1984): 212–18.

Herberholz, B., and Hanson, L. *Early Childhood Art,* 4th ed. Dubuque, Iowa: Wm. C. Brown Publishers, 1990.

Herberholz, D. W., and Alexander, K. *Artworks for Elementary Teachers: Developing Artistic and Perceptual Awareness,* 6th ed. Dubuque, Iowa: Wm. C. Brown Publishers, 1990.

*Hoover, F. Louis. *Art Activities for the Very Young.* Worcester, Mass.: Davis Publications, 1961.

*Jefferson, B. *Teaching Art to Children.* Boston: Allyn & Bacon, 1963.

The Journal of Aesthetic Education, Vol. 21, No. 2 (Summer 1987). A special issue, dealing with discipline-based education.

*Laliberte, N. *The Reinhold Book of Art Ideas.* New York: Van Nostrand Reinhold, 1976.

*Laliberte, N., and Kehl, R. *100 Ways to Have Fun with an Alligator.* Blauvelt, N.Y.: Art Education, Inc., 1964.

*Lanier, V. "To Have Your Cake and Eat It Too: A Response to Beyond Creating." *Studies in Art Education* 25 (1986): 152–53.

*Levete, G. *The Creative Tree: Active Participation in the Arts for People Who Are Disadvantaged.* Great Britain: Michael Russell, 1987.

Linderman, E. A., and Linderman, M. M. *Crafts in the Classroom.* New York: Macmillan, 1977.

Linderman, Marlene. *Art in the Elementary School,* 4th ed. Dubuque, Iowa: Wm. C. Brown Publishers, 1990.

*Linstrom, Miriam. *Children's Art.* Berkeley: University of California Press, 1957.

*Loughram, Bernice. *Art Experiences.* New York: Harcourt, Brace & World, 1963.

Lowenfeld, V., and Brittain, W. L. *Creative and Mental Growth,* 7th ed. New York: Macmillan, 1982.

*Mattil, E. *Meaning in Crafts,* 3rd ed. Englewood Cliffs, N. J.: Prentice-Hall, 1971.

*Montgomery, Chandler. *Art for Teachers.* Columbus, Ohio: Merrill, 1968.

*Read, H. *Education Through Art.* New York: Pantheon Books.

Schuman, Jo Miles. *Art from Many Hands.* Englewood Cliffs, N. J.: Prentice-Hall, 1981.

*Uhlin, D. M., and DeChiara, E. *Art for Exceptional Children,* 3rd ed. Dubuque, Iowa: Wm. C. Brown Publishers, 1984.

*Wolf, D., and Perry, M. "From Endpoints to Repertoires: Some New Conclusions About Drawing Development." *Journal of Aesthetic Education* 22, no. 1 (1988): 17–34.

Lettering and Calligraphy

*Angel, M. *The Art of Calligraphy.* New York: Charles Scribner's Sons, 1978.

*Ballinger, R. A. *Lettering Art in Modern Use.* New York: Van Nostrand Reinhold, 1979. (student edition)

*D'Ancona, P., and Aeschlimann, E. *The Art of Illustration.* New York: Phaidon, 1969.

*Ecke, T. Y. *Chinese Calligraphy.* Philadelphia: Philadelphia Museum of Art and Boston Books and Art, 1971.

*Fairbank, A. *A Handwriting Manual.* New York: Watson-Guptill, 1976.

*Gaitskell, C. D.; Hurwitz, A.; and Day, M. *Children and Their Art,* 4th ed. New York: Harcourt Brace Jovanovich, 1983.

*Goines, D. L. *A Basic Formal Hand,* 3d ed. New York: St. Hieronymus Press, 1976.

Gourdie, T. *Calligraphy for the Beginner.* New York: Taplinger, 1979.

*Harthan, J. *The Book of Hours.* New York: Thomas Y. Crowell, 1977.

*Harvey, M. *Lettering Design.* Barre, Mass.: Barre Publishing, 1976.

*Hassall, W. O., and Hassall, G. *Treasures from the Bodleian Library.* New York: Columbia University, 1976.

*Khibati, A., and Sivelmassi, M. *The Splendour of Islamic Calligraphy.* New York: Rizzoli International Publications, 1976.

*Lancaster, J. *Lettering Techniques.* New York: Arco, 1983.

*Lehman, C. *Italic Handwriting and Calligraphy for the Beginner.* New York: Taplinger, 1982.

*McDonald, B. J. *Calligraphy: The Art of Lettering with the Broad Pen.* New York: Taplinger, 1966.

*Switkin, A. *Hand Lettering Today.* New York: Harper & Row, 1976.

*Whalley, J. I. *The Student's Guide to Western Calligraphy: An Illustrated Survey.* Boulder, Colo.: Shambala Publications, 1984.

Wotzkow, H. *The Art of Hand Lettering.* New York: Dover Publications, 1952.

Color

*Birren, F. *Creative Color.* New York: Van Nostrand Reinhold, 1961.

Itten, J. *The Art of Color.* New York: Van Nostrand Reinhold, 1973.

*Renner, P. *Color, Order and Harmony.* New York: Van Nostrand Reinhold, 1965.

Design

*Bethers, R. *Composition in Pictures,* 2d ed. Belmont, Calif.: Pitman, 1964.

Bevlin, M. E. *Design through Discovery,* 4th ed. New York: Holt, Rinehart & Winston, 1984.

*Lauer, D. A. *Design Basics,* 2nd ed. New York: Holt, Rinehart & Winston, 1985.

Ocvirk, O. G.; Bone, R. O.; Stinson, R. E.; and Wigg, P. R. *Art Fundamentals,* 6th ed. Dubuque, Iowa: Wm. C. Brown Publishers, 1990.

Art Appreciation

Art For Children Series. New York: LRN Company, 1988.

Getting to Know the World's Greatest Artists Series. Chicago: Children's Press, 1988.

Looking at Paintings Series. New York: Hyperion Books, 1993.

Muhlberger, R. *What Makes a . . . Artist Series.* New York: Viking/Metro Museum of Art, 1993.

Understanding the Masters Series. London: Trewin Copplestone, Ltd., 1976.

Paper

*Grater, M. *Paper Faces.* New York: Taplinger Publishing Co., 1968.

Irvine, J. *How to Make Pop-Ups.* New York: Beech Tree Books, 1991.

*Jackson, P., and Frank, V. *Origami and Papercraft.* New York: Crescent Publishers, Inc., 1973.

Johnson, P. *Creating With Paper.* Seattle: University of Washington Press, 1958.

*Newman, T.; Newman, J.; and Newman, L. *Paper as Art and Craft.* New York: Crown Publishers, Inc., 1973.

*Temko, F. *Paper: Folded, Cut, Sculpted.* New York: Collier Books, 1974.

Ceramics

*Ball, F., and Lovoos, J. *Making Pottery Without a Wheel.* New York: Van Nostrand Reinhold Co., 1965.

Ceramics. Menlo Park, Calif.: Lane Books, 1975. A Sunset Book.

*Priolo, J., and Priolo, A. *Ceramics by Coil.* New York: Sterling Publishing Co., Inc., 1976.

———. *Ceramics by Slab.* New York: Sterling Publishing Co., Inc., 1977.

Fiber

Belfer, N. *Batik and Tie Dye Techniques.* New York: Dover Publications, Inc., 1992.

*Guild, V. *Painting With Stitches.* Worcester, Mass.: Davis Publications, 1976.

*Meilach, D. *Basketry with Fibers and Grasses.* New York: Crown Publishers, Inc., 1974.

*———. *Contemporary Batik and Tie-Dye.* New York: Crown Publishers, Inc., 1973.

*Meilach, D., and Snow, L. *Weaving Off-Loom.* Chicago, Ill.: Contemporary Books, 1973.

*Rainey, S. *Wall Hangings, Designing with Fabric and Thread.* Worcester, Mass.: Davis Publications, 1973.

*———. *Weaving Without a Loom.* Worcester, Mass.: Davis Publications, 1966.

*Soboit, M. *Pictures in Patchwork.* New York: Sterling Publishing Co., 1977.

*Sommer, E., and Sommer, M. *A New Look at Felt.* New York: Crown Publishers, Inc., 1975.

Masks

*Tommel, A. *Masks, Their Meaning and Function.* New York: McGraw-Hill Book Co., 1972.

Puppetry

Baird, B. *The Art of The Puppet.* New York: Bonanza Books, 1966.

*Engler, L., and Fijan, C. *Making Puppets Come Alive.* New York: Taplinger Publishing Co., Inc., 1980.

Fijan, C., and Ballard, F. *Directing Puppet Theatre.* San Jose, Calif.: Resources Publications, Inc., 1989.

*Henson, C. *The Muppets Make Puppets.* New York: Workman Publishing, 1994.

*Latshaw, G. *Puppetry, The Ultimate Disguise.* New York: Richard Rosen Press, Inc., 1978.

*Reininger, L. *Shadow Puppets, Shadow Theatres and Shadow Films.* Boston: Publishers Plays, Inc., 1975.

Renfro, N., and Armstrong, B. *Make Amazing Puppets.* Santa Barbara, Calif.: The Learning Works, 1979.

Taylor, B. *Marionette Magic.* Blue Ridge Summit, Pa.: Tab Books, Inc., 1989.

Printmaking

Brommer, G. *Relief Printmaking.* Worcester, Mass.: Davis Publications, Inc., 1970.

*D'Alleva, A. *Native American Arts and Cultures.* Worcester, Mass.: Davis Publications, Inc., 1993.

Herald, J. *World Crafts.* Asheville, N. C.: Lark Books, 1993.

Ross, John, and Romano, Clare. *The Complete Collagraph.* New York: The Free Press, 1980.

———. *The Complete Intaglio Print.* New York: The Free Press, 1974.

———. *The Complete Printmaker.* New York: The Free Press, 1974.

*———. *The Complete Relief Print.* New York: The Free Press, 1974.

*———. *The Complete Screenprint and Lithograph.* New York: The Free Press, 1974.

Saff, Donald, and Sacilotto, Deli. *Printmaking.* New York: Holt, Rinehart & Winston, 1978.

Papermaking

*Mason, John. *Papermaking as an Artistic Craft.* Leicester, England: Twelve by Eight Press, 1963.

A number of books on printmaking also include some information on papermaking.

Video Series

The Big A. A 10-part Video Series. Art for Grades 1–3. GPN, P. O. Box 80669, Lincoln, NE 68501-0669   15 minute programs.

Behind the Scenes. 5 Visual Arts Programs, 40 minutes each. Intermediate grades.

1. Illusion of Depth with David Hockney
2. Color with Robert Gil DeMontes
3. Balance with Nancy Graves
4. Framing with Carrie Mae Weemes
5. Line with Wayne Thiebaud

GPN, P. O. Box 80669, Lincoln, NE 68501-0669

Supplies

A.R.T. Studio Clay Co.
1555 Louis Avenue
Elk Grove Village, IL 60007

Bailey Ceramic Supply
P. O. Box 1577
Kingston, NY 12401

Chaselle
9645 Gerwig Lane
Columbia, MD 21046

Dick Blick
P. O. Box 1267
Galesburg, IL 61402

Minnesota Clay
8001 Grand Ave. South
Bloomington, MN 55420

Nosco Arts and Crafts
901 Janesville Ave.
Ft. Atkinson, WI 53538

Ohio Ceramic Supply, Inc.
2861 St. Rt. 59
P. O. Box 630
Kent, OH 44240

R. B. Walter Art and Crafts
Dept. SA/P. O. Box 6231
Arlington, TX 76005

Sax Arts and Crafts
2405 S. Calhown Rd.
New Berlin, WI 53151

Triaco Arts and Crafts
14650 28th Avenue North
Plymouth, MN 55447

United Art and Education Supply Co., Inc.
P. O. Box 9219
Fort Wayne, IN 46899

Davis Publications, Inc.
50 Portland St.
Worcester, MA 01608

Dover Publications
31 East 2nd Street
Mineola, NY 11501

Sax Visual Art Resources
P. O. Box 51710
New Berlin, WI 53151-0710

Shorewood Fine Art Reproductions
27 Glen Road
Sandy Hook, CT 06482

Audiovisual Resources

Crizmac
Art and Cultural Education Materials
P. O. Box 65928
Tucson, AZ 85728-5928

Crystal Productions
1812 Johns Drive
P. O. Box 2159
Glenview, IL 60025-6159

Dale Seymour Publications
P. O. Box 10888
Palo Alto, CA 94303

Magazines

Arts and Activities
591 Camina de la Reina
Suite 200
San Diego, CA 92108

School Arts
50 Portland St.
Worcester, MA 01615-9959

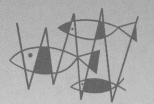

Glossary

Abstract Art   Art that departs from appearances to varying degrees; involves simplification or rearrangement.

Acrylic   Polymers used to produce synthetic rubbers and lightweight plastics. This chemical technology has been applied to the art field in developing a quick-drying medium for painting.

Aesthetics   A search for the nature of pleasing qualities in a work of art. The study of our sensitivity to art forms.

Appliqué   Work applied to, or laid on, another material.

Ascender   The vertical truck of a lowercase (noncapital) letter that rises above its body.

Balance, Formal   Similar or identical images and/or art elements given similar or identical placement on either side of the axis of the artwork so that an effect of pictorial balance is sensed by the viewer. In its extreme form (pure symmetry), one side is the mirror image of the other.

Balance, Informal   Dissimilar elements or images given dissimilar placement, but in such a way that an effect of balance is felt.

Bas-Relief   A low relief in which the design projects less than one half of its proportion or thickness from the background.

Batik   A technique of dyeing fabric by protecting selected portions with wax. The wax serves as a resist (*see* Resist).

Block Print   A print made by lifting off (usually with paper) the ink applied to the uncut areas of a surface (such as a wood or linoleum block). This is a relief printing technique.

Blotto   An image that is duplicated by repeating itself in a symmetrical manner; one side of a sheet of paper is painted and the paper is folded while the paint is still wet.

Brayer   A roller used to spread ink over a printing surface.

Calligraphy   Beautiful and/or decorative writing.

Cast(ing)   The cast is the product that is freed from the mold (*see* Mold).

Ceramics   Usually, though not always, pottery vessels originally made of clay and subsequently fired for permanence.

Chain Stitch   An ornamental stitch in which each stitch forms a loop through the forward end of which the next stitch is taken.

Clay   Viscous earth which, when combined with water, forms a sticky paste that may be modeled into shapes and that hardens as it dries. Used by ceramists and sculptors. Sometimes used with an oil base by sculptors (plastilene).

Coiling   To arrange in rings which lie side by side. A fiber wrap technique.

Collage   An arrangement of objects and materials adhered to a surface (usually a canvas), sometimes as a supplement to drawn and/or painted areas.

Collé   An image created by pieces of paper that are adhered to a surface; often abetted by drawn or painted passages.

Color   Our visual response to wavelengths of light, such as red, green, blue, and so on.

Complementary Colors   Hues opposite each other on the color wheel.

Composition   Arrangement of the elements of art and their resultant images.

Cone   A slightly elongated pyramidal object made of a substance that will cause it to droop at a predetermined temperature as a signal to the ceramist that the proper temperature has been reached. Used in kilns for the firing of ceramic objects.

Core   The innermost part of anything. In coiling, it is the base around which the yarn or material is wrapped.

Descender   The vertical trunk of a lowercase (noncapital) letter that sinks below its body.

Design   A framework or scheme of pictorial construction. The arrangement and handling of the art elements.

Element   In art, a line, a shape, an area of light or dark, a texture, or a color.

Emboss   The producing of protuberances in a planar surface, usually by pressing down the portions between those areas to create a relief-like appearance (*see* Relief)

Encaustic   A painting medium using colored pigments mixed with molten wax and applied to the painting surface.

Engobe   A white or colored coating of clay used to cover pottery, usually for decoration or to aid adhesion of glaze or enamel to the surface of the pottery.

Etching   Engraving by eating into portions of a surface with acid. Printmakers apply an acid-resistant ground, scratch the image through the ground exposing the metal underneath, and bite the image into the metal plate with acid. The technique is part of the intaglio process.

Expression   The manner in which artists try to say something about themselves, their time and/or their environment. They are said to be "expressing" themselves.

Fixative (Fixatif)   A clear, fast-drying liquid substance that is sprayed on delicate artworks to protect them. Commercially available in a pressurized can or for use with an atomizer; hair spray is sometimes used for this purpose.

Form   The total appearance and organization of the visual elements.

Fringing   Ornamental bordering having projecting lengths of thread or cord, either loose or variously arranged or combined.

Geometric   Shapes deriving from geometry, such as squares, circles, triangles, and so on.

Gesso   Plaster or gypsum mixed with water and applied to a surface to serve as a ground for painting.

Glaze   A substance that becomes vitreous at a certain temperature and provides a watertight, glossy (usually), and colorful (often) coating for ceramic articles.

God's Eye   A craft from Mexico in which yarn is wrapped around crossed sticks or metal arms to make a decoration.

Gothic   1. An artistic style of the Middle Ages. 2. A style of typography and calligraphy.

Gouache   A type of opaque watercolor. A pliable adhesive is sometimes added for softness and slower drying.

Harmony   Related elements; the repetition of similar characteristics. A sense of belonging together.

Hue   The common name of a color.

Impressionism   A style of somewhat realistic artwork based on the changing aspects of light.

Incise   Cutting into a surface, usually in a linear manner. Clay may be incised by the sculptor or ceramist as a decorative or definitive effect.

Inlay   The imbedding of a substance in a material of a different character.

Intaglio   A printing process. (*See* chapter on printing.)

Kachina   One of the deified ancestral spirits of the Native Americans of the Southwest. It often refers to the figures created by these people to represent these spirits.

Kiln   A furnace serviced with various fuels and most often used by ceramists to fire clay or other substances to make them more permanent.

Lamination   The adhering of relatively flat, thin materials, usually employing several thicknesses.

Latex   A semirubberized, water-soluble, and relatively quick-drying paint.

Line   The path of a moving point.

Loom   A weaving device through which yarn or thread is made into fabric by crossing the strands known as the warp and weft.

Lowercase   Those letters of the alphabet that are noncapitals; also called miniscules.

Manipulate   Handling of objects for a particular purpose, such as to gain acquaintance with them or to use them in the mastery of some problem or technique.

Maraca   Latin American noisemaker used in rhythm sections of musical groups. Gourds are often used for this purpose.

Marionette   A puppet moved by strings.

Mat   A piece of paper or cardboard surrounding and setting off a work of art or document; often inside a frame.

Mobile   A sculpture piece in which relationships are established by suspending pieces from supporting arms in such a way that they can move with currents of air. Popularized by Alexander Calder.

Mola   A reverse appliqué.

Mold (Mould)   A hollow form into which a liquid or plastic material is poured or pressed and allowed to harden, taking the reverse shape of the mold's interior surface. Duplicate casts (*see* Cast) can be made from certain types of molds.

Monoprint   A print in which the image is created on a smooth surface with paint by drawing through it with various drawing instruments. Paper is pressed over the paint, duplicating the image when withdrawn. A monoprint is usually one of a kind, hence "mono" print.

Mosaic   A technique in which small (usually colored) stones (tesserae) are pressed into cement to form an image.

Mottle   The producing of a patterned appearance with spots or blemishes.

Naturalistic Art   Art which attempts to reproduce the exact nature of things seen.

Neoclassicism   A style attempting an imitation of the works of the Greeks and Romans.

Oxidize   Exposure to the atmosphere will, in time, cause oxides to form on the surfaces of some metals resulting in a darkened appearance. May be artificially induced with chemicals.

Papier-Mâché   Paper ground up or cut into strips and mixed with a gelatinous material such as glue or paste so that it can be molded into desired shapes that are retained as it dries.

Paris Craft   Gauze impregnated with plaster of Paris. Plastr' craft or plaster fabric are names for the same material.

Plaster   Sulphate of lime and gypsum. Ordinarily used in a powdered form and mixed with water. After mixing, the plaster dries and hardens. Used by ceramists, sculptors, dentists, and contractors. Comes in various grades according to use.

Plastilene   Oil-based modeling clay.

Pointillism   A technique of paint application in dots or small swatches. The mixed colors often produce a visual blending.

Polymer   A natural or synthetic chemical compound or mixture of compounds formed by polymerization. This compound is used in the manufacture of a number of art products, such as polymer tempera and modeling paste.

Polyurethane Foam   A type of flexible foam used in upholstery and as carpet padding.

Positive-Negative   An art image, usually made with paper and scissors, in which the void, or cutout shapes, are joined to the positive, or shapes that have been removed, to create a symmetrical design.

Postimpressionism   A style of work following Impressionism that tried to restore more of an expressive meaning to art.

Pot   A vessel, usually made of clay, allowed to dry or fired in a kiln.
Pinch pot   A vessel formed by the pinching together of clay particles.
Slab pot   A vessel constructed by adhering slabs of clay to form its side and base.
Coil pot   A vessel built up from coils (rounded strips) of clay.

Print   A multiple-original artwork on paper that comes into direct contact with an image-bearing surface in such a way that the image is transferred to the paper. Prints may be produced using the intaglio, relief, lithographic, or serigraphic processes.

Quilling   A ribbon, strip of lace, and so on, pleated into small cylindrical folds resembling a row of quills.

Realism   A form of artistic expression, or style, that retains the basic impression of visual observance, but often also attempts to relate and interpret the meanings that lie beneath surface appearances. Approximates camera vision (pure camera vision is "naturalism").

Reed   The tall straight stem of a weed.

Relief   1. The elevation or projection of a design from a flat surface to create the effect of volumes in space. 2. Relief printing—a print made by drawing ink from a raised surface (such as a wood block).

Repoussé   The art of ornamenting metal by making a pattern in relief.

Resist   A material that protects against a chemical or physical action, or fails to be dissolved or penetrated by another material. Used as a block-out by artists who protect the original or subsequent color of a surface from a newly applied one.

Romanticism   A style including experimental, spontaneous, intuitive, and picturesque artwork.

Shape   An area with defined or implied boundaries.

Space (in art)   1. The illusion of distance between elements or images in two-dimensional work. 2. The area surrounding a three-dimensional work or art.

Spectrum   Hues (colors) produced when light is broken into different wavelengths as in a prism or rainbow.

Stabile   A sculpture that is often similar to the mobiles invented by Alexander Calder except that they are stationary rather than in movement.

Subject   1. Persons or things portrayed in artwork. 2. A theme of an artwork. 3. Visual signs employed by the artist.

Symbolic Stage   Representing a quality, situation, or object with another object, emblem, or sign.

Texture   The characteristics of a surface with a degree of roughness or smoothness.

Totem   Something, especially an animal, which members of a totem group have as their sign.

Totem Pole   A column of cedar wood carved with totemic symbols.

Translucent   Limited transparency through which things can be seen, but indistinctly.

Unity   A compatible balance between harmony and variety.

Uppercase   Capital letters of the alphabet, also called "majuscules."

Value   Degrees of lightness or darkness.

Variety   Differences achieved by opposing, contrasting, and changing of the elements to create interest.

Warp   A strand or filament moving in a certain direction that is usually at right angles to another (the weft).

Wash   A highly diluted, liquid application of color, usually over a broad area. Most often thought of in connection with watercolor painting.

Watercolor   A painting medium for which water is the vehicle; most watercolor paintings are characterized by their transparency.

Wedge   As a verb, wedging is the act of using a taut wire for slicing chunks of clay which are later reassembled. This is done in order to render the clay more homogenous and to eliminate air bubbles that could cause the clay to shatter if fired.

Weft   A strand or strands of fabric moving in a certain direction, usually at right angles to the warp (*see* Warp).

Whiting   A finely powdered chalk that has been ground, washed, and refined. It is widely used in the arts for painting, printmaking, and sculpture.

Zonalite   Proprietary name for vermiculite, a free-flowing granular mineral, normally used for insulation.

Chronologies

A Chronology of Western Art (beginning with Greece)

750 B.C.	**Greece**	Archaic age. Sculpture, pottery
470 B.C.		Classical age. Architecture, painting, sculpture
330 B.C.		Ptolemaic age (Egypt)
320 B.C.		Hellenistic age
280 B.C.	**Rome**	Sculpture, architecture, painting, minor arts
140 B.C.		Graeco-Roman art
30 B.C.–A.D. 146		Imperial Rome
100 A.D.		Late imperial Rome and early Christian
300 A.D.	**Medieval Art**	Middle East, *Early Byzantine art;* Egypt, *Coptic art.*
330		*Early Christian art* in western Europe, decline of Rome.
400		Migratory, barbarian arts (Celts, Saxons, Vikings, Huns, Goths).
550		*Muslim* or *Islamic art,* northern Africa, southern Spain (*Moorish art*).
768		*Carolingian art,* France, Germany, northern Italy.
800		*Developed Byzantine art,* Middle East, Greece, Russia, parts of Italy (Venice, Ravenna, Rome, Sicily).
900		*Ottonian art*—mostly in Germany.
1000		*Romanesque art* (Roman-like or modified Roman art in France, England, northern Spain, Italy, and Germany).
1150		*Gothic art* in Europe.
1300	**Renaissance Art**	*Proto-Renaissance,* Italy: Giotto, Duccio, Nicolo Pisano (sculpture).
1400		*Early Renaissance,* Italy: Masaccio, Donatello, Francesca, Leonardo, and so on. Renaissance in West modified by vestiges of Medievalism: van Eyck, Weyden, van der Goes, etc.
1500		*High Renaissance:* Michelangelo, Raphael, Titian, Tintoretto; western Europe influenced by Italy.
1520		*Mannerism and Early Baroque,* Italy: Caravaggio.
1600	**Baroque Art**	*Baroque art* in Europe: Rubens, Van Dyck, Rembrandt, Hals (Netherlands); Velásquez, Ribera (Spain); Poussin, Lorrain (France); Bernini (sculpture, Italy). *Early Colonial art,* Americas.
1700		*Rococo art,* primarily French: Watteau, Boucher, Fragonard, Chardin; but spreads to other European countries: Canaletto, Guardi, Tiepolo (Italy); Hogarth, Gainsborough, Reynolds (England). *Colonial art,* Americas.
1800	**Nineteenth-century Art**	*Neoclassicism:* David, Ingres (France); Canova (sculpture, Italy).
1820		*Romanticism:* Gericault, Delacroix (France); Goya (Spain); Turner (England); Ryder (United States); Barye (sculpture, France).
1850		*Realism* and *Naturalism:* Daumier, Courbet, Manet (France); Homer, Eakins (United States); Constable (England)
1870		*Impressionism:* Monet, Pissarro, Renoir, Degas (France); Sisley (England); Hassam, Twachtman (United States); Medardo-Rosso (sculpture, Italy); Rodin (sculpture, France).
1880		*Postimpressionism:* Cézanne, Seurat, Gauguin, Van Gogh, Toulouse-Lautrec (France).

1900	**Twentieth-century Art**	Sculptors working in a *Postimpressionist* manner: Maillol (France); Lachaise (United States); Lehmbruck, Marcks, Kolbe (Germany).
1901		*Expressionism:* Picasso* (Blue, Rose, and Negro periods). *Les Fauves:* Matisse, Rouault, Vlaminck, Modigliani, Dufy, Utrillo (France). Recent *French Expressionists:* (1930) Soutine, Buffet, Balthus. *German Expressionists:* Nolde, Kirchner, Kokoschka, Schmidt-Rotluff, Marc, Jawlensky, Macke, Beckmann, Grosz, Dix; Munch (Norway). *American Expressionists:* Weber, Shahn, Levine, Avery, Baskin; Orozoco (Mexico). *Sculpture:* Marini (Italy); Epstein (England); Zorach (United States).
1906	**Abstract Art (early phase)**	*Cubism:* Picasso, *Braque, Léger, Gris (France); Laurens (sculpture, France). *Futurism:* Balla, Boccioni (sculpture and painting), Carra, Severini (Italy).
1910–50		*Developed Abstract and Nonobjective art:* Kandinsky, Albers (Germany); Moholy-Nagy (Hungary); *Constructivism:* Larionov, Malevich, Tatlin (Russia); Delaunay (France); Nicholson (England); *DeStijl:* Mondrian, Van Doesburg, Van Tongerloo (Holland); Dove, Marin, Feininger, Frank Stella, O'Keeffe, MacDonald-Wright, Stuart Davis, Demuth, Hartley, Knaths, Diller, Pereira, MacIver, Tomlin, Rothko (United States). *Sculpture:* Brancusi, Archipenko, Arp (France); Epstein, Passmore (England); de Rivera, Nevelson, Hajdu, Noguchi (United States); Gabo, Pevsner (Russian-Constructivists, United States).
ca. 1910	**Fantasy in Art**	*Individual fantasists:* Henri Rousseau (French primitive); de Chirico (Italy); Chagall (France); Klee Switzerland/Germany).
1914		*Dada:* Tzara, Duchamp, Picabia, Arp (France); Ernst, Schwitters (Germany).
1924		*Surrealism:* Ernst (Germany); Delvaux, Masson (France); Dali (Spain, United States); Magritte (Belgium); Bacon (England).
1925		*Sculpture:* Giacometti (Switzerland); González (Spain); Arp (France). *Surrealistic Abstraction:* Picasso* (France); Miró (Spain); Tamayo (Mexico); Matta (Chile, United States); Baziotes, Tobey, Gorky, Rothko, Hofmann, DeKooning (United States). *Sculpture:* Moore, Hepworth (England); Lipchitz (Lithuania, United States, France); Calder (United States).
1930–40	**Traditional Realism**	*Regionalists:* John Sloan, Grant Wood, Thomas Hart Benton (United States); Andrew Wyeth (independent realist, United States).

---

*Artists frequently change their styles, thus some names may appear under more than one category of form-style. Most notable in this respect is Pablo Ruiz Picasso.

1945	**Post–World War II Trends**	*Abstract Expressionism* and *Action painting:* Pollock, Motherwell, Kline, Still, Reinhardt, Frankenthaler, Tworkov, Holty, Rothko (United States); Mathieu, Soulages, Manessier (France); Vieira da Silva (Portugal); de Stael, Appel (Holland); Okada (Japan); Tapies (Spain).
		Sculpture: Roszak, David Smith, Lipton, Lassaw, Lippold, Nakian (United States); Richier (France).
1950	**Post–Painterly Abstraction**	*Color Field* and *Hard-Edge* painters (all United States): Louis, Newman, Kelly Noland, Stella, Poons, Ron Davis.
		Minimalists: Olitsky, Reinhardt (United States); Yves Klein (France).
		Sculpture: Judd, Tony Smith, Rosenthal, Andre (United States).
		Primary-Structurists (some called *Neo-Constructivists* and/or *Environmentalists*): Bontecou, Di Suvero, Nevelson, Bell, Stone, de Witt, Meadmore, Kipp, Katzen, Snelson, Rickey (United States): Paolozzi, King (England); Bill (Switzerland).
1955		*Neo-Dada* and *Funk art* (collage-assemblage): Johns, Rauschenberg (United States); Dubuffet (France).
		Sculpture: Kienholz, Stankiewicz, Mallary, Chamberlain (United States); César (France).
		Pop art and *Happenings:* Warhol, Lichtenstein, Dine, Indiana, Kaprow, Oldenburg, Segal, Grooms, Marisol, Wesselman, Rosenquist (United States); Hamilton, Kitaj, Smith (England).
		Op art: Vasarely (France); Anuskiewicz, Ortmann, Stanczak (United States); Agam (Israel); Riley, Denny (England).
1965–80		*New Realism:* Pearlstein, Ramos, Katz, Theibaud, Lindner, Close, Cottingham, Estes (United States).
		Sculpture: Gallo, de Andrea, Hanson (United States).
		Technological art (kinetics, neon, sound): Wolfert (color organ, 1930–63); Tinguely (Switzerland, United States); Chryssa (Greece); Samaris, Sonnier, Riegack, Flavin, Rickey (United States); Hess (Germany, United States); Soto (Venezuela); Castro-Cid (Chile); Le Parc (Argentina); Takis (Greece).
		Environments, Land art, or *Earthworks; Process and Conceptual art:* Lansman, Andre, Christo, Smithson, Serra, Lewitt, Heizer, Oldenburg, Kipp, Di Suvero; Katzen, Snelson, Rickey, Woody, Nauman (United States): Beuys, Kiefer (Germany).
1980–96		*Neo-Expressionism:* Schnabel (United States); Cucchi, Chia (Italy); Penck, Kiefer, Baselitz (Germany).
		Other artists, irrespective of style, who have created significant artworks since 1980 (some may be repeats): Chuck Close, Duane Hanson, John De Andrea, Philip Pearlstein, Janet Fish, Miriam Schapiro, Joyce Kozloff, Pat Steir, Georg Baselitz, A. R. Penck, David Salle, Eric Fischl, Leon Golub, Richard Long.

A Chronology of Non-Western Art

This section is included as a diversion from geographically familiar art and to mark the breadth and depth of the creative spark. An attempt to be exhaustive would be suicidal for the authors; only truly significant art forms are noted and all regions are not covered. Dates are very general (c. for "circa"—approximate). The earliest dates indicate that art products have been found from periods when human beings first found refuge and the security and time to produce those works.

Schoolroom displays of "exotic" works from ancient and distant cultures may replace a provincial outlook with a worldview.

c. 500,000–12,000 B.C.	**Paleolithic Period**	Crude fetishes, utility instruments, and cave paintings
c. 12,000 B.C.–circa 7,000 B.C	**Neolithic Period**	Tombs, sculpture, pottery
	Egypt	Pyramids, architecture, painting, sculpture, pottery, minor arts
3000 B.C.	Old Kingdom	
1500 B.C.	New Kingdom	
	Mesopotamia	Primarily architecture, sculpture
2850–1900 B.C.	Sumerian	
1600–1143 B.C.	Babylonian	
883–c. 745 B.C.	Assyria	
550–336 B.C.	Persia (Iran)	
	Aegean or Minoan	Architecture, fresco paintings, pottery
3000–1100 B.C.		
	India	Sculpture, painting, pottery, minor arts
3300–1500 B.C.	Dravidian	
1500–660 B.C.	Aryan	
650–300 B.C.	Saisumega/Nanda	
300–200 B.C.	Mauryan	
200 B.C.–A.D. 1	Sunga	
A.D. 1–300	Kushana, later Andra	
A.D. 1–400	Gandara	
A.D. 300–600	Gupta	
	China	Architecture, sculpture, painting, pottery, fabrics
3000–2205 B.C.	Patriarchal	
2205–1766 B.C.	Hsia dynasty	
1766–1122 B.C.	Shang	
1122–255 B.C.	Chou	
255–206 B.C.	Ch'in	
206 B.C.–221 A.D.	Han	
A.D. 221–265	3 states	
265–618	6 dynasties	
618–907	T'ang	
3th–14th centuries	Yuan	
14th–17th centuries	Ming	
17th–20th centuries	Ch'ing	

	Japan	Architecture, painting, fabrics, sculpture, minor arts
A.D. 645–710	Mahayana Buddhism	
710–794	Nara	
794–897	Jogan	
897–1192	Yamato Ye	
1336–1603	Zen (Ashikaga)	
1603–1868	Tokugawa (Ukiyoye)	
	Mohammedan/Muslim	(Saracenic) Architecture, calligraphy, nonfigurative painting, textiles, ceramics, mosaics
A.D.700–present	**Egypt, Constantinople, Asia Minor, Persia, India, Spain**	
3900 B.C.–A.D.	**Africa** 1500 Nubia (Egyptian influence)	
	"A" Group	Minor arts
2300 B.C.	**"B" Group**	Sculpture, painting, minor arts
12th–11th centuries B.C.		Kush Architecture, sculpture
1500 B.C.–A.D. 1500	**West Africa**	Sierra Leone, Dahomey, Senegal, Mali, Ghana, Benin, Ife Bronze, copper, brass sculpture, minor arts
A.D. 100–1500	Bantu, Congo, East coast, Zimbabwe, and Swahili	Swahili and Zimbabwe—iron, copper, brass casting, architecture, and sculpture
	Oceanian	(Pacific) Assembled and painted masks, pottery Migrations from South East Asia began about A.D. 400 Nearer islands (Indonesia), then New Guinea, Australia (Melanesian), Micronesia, and Polynesia
	Native American	Art varies with sites
A.D. 1–1600	Mayan and Aztec art of Yucatan, Honduras, Mexico	Inca art of Peru Prehistoric and historic art of the Southwest, the Plains, Pacific coast, and Eskimos

Index